Instantaneous User Identification for Personalized Interaction on Shared Surfaces

Dominik Schmidt

Diplom-Medieninformatiker
Ludwig-Maximilians-Universität, München, Germany

Thesis submitted for the degree of
Doctor of Philosophy

School of Computing and Communications
Lancaster University

June 2012

Instantaneous User Identification
for Personalized Interaction
on Shared Surfaces

Dominik Schmidt

Thesis submitted for the degree of Doctor of Philosophy
June 2012

Abstract

Interactive surfaces facilitate direct and expressive multi-touch, multi-user interaction, providing a compelling platform for co-located collaboration. Surface computing systems, however, are typically unaware of different users. Consequently, touch input from different users remains indistinguishable and anonymous. In this thesis, we contribute to the body of surface computing research by proposing novel methods for user identification, and by demonstrating how the so enabled personalization facilitates new types of interaction. If touch input is associated to users, applications can personalize individual interactions—without constraining other concurrent users. Personalization allows for a wide range of interaction techniques that are not obvious to realize without user identification. For instance, personal clipboards may enable independent copy-and-paste operations on a shared surface. User identification for surface computing must be immediately available and smoothly integrated with direct-touch input in order to not impede the prevailing fluid multi-touch interaction style. We present three novel methods for instantaneous user identification on vision-based interactive surfaces: *IdWristbands* uses bracelets that emit infrared codes to identify individual finger touches, *HandsDown* is based on biometrics and allows users to identify by placing their hand flat on the surface, and *PhoneTouch* employs mobile phones in a stylus-like fashion for identified direct-touch interaction. Albeit following distinct identification strategies, either method allows users to spontaneously identify at arbitrary locations directly on an interactive surface. We use IdWristbands, HandsDown, and PhoneTouch as basis for analyzing and exploring the design space of personalized interaction. We illustrate its opportunities and benefits by introducing a wide range of novel user-aware interaction techniques. In a user study, we show that instantaneous user identification and personalization conveniently facilitate interaction techniques that are otherwise not immediately accessible or difficult to realize.

Acknowledgments

I would like to take this opportunity to thank you all who accompanied and supported me in countless ways on this journey—thank you for a wonderful, exciting, and enjoyable four years in Lancaster. I especially admire and value the passion and inspiration of my supervisors, Hans Gellersen and Enrico Rukzio, who guided me with great knowledge and patience—thank you! It is not easy to find an environment as welcoming, friendly, and helpful as the EIS group with its amiable members and acquaintances; I will definitely miss you and the many great times we had. A big thanks also goes to all others in the School of Computing and Communications who substantially helped making my Lancaster-period a time to remember—thank you for all the support! I would also like to thank Tobias Meyer for his valuable contribution to parts of this work, as well as Lucia Castellanos and Ming Ki Chong for proofreading and feedback. Last but not least, I am deeply grateful for the love and help I always received from my family who encouraged, trusted, and supported me in so many different ways and made all this possible—vielen, vielen Dank!

Related Publications

[1] T. Meyer and D. Schmidt. IdWristbands: IR-based user identification on multi-touch surfaces. Poster ITS, 2010.

[2] D. Schmidt. Design and realization of an interactive multi-touch table. Technical report, Lancaster University, 2009.

[3] D. Schmidt. Know thy toucher. CHI Workshop: Multitouch and Surface Computing, 2009.

[4] D. Schmidt. Towards personalized surface computing. UIST Doctoral Symposium, 2010.

[5] D. Schmidt. PhoneTouch: Seamless cross-device interaction. CHI Workshop: Looking into wow products, from analysis to heuristics, 2012.

[6] D. Schmidt, F. Chehimi, E. Rukzio, and H. Gellersen. Computer interface method. Patent application US13/151554. 2011.

[7] D. Schmidt, F. Chehimi, E. Rukzio, and H. Gellersen. PhoneTouch: A technique for direct phone interaction on surfaces. In *Proc. UIST*, pages 13–16, 2010.

[8] D. Schmidt, M. Chong, and H. Gellersen. HandsDown: Hand-contour-based user identification for interactive surfaces. In *Proc. NordiCHI*, pages 432–441, 2010.

[9] D. Schmidt, M. Chong, and H. Gellersen. IdLenses: Dynamic personal areas on shared surfaces. In *Proc. ITS*, pages 131–134, 2010.

[10] D. Schmidt and H. Gellersen. Show your hands: A vision-based approach to user identification for interactive surfaces. Poster ITS, 2009.

[11] D. Schmidt, J. Seifert, E. Rukzio, and H. Gellersen. A cross-device interaction style for mobiles and surfaces. In *Proc. DIS*, pages 318–327, 2012.

[12] J. Schöning, J. Hook, T. Bartindale, D. Schmidt, P. Oliver, F. Echtler, N. Motamedi, and P. Brandl. *Tabletops–Horizontal Interactive Displays*, chapter Building interactive multi-touch surfaces, pages 27–50. Springer, 2010.

[13] J. Schöning, J. Hook, N. Motamedi, P. Oliver, F. Echtler, P. Brandl, L. Muller, F. Daiber, O. Hilliges, M. Löchtefeld, M. Roth, D. Schmidt, and U. von Zadow. Building interactive multi-touch surfaces. *Journal of Graphics, GPU, & Game Tools*, 14:35–55, 2009.

Table of Contents

List of Figures

List of Tables

List of Listings

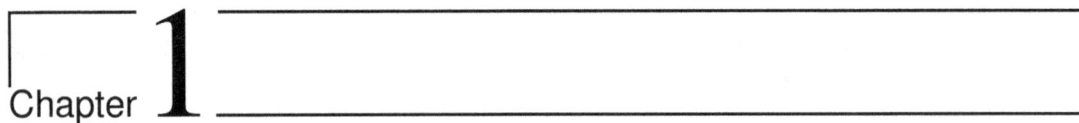

Introduction

Surface computing has emerged as a new type of graphical user interface (GUI) that appeals through its direct, expressive, and natural style of interaction, while providing a compelling platform for multiple simultaneous users. By turning passive screens into interactive displays, surface computing allows people to immediately interact with applications through direct finger touch. Figure 1.1(a) shows an example of multiple children jointly using an interactive table. Unlike traditional touch screens, interactive surfaces sense multiple contact points at the same time, and hence allow for expressive gestural input. Leaving traditional input devices like keyboards and mice behind, surface computing promotes rich and natural interaction with increased degrees of freedom. Input is no longer restricted to a single cursor but may comprise numerous contact points. At the same time, interactive surfaces facilitate co-located collaboration as they are equally accessible to multiple concurrent users. The unrestricted multi-touch input makes surface computing a compelling multi-user interface for natural and expressive interaction.

Despite the prevailing focus of surface computing on multi-user scenarios, typical surface systems cannot distinguish different users. They detect multiple contact points at the same time, but input remains anonymous. Figure 1.1(b) shows the system view of an input situation such as illustrated in Figure 1.1(a). From this view, assigning touches to individual users is challenging as touches look alike and their spatial layout does not allow for inferring corresponding users without ambiguity. Consequently, surface computing applications are unaware of different users and cannot distinguish their input.

Being aware of different users broadens interaction and application possibilities for surface computing. For instance, on the basic level of touch input, user identification helps to correctly interpret multi-finger, multi-hand, or multi-user gestures, which otherwise suffers from ambiguities. On the application level, customizing functionalities or the appearance of interface elements as a function of the user requires prior identification as well. For instance, to restrict access to critical operations to authorized personnel, the initiating user has to be known. Likewise, touches need to be associated to individual users in order to create an audit trail for security-sensitive environments.

In this thesis, we aim at both contributing *instantaneous user identification* methods and at exploring the design space of *personalized interaction* on shared surfaces. This serves the dual goal of enabling and exploiting user-awareness in surface computing, as detailed in the following:

(a) Multi-user interaction on the surface*   (b) Possible system view of the same scene

Figure 1.1:   Surface computing facilitates expressive multi-touch, multi-user interaction. Assigning touches to individual users, however, is challenging as touches look alike.

*Application developed by DOKLAB, photo © 2010 by Museum Rotterdam

- *Instantaneous user identification* allows users do identify immediately (i.e., integrated with a touch interaction, without the need for additional steps) and directly on the surface (i.e., the touch location determines the spatial scope of identification). This is to minimize workflow interruptions, while preserving the directness of typical surface interaction.

- *Personalized interactions* are enabled by instantaneous identification. They are individually tailored to a particular user without impeding others who simultaneously share the same interface.

To this end, we contribute three novel methods for instantaneous user identification on interactive surfaces—IdWristbands, HandsDown, and PhoneTouch. Based on fully functional prototype systems, we demonstrate their feasibility for the task at hand, and propose a wide range of novel interaction techniques to explore the design space of personalized interaction. This combination of introducing new enabling methods and exploring the surrounding interaction space illustrates benefits and deepens the understanding of user-awareness for surface computing.

1.1 Background

Surface computing allows for expressive and natural direct-touch interaction with visual content. Interactive surfaces are devices that fuse input and output spaces; their display doubles as input device. Instead of using indirect pointers, such as provided by a computer mouse in conventional interfaces, users manipulate a GUI directly by touching it with multiple fingers at the same time. In analogy to real-world environments, all that a user sees on the display can be directly touched and manipulated, without the previous restriction to a single point of contact. This physical metaphor of surface computing results in low learning curves and leads to a more immediate and expressive way of interaction compared to traditional desktop computing.

The immediate and unrestricted access to the user interface makes interactive surfaces a desirable platform for co-located collaboration. Unlike the small displays of single-user touch-enabled devices (e.g., smart phones or tablets), the larger displays of interactive surfaces lend themselves to multi-user scenarios. As in traditional meetings around a physical table, users can jointly interact with the shared interface—but can now fuse virtual and real-world interactions. This equal interaction opportunity democratizes access to the computer system.

(a) Gaming: Poker surface [144]

(b) Complementing museum exhibitions [64]

(c) Surface as musical instrument [75]

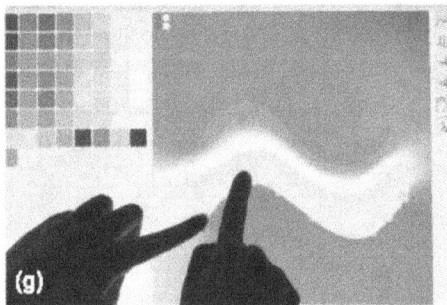

(d) Creative multi-touch design [153]

Figure 1.2: Examples of surface computing applications

In contrast to traditional touch screens, surface computing promotes continuous, unrestricted, rich, and expressive interaction through multi-touch input. Being able to simultaneously use multiple fingers, hands, or both substantially increases the available degrees of freedom and thus facilitates expressive direct manipulation. Instead of a single cursor, multiple points of contacts are at the users' disposal. For example, in a graphics editor as shown in Figure 1.2(d), it is straightforward to adjust various points on a curve at the same time, using multiple fingers. Depending on the surface size, interactions do not only involve finger but may also extend to hand and arm movements, thus addressing different muscle groups. Moreover, touch input is not restricted to just finger contacts. In fact, interactive surfaces can react naturally to arbitrary touch input, such as swiping across multiple sliders with the back of a hand for simultaneous adjustment [29].

Interactive surfaces lend themselves to a multitude of application domains, thereby playing out their strengths in co-located multi-user settings (Figure 1.2). For instance in the area of gaming, Poker surface, a digital version of the popular card game, uses a multi-touch table as public space in combination with mobile phones to display the cards in hand [144]. Supporting walk-up scenarios and large-scale visualizations, interactive surfaces are a compelling platform for exhibits such as found in museums (e.g., [64]). In the area of education, surface computing facilitates collaborative learning in the classroom (e.g., [126]). Also the creative domain benefits from expressive multi-touch input, for example by using an interactive table as musical instrument for live performances [75], or for efficiently designing 2D vector graphics [153]. As suggested by these examples, the multi-touch input and large display size makes surface computing a compelling choice for multi-user applications that benefit from unrestricted and expressive input.

1.2 Problem Space

User identification for interactive surfaces poses new challenges compared to identification for traditional single-user or previous co-located multi-user systems. Surface computing follows a new interaction paradigm that promotes simultaneous collaboration of multiple users through direct access to a single, shared interface. Never has there been a platform that provided an easier and more equal access to GUIs for multiple concurrent users. On the system side, however, such freedom complicates keeping track of different users.

Considering single-user devices in contrast (e.g., desktops, laptops, tablets, or mobile phones), user identification is seldom an issue. Although such devices support multiple users by means of individual user profiles, they are rarely used by more than one person at a time. Typically, users log in at the beginning of a session, for example by providing a password or pin (Figure 1.3(a)). All subsequent input is interpreted in the context of the current user, and any action associated to the corresponding profile, for example to authorize access to personal data. Depending on the usage scenario and its security requirements, an explicit authentication may not even be desired. For instance, many users prefer a shared profile for their family computers [42], which often loads automatically at startup without someone's help.

(a) Mobile device login   (b) SDG with multiple mice [116]   (c) Multi-touch surface [64]

Figure 1.3: Identifying users in different scenarios: (a) From single-user login, (b) to individual input devices, (c) to unrestricted direct-touch input.

In comparison, conventional single display groupware (SDG), a general class of multi-user systems for simultaneous co-located collaboration, provides individual input devices for each user while sharing a single display (see section 2.1). In doing so, it is straightforward to assign actions to their originator, as each input event is delivered via a dedicated channel that can be registered to a user in advance (Figure 1.3(b)). By virtue of individual and identifiable input devices, such systems are inherently aware of different users and can treat their input appropriately (e.g., by restricting access to particular controls to authorized users). The prevailing style of multi-touch interaction in surface computing, however, results in highly interwoven streams of indistinguishable input from different users as they interact directly with the shared interface at the same time

(Figure 1.3(c))—thus introducing specific challenges for user identification on interactive surfaces.

Carrying over traditional methods of user identification is typically not desirable; surface computing calls for new means of identification that are closely integrated with purposeful touch interaction. In particular, traditional methods are designed with different usage scenarios in mind. For instance, session-based logins, while appropriate for single-user devices, oppose the concept of simultaneous and instantaneous access to a shared interface. First, all input within the entire surface, or sub-areas thereof, are associated to a single user, thus making such areas unusable for others. Secondly, conventional identification credentials (e.g., passwords or pins) are difficult to enter on a large interactive display where bystanders can easily observe any input. Note that there has been isolated work on making such methods suitable for surface use [79]. They remain, however, interruptive as they involve separate and time-consuming steps for identification and hence hold up the general workflow.

In contrast, successful identification methods for multi-user scenarios in surface computing need to integrate identification and purposeful interaction without restricting the prevailing interaction style. Consider the following example application scenarios, which illustrate advantages of instantaneous and direct user identification:

- *Access Control.* In security-sensitive applications, such as emergency response systems for disaster recovery, a user's level of authority typically determines the range of functionalities that are accessible. As this authorization level varies with different roles, not all team members must be able to manipulate all data alike. Using an interactive surface, however, all interface elements are initially accessible without restrictions. To safeguard critical functions without impeding the fluid interaction style of direct-touch, user identification for surface computing has to be instantaneous and embedded in the actual interaction. At the same time, instantaneous identification allows for creating audit trails that document interactions of individual users.

- *Personal Data.* In collaborative tasks, users typically bring in personal data to support the teamwork. For example, to jointly prepare a presentation, different team members may contribute material that they have individually prepared in advance. Using an interactive surface to facilitate such meetings, participants require effortless and secure access to their personal files. Likewise, they often wish to take with them material that has been created as outcome of a group activity. Both cases benefit from a fluid user identification approach that allows users to instantly retrieve and store personal data without interrupting their workflows.

- *Input Sequences.* Independent input sequences, a common paradigm in direct manipulation interfaces, consist of first selecting a tool or parameter to then apply it in a second step. For example, in a drawing application, users initially select a color to then draw using the chosen color. Such a behavior mirrors our experiences with physical environments. To implement independent input sequences for multi-user scenarios in surface computing, however, applications need to instantly link individual touch input to users. Otherwise, they cannot keep track of parameter selections and thus fail at producing the expected result, such as drawing with the previously selected color.

Instantaneous user identification for surface computing allows users to immediately identify on interactive surfaces, integrated with typical multi-touch input to minimize workflow interruptions compared to knowledge-based approaches (e.g., [79]). Identification may be either transparent in that any touch interaction is implicitly associated to a user, or may be explicit but immediately available on-demand. In either case, instantaneous user identification implies an identification scope that is limited in both time and space. Unlike traditional session-based login mechanisms, it takes place in the context of individual interactions. Therefore, it enables personalized interaction, that is interaction tailored to a particular user. By exploiting associated information, for instance individual preferences, applications can customize their response in the context of the interacting user—in presence of other users who are simultaneously active on the same interface.

1.3 Contributions

This thesis makes several original contributions to the area of human-computer interaction (HCI). It advances the state-of-the-art of user identification on interactive surfaces and contributes to a deeper understanding of personalized interaction for surface computing. Our work centers around the three identification methods that we propose: IdWristbands, HandsDown, and PhoneTouch.

We chose these identification methods guided by the typical classification of authentication factors, which are grouped into three categories: knowledge-based, ownership- or object-based, and inherence- or identity-based factors [111]. We do not consider knowledge-based methods as they require users to recall memorized information in order to provide it to the system, which interrupts the flow of ongoing interaction (e.g., by entering a password) and thus contradicts our goal of instantaneous identification. We therefore focus on the remaining two factors: HandsDown is an inherence-based method and relies on something users are, while both IdWristbands and PhoneTouch are ownership-based methods and rely on something users have.

We demonstrate the suitability of all three methods for instantaneous user identification and exploit them for realizing concrete user-aware interaction techniques to explore the design space of personalized interaction. Our contributions are summarized as follows:

1. Enabling instantaneous user identification

   (a) Design and implementation of three novel methods for instantaneous user identification on interactive surfaces

       i. *IdWristbands* are wrist-worn bracelets that continuously emit infrared identifiers to identify finger touch input of the same hand.

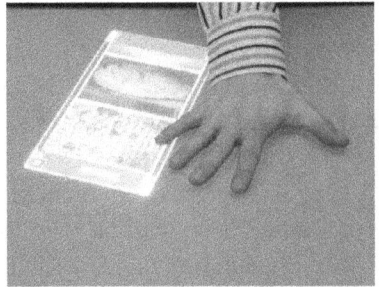

ii. *HandsDown* is a biometric method based on hand-contour analysis that allows users to directly identify by placing a hand on the surface.

iii. *PhoneTouch* uses mobile devices as proxies for their users by means of stylus-like direct-touch interaction.

    (b) Demonstration of feasibility and assessment of identification performance through fully-functional prototypes and evaluation of the proposed methods

2. Exploration of personalized interaction

    (a) Framing of the personalized interaction concept with respect to uses of and immediate access to personal information

    (b) Conceptual and systematic exploration of the design spaces of the three proposed enabling methods, comprising an in-depth analysis of input and output characteristics of HandsDown and PhoneTouch

    (c) Design and implementation of a wide range of novel interaction techniques for HandsDown and PhoneTouch to populate the design space and illustrate benefits of personalized interaction

3. Evaluation of user experience

    (a) Introduction of personal clipboards for surface computing to illustrate benefits of instantaneous user identification and personalized interaction

    (b) Demonstration of IdWristbands, HandsDown, and PhoneTouch as suitable methods for personalized interaction and qualitative analysis of interaction particularities

In addition to these three major contributions, we present practical guidelines for designing and building interactive surface systems in the appendix. Such systems are a prerequisite for undertaking this research, but the resulting report stands as a minor contribution on its own. It provides detailed information for researchers and practitioners alike who wish to build their own devices for surface computing.

1.4 Methodology

As the problem space spans multiple levels, from system-level enabling methods to application-level integration, so does our methodology. We take a multi-faceted approach to this research that comprises prototyping, design space exploration, interaction design, and laboratory-based, empirical evaluation, following the course outlined in Figure 1.4.

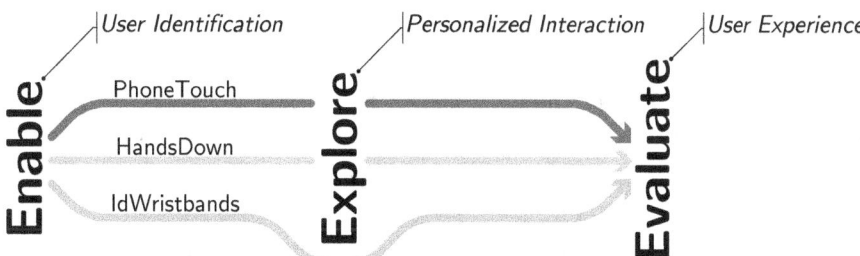

Figure 1.4:   Thesis course and methodology

Enable.   To develop, test, and refine novel user identification methods, we implemented several fully functional prototype systems. This combined effort of building new hardware devices and devising corresponding software concepts allowed for demonstrating the feasibility of IdWristbands, HandsDown, and PhoneTouch. For each method, we ran a user study to access the corresponding identification performance. At the same time, the resulting proof-of-concept systems served as underlying platform for explorations on the interaction and application level.

Explore.   Exploring the design space of personalized interaction comprises both conceptual analysis as well as demonstration of concrete example techniques. On a conceptual level, we systematically analyzed interaction characteristics as well as input and output spaces of IdWristbands, HandsDown, and PhoneTouch. Informed by these analysis, we designed a wide range of novel user-aware interaction techniques based on HandsDown and PhoneTouch, thereby populating the design space of personalized interaction with concrete examples. To investigate benefits of personalized interaction, we implemented these techniques as fully-functional interface prototypes. Further, we continuously gathered informal user feedback to test our ideas and inform design iterations.

Evaluate.   To compare and evaluate IdWristbands, HandsDown, and PhoneTouch as enabling methods for personalized interaction, we conducted a formal laboratory experiment. Participants in groups of two applied each method to the same task, consisting of individual copy-and-paste activities with personal clipboards on a shared surface. We performed an in-depth analysis to assess qualitative differences in using the three methods for personalized interaction, which was based on observations (simultaneous and post-hoc using video recordings) as well as on user feedback (gathered through questionnaires and open-ended interviews).

1.5 Thesis Roadmap

The just outlined thesis course and methodology maps to chapters as follows:

Chapter 2: *Related Work* examines surface computing in the context of groupware to highlight benefits and challenges of user identification. We also provide an overview of technologies for interactive surfaces with a focus on multi-touch detection. Finally, we review and contrast existing methods of user identification for surface computing.

Chapter 3: *Enabling User Identification* describes the functional principles, implementation, and evaluation of IdWristbands, HandsDown, and PhoneTouch, and demonstrates how they enable instantaneous user identification on interactive surfaces. This chapter covers issues on the level of touch detection and system implementation. We further compare key characteristics of the proposed methods. Related publications: [1, 3, 4, 7, 8, 10].

Chapter 4: *Exploring Personalized Interaction* investigates the design space of personalized interaction on the basis of the just proposed user identification methods. We frame the concept of personalized interaction before analyzing input and output characteristics of HandsDown and PhoneTouch. The main contribution of this chapter lies in the wide range of novel user-aware interaction techniques that populate the personalized interaction design space. Related publications: [3, 4, 5, 9, 11].

Chapter 5: *Evaluating User Experience* contributes an in-depth qualitative analysis of personalized interaction based on IdWristbands, HandsDown, and PhoneTouch. In a laboratory experiment, we compare these three methods using personal clipboards for shared surfaces, a novel user-aware interaction technique, to gather insights on particularities of identified interaction.

Chapter 6: *Conclusions* summarizes the contributions of this work from different viewpoints. We further discuss promising future research directions.

Appendix A: *Prototype Platform* contains practical guidelines for building interactive surface devices on the system level. In particular, we describe and illustrate the design and implementation of three interactive tables that serve as flexible research platform for exploring instantaneous user identification and personalized interaction. Related publications: [2, 12, 13].

Appendix B: *Supplementary Material* contains questionnaires used to gather feedback for the various studies.

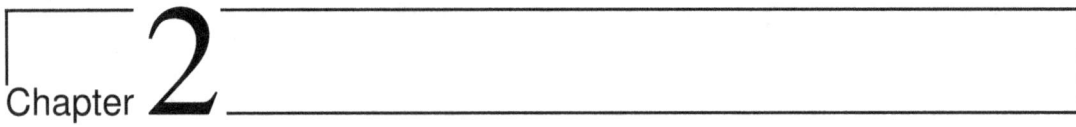

Chapter 2

Related Work

Unlike conventional single display groupware (SDG), surface computing is based on a single shared input channel for direct-touch interactions. Such joint input poses new challenges for identifying concurrent users in order to facilitate personalized interaction. We set out to examine surface computing in the context of previous systems for co-located collaboration and highlight the impact of changing input paradigms on user identification. As input sensing and user identification are closely interleaved on interactive surfaces, we analyze common touch detetection techniques with a focus on vision-based approaches. Finally, we review existing methods for user-awareness on interactive surfaces and compare their characteristics.

2.1 New Challenges for Surface Computing

Interactive surfaces facilitate co-located collaboration in the tradition of groupware. Ellis et al. define groupware as "computer-based systems that support groups of people engaged in a common task (or goal) and that provide an interface to a shared environment" [43]. Such systems are typically viewed along the dimensions of time (synchronous or asynchronous) and space (same or different place), resulting in four categories (Figure 2.1). Within the category "same time—same place", Stewart et. al position single display groupware (SDG) as a specific type of groupware, which they define as "computer programs that enable co-present users to collaborate via a shared computer with a single shared display and simultaneous use of multiple input devices" [148]. According to Stewart et al., sharing a single display facilitates interaction that requires simultaneous input from multiple users, enriches existing computer-supported collaboration by making it more efficient and enjoyable, and encourages peer-learning as well as peer-teaching. As surface computing and SDG share most characteristics, we consider surface computing a specific type of SDG, which is in accordance with related work (e.g., [36, 103]). Instead of using "multiple input devices", however, surface computing is based on a single input channel.

Before the introduction of surface computing, user identification was successfully applied to SDG applications, facilitating various interaction concepts. The Multi-Device Multi-User Multi-Editor (MMM), an early SDG system, is aware of different users. It supports parallel input without interference (e.g., keeping track of independent tool

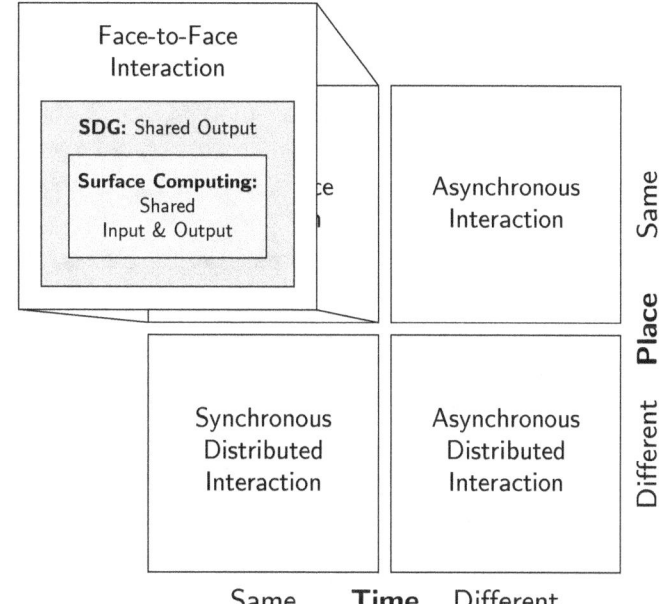

Figure 2.1: "Same time—same place" classification of surface computing as type of SDG [148] in the general groupware framework introduced by Ellis et al. [43].

selections), individual feedback (Figure 2.2(a)), and per-user settings [21]. Another SDG system, Pebbles, allows several users to work together using individual handheld devices for input on a shared display [109]. In the drawing application shown in Figure 2.2(b), user identification is indispensable to enable simultaneous drawing in different modes as well as a per-user undo function. As last example, Dynamo is designed to support occasional meetings in unfamiliar public spaces [72]. It provides personal palettes and workspaces on a shared display (Figure 2.2(c)).

These examples illustrate the relevance of user-awareness for many widespread and familiar direct manipulation concepts. Particularly independent interaction sequences, which consist of first selecting or parameterizing a tool (e.g., a drawing color) for later application, require systems to preserve a per-user state. Beyond that, iDWidgets, a framework for personalized interface components, sees user identification as a key requirement for a wide range of compelling interaction concepts [133]. This framework illustrates benefits of user-awareness along the four dimensions: function (i.e., same appearance but different behavior for different users), content (i.e., different content for different users), appearance (i.e., different appearance for different users), and group input (i.e., combining input from multiple users). For instance, a button can execute different commands depending on the user, or an application can personalize photo captions (e.g., a caption reads "dad" only for the person whose father is shown [134]).

As a matter of fact, such concepts are straightforward to implement for single-user interfaces, but also traditional SDG readily provide the necessary information. Since each input device (e.g., mice, keyboards, or—in case of Pebbles—personal digital assistants (PDAs)) uses a dedicated communication channel, applications can directly associate input events to individual users; therefore, user-awareness is taken for granted. Typically, works concerned with user identification for SDG focus on facilitating application development.

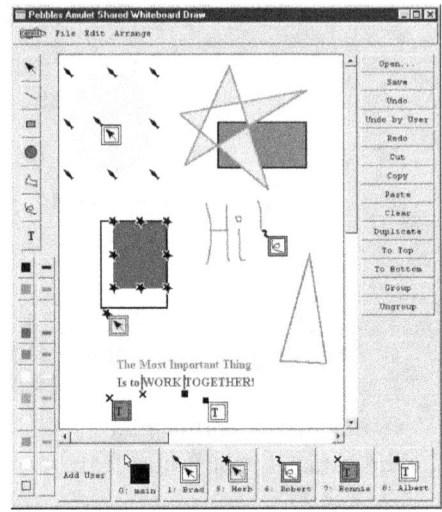

(a) Individual feedback of the MMM: Selections are marked by the users' color (colorized ex post for clarity) [21].

(b) Early version of the PebblesDraw user interface: Users can interact independently; each user is assigned a shape to mark both cursor and selection [109].

(c) Access control to personal workspaces in Dynamo [72]

Figure 2.2: Early applications of user identification in SDG

For example, MID, a Java-based package, enables addressing multiple input devices on a single computer by adding device identifiers as input event parameter [69]. Similarly, the SDGToolkit for rapid prototyping manages multiple mice and keyboards to associate input events with a unique source identifier [157]. Beyond that, it provides multi-user-aware controls to implement behavior that depends on the interacting user.

The challenge for surface computing, however, lies in associating input events to different users in the first place. As shown in Figure 2.3(a), traditional SDG employ individual devices and thus provide private input channels, whereas users of interactive surfaces share a single input space (Figure 2.3(b)). After prior registration, device identifiers in conventional systems directly correspond to users, and applications can associate input events without difficulties (unless users change their devices). Researchers proposed hybrid approaches for surface computing [59], which integrate conventional input devices (i.e., mice and keyboards), but touch input remains anonymous in general. While touching with bare fingers allows for rich interaction and equal interface access, such unrestricted input presents new challenges for user identification.

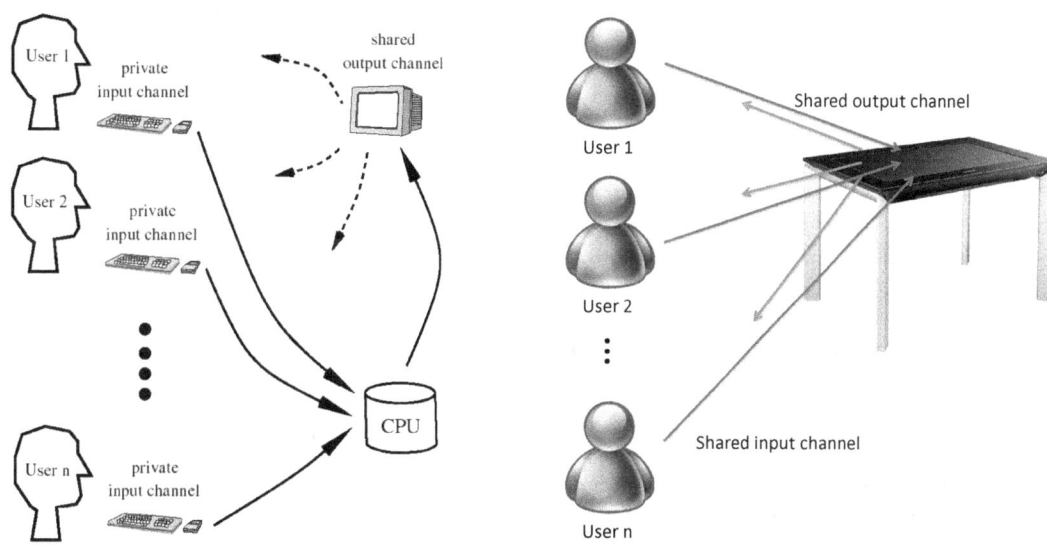

(a) Traditional SDG combine multiple input devices with a single shared display [148].

(b) Users of interactive surfaces share both input and output space.

Figure 2.3:   Input and output channels in traditional SDG and surface computing

User identification is a prerequisite for a wide range of compelling interactions on interactive surfaces. For example, it can facilitate document sharing and spontaneous transfer of access privileges [127]. As shown in Figure 2.4, handing over a document is seamlessly integrated into the workflow and does not impede fluid interaction, once users and their input are identified.

2.2 Enabling Techniques

User identification on interactive surfaces is inseparably connected to touch detection. We therefore set out to review enabling techniques for surface computing with a focus on multi-touch sensing. This section provides the necessary technical background for both

Figure 2.4: The "release" technique facilitates document sharing on interactive surfaces: Identifying users is required to transfer access privileges [127].

the discussion of existing methods for user identification in section 2.3 as well as for the novel methods that we introduce in Chapter 3.

The first system capable of detecting multiple independent touches for human input, the Flexible Machine Interface [91], was introduced in 1982 [136, p. 8]. From there on, various approaches and systems of different form factors using different touch sensing techniques have emerged in research and as commercial products [27]. In the following, we emphasize vision-based touch detection, a family of techniques widely used especially for large interactive surfaces. Vision-based techniques provide rich input information, readily scale to large displays, and are cheap as well as easy to implement [12]. We complete our review of input sensing for surface computing by considering alternative touch detection techniques (i.e., not based on computer vision). Finally, we highlight novel techniques for delivering individual output on a shared surface, which are of particular interest to the design space of user-aware interfaces.

2.2.1 Vision-Based Touch Detection

Vision-based input detection provides rich information and has therefore attracted researchers early on. VIDEOPLACE, introduced in 1985, is an example for camera-based interaction tracking [83]. In addition to merging live silhouettes of the user with computer-generated content, the system allows for directly interacting with virtual objects through movement in real-time (Figure 2.5). For example, users can point and perform selections with their bare hands and fingers. VIDEOPLACE does not detect direct-touch contacts with a surface, but allows for interaction in the air from a distance with the users' silhouettes as visual reference. In contrast, HoloWall, a wall-sized vertical display, detects the users' whole body, physical objects, and direct finger touch interaction, using an infrared camera and illumination mounted behind the screen [89]. DigitalDesk and EnhancedDesk use horizontal displays and are thus more similar to current interactive tabletop setups. DigitalDesk projects electronic documents and applications onto a physical desk, allowing for interactions with fingers and pens [164]. A video camera tracks hands from above while an additional microphone detects taps (Figure 2.6(a)). Using a similar configuration, the EnhancedDesk supports improved realtime tracking of fingers and hands using an infrared camera and template-based matching [82].

Vision-based systems also facilitate tracking of tangible objects, typically by using visual markers, which was initially explored independent from finger touch detection. For example, the metaDESK, an interactive back-projected tabletop, tracks tangible objects with an integrated camera and infrared illumination, but does not allow for finger touch input [158]. Likewise limited to marker tracking, the ARToolkit is targeted at both

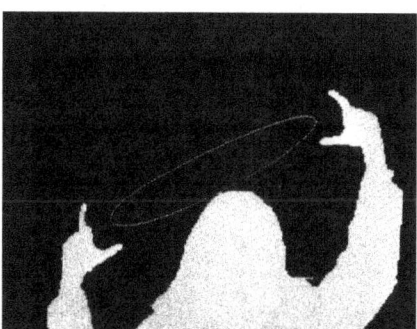

Figure 2.5: VIDEOPLACE: Rendering live silhouettes for direct interaction with digital content, such as manipulating four control points simultaneously to change a shape [83].

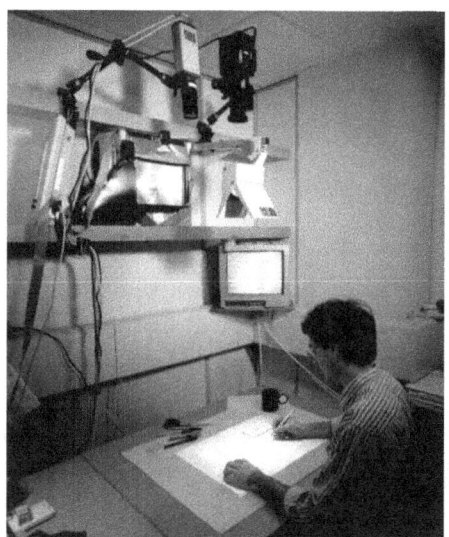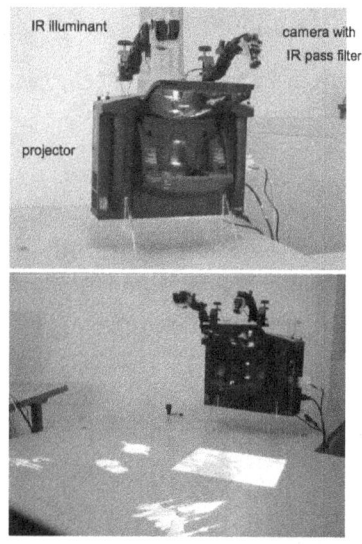

(a) The DigitalDesk uses a video camera to track hands from above and a microphone to detect taps [164].

(b) PlayAnywhere turns any existing table into an interactive surface [165].

Figure 2.6: Two vision-based interactive surface systems

tangible user interfaces and augmented reality, using a ceiling-mounted camera above a tabletop [78]. Going beyond a single display, augmented surfaces integrate portable computers, equipped with visual markers, into spatially continuous workspaces that span across multiple table and wall displays [124]. Here, all interaction relies on the input devices (e.g., touchpad or mouse) of the portable computers (e.g., hyperdragging to transfer information directly in between computers). In contrast, reacTIVision, an open-source computer-vision framework, combines tangibles with touch input by tracking both visual markers and fingers simultaneously on the same surface [76].

Current vision-based interactive surfaces use cameras or other photosensors that operate in the infrared spectrum (for increased robustness in presence of changing environmental light) in conjunction with image processing for touch detection. Typically, such systems consist of a dedicated surface for both detecting input and presenting output. PlayAnywhere (Figure 2.6(b)), a portable and self-contained system, is an exception however, as it can turn any existing table into an interactive surface [165].

To track fingers and other objects on the software side, the provided images are processed in a tracking pipeline, which typically starts with preprocessing steps to remove noise, to mitigate lens distortion, and to increase contrast (e.g., by applying a binary threshold). This is followed by extracting blobs that correspond to touches (e.g., using a connected components algorithm) which are then correlated over time (i.e., corresponding blobs in subsequent frames are associated to enable continuous tracking).

In the following, we review techniques for vision-based touch detection, grouped by general approach: first, techniques using cameras that point at the surface from behind or above (usually in conjunction with a projector, which makes such systems rather bulky), secondly, visual hull techniques (using cameras or photosensors from the side), and thirdly, techniques based on photosensors integrated with flat-panel displays. In addition, we briefly discuss sensing techniques that reach beyond the two-dimensional surface plane.

External Camera Techniques

FTIR. The introduction of frustrated total internal reflection (FTIR) for multi-touch sensing has pushed the prevalence of vision-based surfaces [52]. Although previously used in biometric finger print scanners, the application of FTIR to interactive surfaces was new, and facilitated constructions of large surfaces at low costs.

In an FTIR setup, a series of infrared light-emitting diodes (LED) are mounted along the edges of a transparent acrylic sheet, injecting light into the surface (Figure 2.7(a)). As air has a lower index of refraction than acrylic, and as the angle of incidence is sufficiently small, the light experiences total internal reflection. If a user touches the surface, however, the finger frustrates the total internal reflection. Therefore, light can escape and is reflected by the finger. An infrared-sensitive camera pointed at the surface from behind clearly sees this reflection as a bright dot, and makes extraction by basic computer-vision algorithms straightforward. To allow for projecting images onto the transparent acrylic sheet, a diffusing back-projection film is added. Typically, a compliant layer is placed between acrylic and projection layer, made of a soft and transparent material (e.g., silicone or latex), to increase the robustness of finger tracking [13]. Inverted FTIR is a variation that places the camera in front of the surface and hence allows for using flat-panel displays [40].

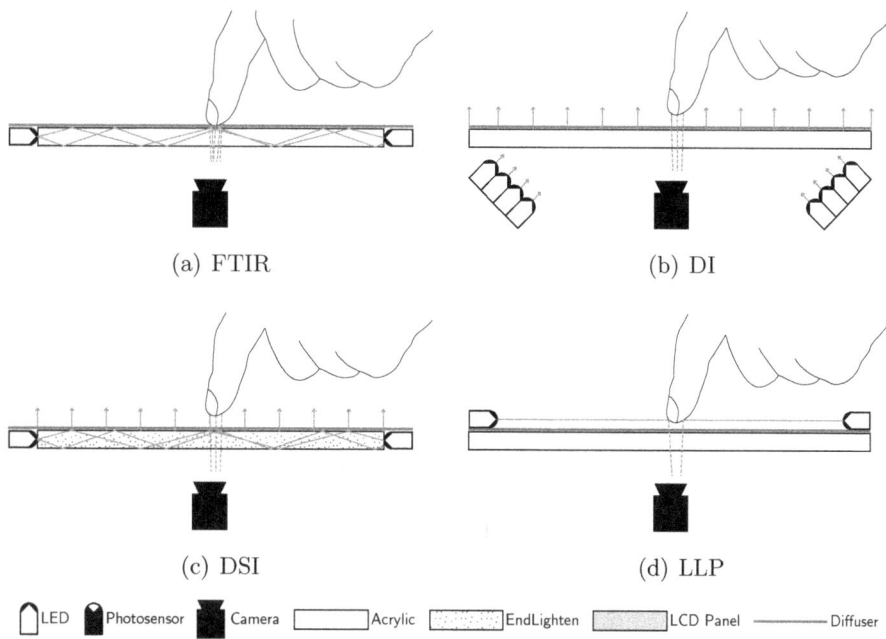

Figure 2.7:   External camera techniques

DI and DSI. In contrast to FTIR, diffused illumination (DI) systems use infrared illumination from behind the surface (Figure 2.7(b)). The surface is covered with a diffusing layer to blur and conceal objects at a distance and to provide a projection background at the same time. Fingers and objects in close proximity to the surface reflect the light and thus become detectable for a camera mounted on the opposite side. Microsoft's Surface 1.0 platform is a prominent example of a DI system [93]. Diffused screen illumination (DSI), a variation of DI, injects light through the edges (similar to FTIR), but uses EndLighten acrylic [46]. This special type of acrylic contains small reflective particles that diffuse the light and emit it uniformly across the entire surface (Figure 2.7(c)). DSI allows for a simpler system setup compared to DI as no distant light sources are required.

In contrast to FTIR, both DI and DSI enable the detection of arbitrary objects (i.e., their shapes and surface properties), for example to track visual markers of tangibles, and can sense hovering interactions in the space above a surface. On the other hand, FTIR enables more robust finger tracking due to a higher contrast between touches and the surrounding surface area.

LLP. Systems based on the laser light plane (LLP) technique span a thin plane of infrared light as close to the surface as possible (Figure 2.7(d)). Objects or fingers intersecting this plane reflect light and are seen by the camera used for detection. Z-touch extends this concept to detect three-dimensional interaction by using multiple stacked light planes synchronized with a high-speed camera, thus enabling basic depth sensing [154].

Vision-Hull Techniques

Corner Cameras. Positioning two or more cameras in the corners of a surface provides different perspectives and allows for reconstructing the input space for touch detection (Figure 2.8(a)). In general, such systems require an additional camera for each additional touch point to be detected simultaneously. For example, DViT, a commercial solution by Smart Technologies, Inc., uses four cameras and can hence track four touch points at the same time [146].

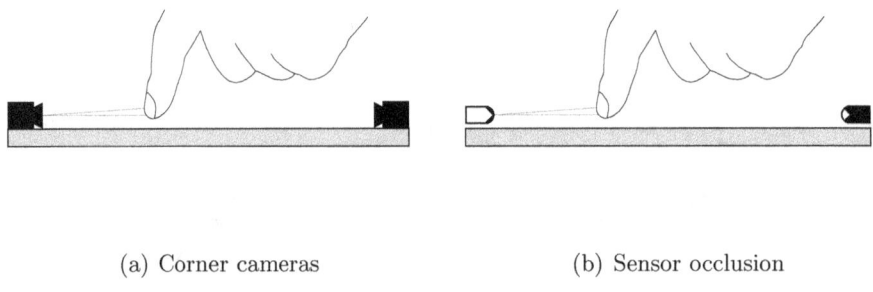

(a) Corner cameras   (b) Sensor occlusion

Figure 2.8:   Vision-hull techniques

Sensor Occlusion. Instead of using a single light source and few cameras, techniques based on sensor occlusion surround the surface with an array of both light sources and sensors (Figure 2.8(b)). Light sources are switched on one at a time, thus providing independent perspectives for the sensors in range. For example, ZeroTouch uses modulated infrared light sensors to detect up to 30 touch points simultaneously [99]

Integrated Techniques

ThinSight. ThinSight combines the advantages of rich input with a compact and thin form factor [65]. Retro-reflective optosensors that consist of both infrared light emitter and detector are arranged in a two-dimensional grid behind a regular liquid crystal display (LCD) panel (Figure 2.9(a)). Similar to DI, those objects that come close to the screen reflect more infrared light. The intensities measured by the different sensors are combined into a single image for further processing.

PixelSense. The Samsung SUR40 device for Microsoft's Surface 2.0 platform, a commercial interactive surface, uses PixelSense for touch detection [94]. PixelSense is similar to ThinSight, but fully integrates infrared backlight and sensors with the LCD panel (Figure 2.9(b)).

FLATIR. FLATIR uses an array of infrared sensors mounted behind an LCD panel [66]. Unlike ThinSight, the light source is positioned in front of the panel, using an edge-lit acrylic sheet to exploit the FTIR effect (Figure 2.9(c)).

Techniques for Sensing Beyond the Plane

By adding a depth camera, vision-based systems enable precise manipulations also in the space above the surface, for example to manipulate 3D content [61]. SecondLight follows

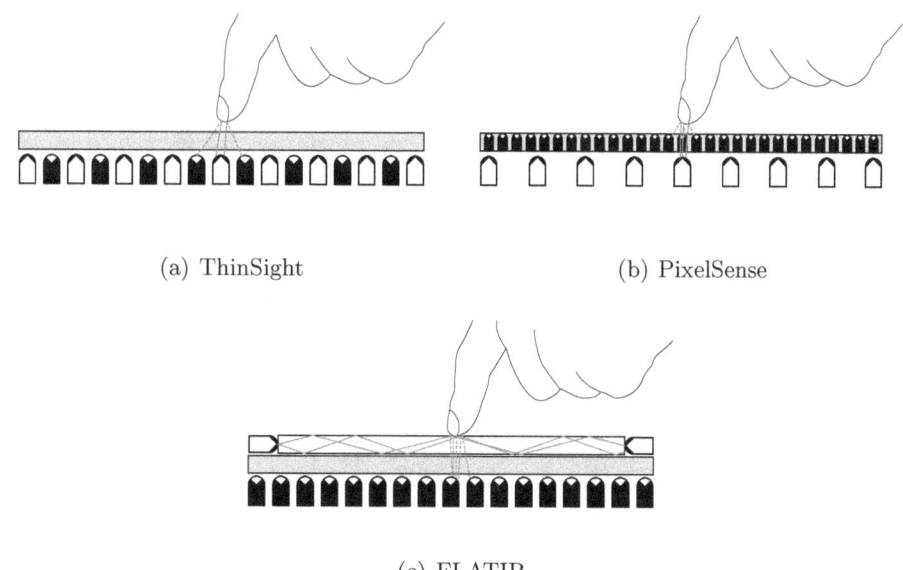

(a) ThinSight   (b) PixelSense

(c) FLATIR

Figure 2.9:   Integrated techniques

a different approach to extend interaction sensing beyond the surface [73]. Electronically controlled, the screen switches between clear and diffused states at high speeds. Two synchronized cameras detect both touch input on the surface (diffuse) and interactions in the space above (clear). On the output side, two equally synchronized projectors can simultaneously display content directly on the screen (diffuse) and on objects located on top of it (clear). Expanding the interaction space even further, LightSpace uses multiple depth cameras and projectors to turn an entire room into an interactive space [166]. This allows for mid-air interaction and using arbitrary surfaces—including the user's body— as interactive displays. Sharing a similar goal, OmniTouch is a wearable system that combines a shoulder-worn depth camera and projector to enable multi-touch interaction on everyday surfaces [55].

2.2.2   Miscellaneous Touch Detection

In the following, we provide a brief overview of alternative touch detection techniques, which do not use optical tracking. Such techniques are currently integrated mainly into single-user consumer devices.

Resistance-Based Techniques

Resistive touch screens are generally durable and low cost [39]. Compared to other sensing techniques, they require users to apply more pressure for activation, but directly allow for non-finger interaction with arbitrary objects (e.g., pens). Resistive touch screens consist of two transparent layers coated with electrically conductive materials (e.g., indium tin oxide), which are separated by invisible spacers. A glass or acrylic panel serves as insulating back layer. The touch-screen controller applies voltage to one and reads it from the other conductive layer, alternating between the two in order to determine the X and Y coordinates of a touch.

Capacitive-Based Techniques

Capacitive-based techniques can detect fingers or other conductive and grounded objects, but are more difficult to manufacture and integrate compared to vision-based techniques. The number of simultaneously detectable touches is limited by firmware or controller design or both. Two variations are commonly found as described in the following.

Surface Capacitance. Surface capacitive techniques use a conductive coating on one side of an insulating pane (e.g., glass) to set up an uniform electric field across the conductive layer. Touching with conductive objects transfers small amounts of charge from the electric field of the panel to the electric field of the touching object. The resulting different effective capacitance is measured by sensors in the corners, and a microprocessor interpolates the touch position.

Projected Capacitance. In comparison, projected capacitive techniques are more expensive, but facilitate multi-touch sensing and provide an increased mechanical resilience as they can be covered with non-conductive material for protection. Here, a grid of wires is laid out between two glass layers. For example, SmartSkin, a sensor architecture for interactive surfaces, uses copper wires as transmitter and receiver electrodes, laid out in a grid [122]. The vertical wires transmit a wave signal, which is received by the horizontal wires, as each crossing point acts as capacitor. Two independent microprocessors are used to generate and measure the signals. The measured amplitude decreases when a conductive and grounded object comes close to a wire crossing point as the object capacitively couples to the electrodes. By interpolating the received signals, the system cannot only determine two-dimensional locations of multiple objects, but can also estimate their distance from the surface. Further, a finer grid allows for sensing detailed object shapes.

Acoustic-Based Techniques

Using passive acoustic sensing, Paradiso et al. detect knocks on a glass window with four contact microphones in its corners [114]. The system locates hits using a time difference of arrival approach. By analyzing additional signal properties, it can also identify different types of knocks (e.g., knuckle knock versus metal tap). Similarly, both Harrison et al. [57] and Lopes et al. [85] identify various touch types, such as different parts of a human finger or a set of passive tools. Here, acoustic-based techniques take a supplementary role as they work in tandem with an independent touch detection already in place.

2.2.3 Personalized Output

In addition to multi-touch sensing, researches also looked into user-aware output techniques, which can present individual content to concurrent users. In this context, Shoemaker et al. coined the term Single Display Privacyware, describing systems that allow for private information to be shown in the context of a shared display [145]. The authors suggest that using private information may help to solve clutter-related problems and reduce some awareness information. The presented prototype system consists of a single monitor and two mice, using shutter glasses for providing private output to two simultaneous users.

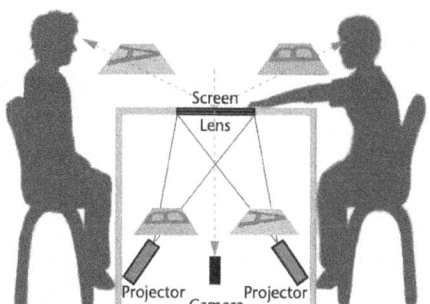

Figure 2.10: The Lumisight Table presents different information to individual users on the same surface [71].

Doing without additional wearable devices, Lumisight is an interactive table that presents individual information on the same surface to its users [88]. Here, four projectors provide different images, which is enabled by Lumisity, a film that is either transparent or translucent depending on the view angle (Figure 2.10). Also using Lumisity film, Tangible Private Spaces (TaPS) provide a more flexible solution for displaying private information that does not restrict a user's position around the surface [100]. TaPS, made of an acrylic sheet with the film on top, are continuously tracked by the system. Information displayed on the screen directly underneath a tangible is only visible from a specific viewing direction. By additionally using polarized light sources and modified LCD, PiVOT provides multiple collocated personalized views to individual users, while showing a shared view to all users [77].

2.3 Methods for User-Awareness

In this section, we set out to review related works concerned with user-awareness for surface computing. We first analyze methods that *differentiate* users before proceeding to methods that *identify* them. User-differentiation methods correlate touch input with distinct users (e.g., based on geometrical properties), thus making applications aware of multiple concurrent users regardless of their identity. Relating input to users over time, however, is not possible; a returning user's input is treated as unknown. In contrast, user identification methods associate touch input to specific users that have been identified based on some factor (e.g., an identification token). Consequently, a returning user is recognized by such methods.

Following the common terminology of authentication factors, we distinguish identification methods that are based on *ownership* (i.e., something a user possesses), *inherence* (i.e., something a user is or does), and *knowledge* (i.e., something a user knows). To further group similar methods, we introduce additional sub-categories (e.g., combining methods that are based on related sensing approaches). Figure 2.11 depicts this taxonomy. In analyzing related works, our focus lies on the sensing methods used to acquire identifying information, but we also discuss concepts for user-aware interactions where available.

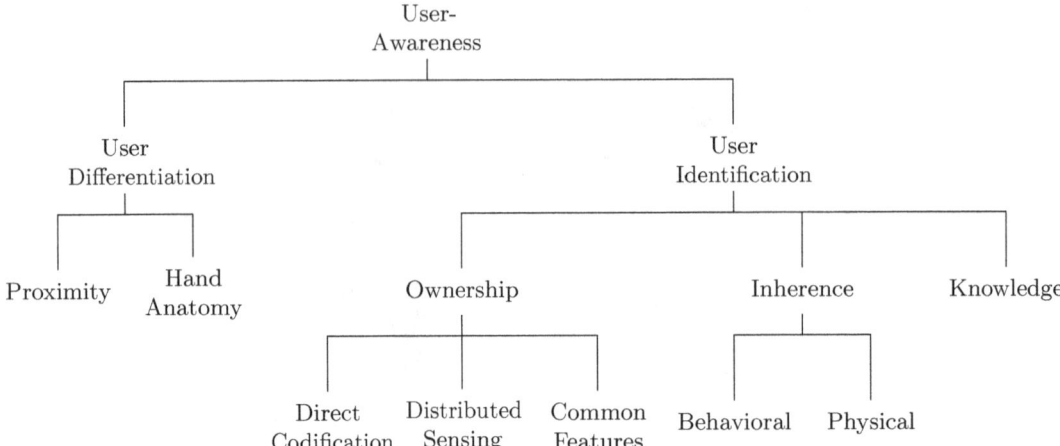

Figure 2.11:   Taxonomy of enabling methods for user-awareness on interactive surfaces

2.3.1 User Differentiation

User differentiation is a first step beyond isolated touch input. Being aware of different users allows to correctly interpret multi-touch input, for instance by differentiating between a multi-finger gesture from a single user and several independent gestures from multiple users. The users' actual identities, however, remain unknown; it is therefore not possible to personalize interactions nor to recognize returning users. Some methods, however, allow users to manually identify in a separate, independent step. In the following, we review related works grouped by the general approach they take to distinguish users.

Proximity

Proximity sensing is concerned with detecting the presence and location of users close to an interactive surface. Such methods vary in the type and number of employed sensors, and hence the resulting detection granularity (e.g., ranging from detecting a user's body around the table to detecting individual hands above the surface). Walther-Franks et al. add a set of infrared proximity sensors around the sides of an interactive tabletop [161]. This allows for detecting the presence and location of surrounding users, for example to provide individual toolboxes. Similarly, Klinkhammer et al. equip a custom-built interactive table with 96 infrared distance sensors to track users around the table and provide personal territories for a museum application [81]. These two methods do not facilitate implicit user differentiation of individual finger touches, but rely on providing user-specific proxy elements within the graphical user interface (GUI).

In contrast, Medusa, a proximity-aware tabletop based on Microsoft Surface, goes a step further by associating individual touch points to different users [15]. Its 138 infrared proximity sensors (Figure 2.12) are arranged to not only sense the users' physical location and distance around the table (using outward-facing sensors), but to also detect interaction taking place above the surface (using upward-facing sensors). Therefore, the system can track arms to distinguish left from right hands and to map users to touch points. This represents a mixed approach exploiting both proximity and hand anatomy (the latter being subject of the next section). Specific situations, however, such as crossing arms could lead to associating touches to the wrong user. Medusa extends user differentiation and allows users to log in by manually selecting their account from a list. Note that the actual user identification, however, is independent from proximity sensing. On the surface, users are represented by glowing orbs that follow them around the table. They can further use the orb to retrieve and store personal files. Logging out is explicit or happens after walking away.

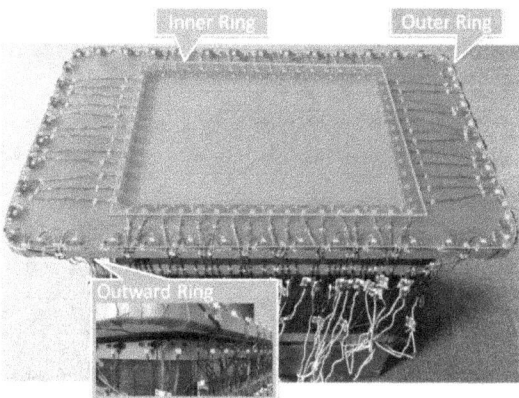

Figure 2.12:   Medusa is a proximity-aware tabletop based on Microsoft Surface augmented with 138 infrared proximity sensors [15].

Hand Anatomy

The following methods either detect hands above the surface or directly exploit finger touch characteristics to correlate input events based on known anatomical properties. Detecting hands allows for grouping finger touches, for example to distinguish between a single-handed two-finger gesture and a two-handed gesture, which uses a single finger per hand. Dohse et al. augment a rear projection touch table with an overhead camera to track hands in order to assign touches to users [38]. Interactive surfaces based on standard DI (which can see beyond the actual surface layer and hence detect interaction up to a certain level above the surface) also allow for deriving information about hovering hands and their orientation. For example, Walther-Franks et al. propose an empirical model and heuristics based on anatomical properties for real-time distinction of hands [160].

In contrast exclusively relying on finger touch characteristics, Dang et al. map fingers to their joined hand based on finger location and orientation with the goal to improve gesture recognition [34]. Similarly, Wang et al. infer higher-level information about hands and users from finger input alone [162]. Their algorithms determine if two fingers belong to the same hand and further estimate a user's position around the table, thereby providing a lightweight approach for distinguishing users. See Me, See You also facilitates user differentiation by exploiting finger location and orientation, but uses support vector machines (SVM), a machine learning approach, to predict user positions around an interactive table [170]. Murugapaan et al. use a depth camera to extract touches, hand postures, and corresponding users [106].

2.3.2 Ownership-Based Identification

Ownership-based identification methods use a token that holds the information to identify users. The large variety of methods in this category illustrate that such tokens can take various shapes. According to their detection strategy, we split ownership-based methods into thee sub-categories: *direct codification*, *distributed sensing*, and *common features*.

Direct Codification

Methods based on direct codification employ dedicated tokens, which are immediately detected to retrieve the contained identifying information. Such a token may be worn by the user or may present itself as a wired connection to the corresponding system.

Connected. Albeit different from typical tokens, connected identification methods also require users to be in possession of—or rather in connection with—a specific entity. The following examples use capacitive coupling to transmit a signal, carrying identifying information, through the users' body. Upon touching the surface, at the contact point between user and device, this signal is detected to recover the embedded identifier and to immediately associate individual touches to users.

DiamondTouch, an interactive tabletop, pioneered multi-user aware touch technologies [37]. During interaction, users have to be in constant contact with an individual receiver (e.g., integrated in a chair as shown in Figure 2.13(a)) to allow for capacitive coupling through the body: "When a user touches the table, a capacitively coupled circuit is completed. The circuit runs from the transmitter, through the touch point on the table surface, through the user to the user's receiver and back to the transmitter." Originally introduced as a small research prototype of $20\,\mathrm{cm} \times 20\,\mathrm{cm}$, Circle Twelve Inc., a company holding the exclusive licenses to the technology, now sells two commercial versions with surface areas up to $86\,\mathrm{cm} \times 65\,\mathrm{cm}$ [32]. DiamondTouch offers robust touch detection and user identification, even in presence of debris, but relies on front-projection. In addition, the number of concurrent users is limited to four, and they cannot move freely around the table to change positions. Using the same user identification principle as DiamondTouch but based on a LCD screen, a table for arcade games was recently exhibited [155]. Instead of using receivers integrated into the chairs, users have to touch one of the four electrodes located around the table while interacting.

On the software side, DiamondTouch's user identification has been regarded as a key feature for developing early prototypes for multi-user tabletop applications [101]. For example, cooperative gestures that integrate input from multiple users [102] or multi-user coordination policies [105] rely on this feature. On a toolkit level, DiamondSpin was developed to facilitate prototyping for multi-user surface applications with Diamond-Touch [143], for example used by UbiTable, a surface application that allows users to integrate their mobile devices with a shared tabletop [141].

Untethered. The following ownership-based identification methods require users to wear the token used for identified input. Targeted at rapid prototyping, the TouchID toolkit augments ordinary gloves with strategically placed fiducial markers [86]. This does not only allow for distinguishing between input from different users, but also provides information to discriminate hands from a single user (i.e., left or right) and detect different finger or hand parts (e.g., knuckles or back of hand). The prototype is based on Microsoft

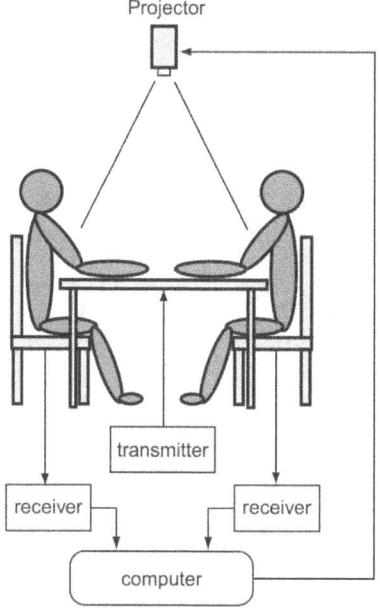
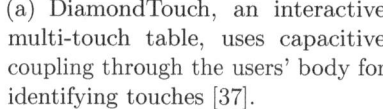

(a) DiamondTouch, an interactive multi-touch table, uses capacitive coupling through the users' body for identifying touches [37].

(b) By attaching fiducial markers to a glove, the TouchID toolkit cannot only distinguish users but also different hand parts [86].

Figure 2.13:   Two identification methods using direct codification for user identification

Surface, using 2 cm × 2 cm fiduciaries, and comprises a calibration tool that registers the required mapping between tag identifiers and users as well as hand parts. The toolkit features an event-driven API to develop prototypes, as well as a posture and gesture recognition tool. User identification takes place at the granularity of single touches, but requires users to wear gloves and register them with the application.

With a focus on secure user authentication rather than continuous and fluid identification, the IR Ring, a small ring equipped with a circuit board, continuously emits a Manchester-encoded pseudo random bit sequences using infrared light pulses to be detected by a vision-based surface [130]. Fingers close to a detected ring are associated to the corresponding user and thus identified. Vu et al. present another ring-based approach, but for capacitive touch screens [159]. In contrast to DiamondTouch, no physical connection is required; the battery-powered ring transmits a modulated electrical identification signal once in contact with the screen (either directly or indirectly through the finger).

Distributed Sensing

In contrast to the methods introduced in the previous section, the following systems do not directly transmit identification information to the surface, but rely on distributed sensing to correlate touch input with data from complementary sources. Typically, the interactive surface detects touch locations of all users, while independent sensors separately detect touch events of individual users. As both sources observe the same physical touch events, they can be correlated to assign touches to users.

Event-Based Sensing. Several systems correlate discrete events to associate user identities to touch input. For example, BlueTable allows users to place their phones on the interactive table to establish a connection [167]. Phones act as proxies for their users, for instance to retrieve personal data by immediately spilling out photos stored on the phone onto the table. Interaction is primarily based on (non-identified) finger input, however, while the phones remain passive. BlueTable uses a camera to detect phones based on their shape and requests infrared activity on all devices in Bluetooth range to match wireless and optical channels.

Enabling more fine-grained and dynamic interaction with mobile phones directly on the surface, Schöning et al. identify and authenticate users that wish to execute critical operations on a multi-touch wall [138]. Phones independently detect a touch with their accelerometers or microphones, and simultaneously send a bright flash (using built-in flash lights) as well as a user identifier via Bluetooth. If the surface system receives both events within a short enough time frame to unambiguously associate them, touch identification is successful. In contrast to BlueTable, phones are permanently held in the users' hands for spontaneous and immediate direct-touch interaction (Figure 2.14). Following a similar sensing approach, Hutama et al. attach two contact prongs to the phone's top, which are detected as two blobs by the vision-based surface [70]. At the same time, each phone transmits its current orientation (measured by inertial sensors) over a wireless link. To associate phone-surface contacts with particular phones, the system correlates tilt information. Like fingers, phones are used for direct-touch interaction and allow for identified input on the surface, acting as proxies for their users. As the phone orientation is restricted to using its top edge for touching, however, the input resolution of touches is less fine-grained.

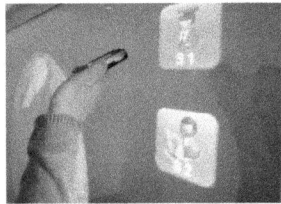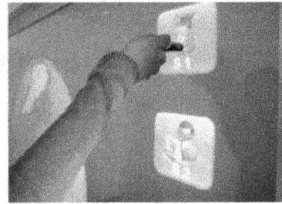

Figure 2.14:   Spontaneous authentication using phones [138]

Instead of phones, uPen uses a dedicated stylus equipped with a switch at its tip to detect contact events, which it transmits wirelessly together with an identifier [20]. Such events are matched with detected input on the surface for associating pens with touches. Besides direct-touch interaction, uPen also supports remote interaction with an integrated laser pointer using a video camera for detection.

Other systems employ radio-frequency identification (RFID) tags as the identification source. For example BlueBoard, a large touch-sensitive wall display, allows users to swipe RFID badges to bring up a personal icon on the display, which acts as storage bin for content to be transmitted via email after a session has finished [131]. This approach, however, uses an external RFID reader and does not integrate identification with direct surface interaction. In contrast, SurfaceFusion, a rear-projected tabletop system, allows for interaction with RFID-equipped tangible objects directly on the surface [113]. A camera detects when objects are placed on or removed from the surface to correlate such events with information acquired by an integrated long-range RFID reader. In an example application, users can copy digital content, such as photos, to a personal network folder by dragging them towards a badge placed on the table. A different approach to using RFID on a vision-based interactive surface is presented by Rabbit, a tangible mediator, which translates RFID values into visual two-dimensional codes [62]. It reads the RFID tag of objects placed on top of it and translates it into a visual representation using a series of infrared LED.

Continuous Sensing. ShakeID continuously matches accelerometer data (sensed by a phone in the user's hand) with three-dimensional body tracking from a Kinect depth camera [128]. The phone is not used to directly interact with the multi-touch display, but to capture continuous motion data. ShakeID associates touch contacts on the screen with the user's body and their other hand, which holds the phone (by matching touch-screen readings with Kinect-based skeleton tracking), and in turn correlates this hand with the phone itself (by matching Kinect and acceleration data). Note that the phone has to be in motion for successful matching, and all users need to be visible to the external Kinect camera.

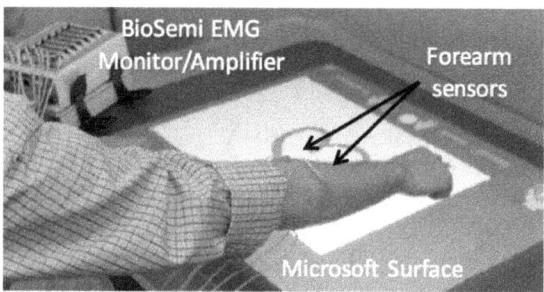

Figure 2.15:   Using forearm EMG to sense muscle activities [19]

Other approaches require users to wear devices in order to provide an individual information channel for correlation with touch input. For example, IdenTTop, a top-projected interactive tabletop, employs a Polhemus FASTRAK electromagnetic motion tracker as supplementary source to associate touch input to specific users [115]. Benko at al. use forearm electromyography (EMG) (Figure 2.15) to sense muscle activities [19]. Despite their current focus on single-user applications (e.g., to detect which finger performed a touch), such sensing can support user identification by correlating muscle activity with surface touch input.

Common Features

Instead of asking users to wear or use dedicated devices, the following two approaches rely on common features, namely apparel typically worn. Moving away from hands and fingers, Bootstrapper distinguishes users based on the shoes they wear [125]. A set of depth and color cameras, mounted around a Microsoft surface, capture shoe images and compare them to a database of registered users (Figure 2.16). Once a user is recognized, shoes are associated to finger touches based on the user's position, supported by hand information available from the surface's DI sensing. Bootstrapper is suitable for non-critical low-security applications as users may wear similar or identical shoes. Also looking at shoes, but from below, Multitoe, a back-projected multi-touch floor, allows users to tap with the ball of their feet for selection, or jump to invoke menus [16]. The foot detection is based on a combination of DI and FTIR to extract sole patterns, which are used for identification. For precise pointing, each foot is mapped to a single, user-customizable hotspot. As foot touch is the only interaction modality, Multitoe implicitly identifies all interaction.

Figure 2.16:   Bootstrapper distinguishes shoes for user identification [125].

2.3.3 Inherence-Based Identification

The following inherence-based approaches use either *behavioral* (e.g., touch gestures) or *physical* biometrics (e.g., fingerprints) for user identification.

Behavioral

Applying the technique proposed by Sae-Bae et al. [135], users authenticate by performing pre-defined gestures consisting of palm and finger movements (e.g., a closing gesture, moving all five fingertips towards the center). The system analyzes movement characteristics of the center of the palm and fingertips for pattern recognition and authentication. This approach relies on explicit user interaction for identification, and is not integrated with ongoing touch interaction. Although implemented for the iPad, a single-user device, it is also applicable to larger multi-user surfaces. In contrast, Eoff et al. propose an implicit identification approach based on pressure, tilt, and speed of pen strokes [44]. Using a Wacom tablet for input, identification is handled on a per stroke basis without the need for additional context data (i.e., a single stroke—from putting the pen down to lifting it up again—can be identified). As this approach relies on stroke data provided by pens, however, it is not applicable to finger touch input.

Physical

The first interface to consider fingerprints for direct interaction with GUIs was presented by Sugiura et al. [152]. It allows users to assign different commands to their fingers, or to use them as virtual data storage, even between remote networked computers. As a result, fingers seem to actually hold the commands or objects. The presented prototype relies on an optical fingerprint scanner that is externally attached to a laptop. Consequently, identification is separated from typical user input. Neither does this setup allow for direct-touch interaction nor is the scanner integrated with existing controls (e.g., buttons).

Capacitive Fingerprinting is an approach that measures the impedance of a user to the environment across a range of alternating current (AC) frequencies [56]. Due to varying body characteristics, different users yield different impedance profiles, which allows for distinguishing them using machine learning. The impedance profile is read 33 times a second during regular touch interaction, and no user instrumentation is required. For registration, the system initially scans the impedance profile of a user. The current prototype is limited to single-touch interaction and was evaluated with two concurrently registered users only.

Rather than focusing on user identification per se, but aiming at improving general touch accuracy, RidgePad uses a fingerprint scanner to deduce finger posture and user identity in order to more reliably determine the intended touch location [68].

Instead of using fingers, Carpus identifies users based on features extracted from their hands' dorsal regions (i.e., the upper side) [119]. This approach allows for transparent and unobtrusive identification, as individual finger touches can be associated to identified hands, but requires an additional overhead camera.

2.3.4 Knowledge-Based Identification

In general, knowledge-based user identification for interactive surfaces is different from both ownership- or inherence-based identification as it requires the user to explicitly retrieve and input information, thus impeding transparent and fluid identification of arbitrary touch input. Kim et al. explored five such approaches, which are designed to prevent observation (i.e., shoulder-surfing) attacks, for example by using varying finger pressure as input modality [79]. These approaches enable explicit authentication (requiring users to recall a pass phrase), but do not lend themselves to spontaneous and quick user identification integrated into ongoing interactions.

| Method | Identification Characteristics | | Detection Characteristics | User Requirements |
	Identifier Origin	Identification Granularity	Identification Principle and Integration	
Ownership-Based				
Direct Codification: Connected				
DiamondTouch [37]	Capacitive signal from table	Fingertip	Decodes modulated electrical signal transmitted through finger (capacitive-based)	Connect to table receiver
Direct Codification: Untethered				
TouchId Toolkit [86]	Fiducials on glove	Finger and other hand parts	Detects fiducial markers on glove (vision-based)	Wear glove
IR Ring [130]	Light pulses from ring	Fingertip	Associates touches to light pulses emitted by ring based on proximity (vision-based)	Wear ring
Capacitive ring [159]	Capacitive signal from ring	Fingertip	Decodes modulated electrical signal transmitted through finger (capacitive-based)	Wear ring
IdWristbands [1]*	Light pulses from wristband	Fingertip	Associates touches to light pulses emitted by wristband based on proximity (vision-based)	Wear wristband
Distributed Sensing: Event-Based Sensing				
BlueTable [167]	Phone	Phone back	Detects shape of phone placed on surface (vision-based) and triggers infrared activity on phone via wireless channel (Bluetooth) for correlation	Hold phone
Spontaneous authentication [138]	Phone	Phone edge	Inertial-based sensing of touch impact on phone makes it flash (vision-based detection) and send wireless message (Bluetooth) for correlation on surface	Hold phone
Tilt correlation [70]	Phone	Phone edge	On inertial-based sensing of touch impact on phone, correlates device tilt independently detected by surface (vision-based) and phone (inertial-based); wirelessly connected	Hold phone
uPen [20]	Stylus	Stylus tip	Pen detects touch with switch at its tip, time-based correlation with touch detection on surface; wirelessly connected	Hold stylus
BlueBoard [131]	Badge	n/a	Swiping badge on external RFID reader brings up personal icon on surface; not integrated with touch input	Swipe RFID badge
SurfaceFusion [113]	Tangible	Tangible	Time-based correlation of vision-based detection and RFID events from integrated reader	Hold tangible
Rabbit [62]	Tangible	Tangible	Converts RFID into visual markers to be directly detected by surface	Hold tangible
PhoneTouch [7]*	Phone	Phone corner	Detects touch on phone (inertial-based) and surface (vision-based) for time-based correlation	Hold phone

31

Method	Identification Characteristics		Detection Characteristics	User Requirements
	Identifier Origin	Identification Granularity	Identification Principle and Integration	
Distributed Sensing: Continuous Sensing				
ShakeID [128]	Phone	Finger	Two-step association: Continuously correlates phone motion observed by phone (inertial-based) and Kinect (vision-based), and then touches observed by Kinect (via anatomy inference) and surface	Hold phone
IdenTTop [115]	Tracker sensor	Finger	Correlates motion detected by electromagnetic motion tracker (Polhemus FASTRAK) with surface-based touch input	Wear tracker sensor
Muscle Sensing [19]	Muscle-sensing device	Finger	Can correlate finger movement sensed by forearm electromyography with surface-based touch input	Wear muscle sensor
Common Features				
Bootstrapper [125]	Shoe (top)	Finger	Stationary cameras detect shoe features for association with touch input based on location	Wear shoes
Multitoe [16]	Shoe (sole)	Foot	Interactive floor with foot-based interaction, extracts sole patterns	Wear shoes
Inherence-Based				
Behavioral				
Multi-touch gestures [135]	(Finger/hand) motion	n/a	Analyzes multi-touch gestures; no identification of individual touches	None
Pressure and tilt pen data [44]	(Stylus) motion	Stylus tip	Analyzes pressure and tilt data for identified stylus interaction	Hold stylus
Physical				
Fingerprint UI [152]	Fingerprint	n/a	External fingerprint reader; no integration with touch input	None
Capacitive Fingerprinting [56]	Body composition	Finger	Analyzes impedance profile of a user	None
Carpus [119]	Hand dorsal region	Finger	Additional camera extracts hand features, associates hands to touches based on anatomy	None
*HandsDown [8]**	Hand contour	Hand	Extracts contours of hands placed on surface, no direct integration with finger touch	None
Knowledge-Based				
Multi-touch authentication [79]	Knowledge	n/a	Authentication on surface via touch input; no integration with touch input	None

Table 2.1: Summary of user identification methods. *The new methods introduced in this thesis (IdWristbands, HandsDown, and PhoneTouch) are included for comparison.

2.3.5 Discussion

Table 2.1 provides a summary of the user identification methods reviewed in this chapter. We also included the new methods to be introduced in the next chapter—IdWristbands, HandsDown, and PhoneTouch—to illustrate their fit into the body of related work. This table lists *identification* and *detection* characteristics, which are both detailed in the remainder of this section. Identification characteristics are concerned with the origin of identifiers (e.g., fingerprint or phone) and the granularity of identified interaction (e.g., fingertip or phone corner). Detection characteristics on the other hand comprise the functional principle of identification and touch integration as well as potential requirements on the user side (e.g., equipment users have to wear).

Identification Characteristics

The particular information that identifies a user may originate from a variety of sources, as outlined by our distinction of methods based on ownership, inherence, or knowledge, and as illustrated by the above reviewed systems. Conceptually, inherence-based methods rely on biometric features (i.e., properties inherent to a person) while ownership- and knowledge-based methods use selectable identifiers (e.g., mobile phones, represented by a numeric identifier, or passwords). When designing user-aware systems it is important to consider that biometric features uniquely identify an actual person. Therefore, they cannot be changed, which may raise privacy concerns. Moreover, systems based on such identifiers require prior enrollment. In contrast, invalidating a compromised identifier using an ownership-based method may be as easy as reprogramming the device used as token.

Some methods appropriate the same entity for both providing identifying information and enabling user-aware interaction. For example, mobile phones can serve as identification token while being used for direct-touch interaction [70]. These two roles, however, may also be separated. For example, the IR Ring provides user identity, but fingers are used for identified interaction; light pulses from the ring and finger touches are associated in a separate step based on proximity [130]. Similarly, Bootstrapper identifies users based on their shoes, but allows for identified finger input by means of associating identified and interaction entities [125].

The entity—or agent of control—available for identified touch interaction (e.g., finger or phone) determines the possible input granularity, which in turn impacts the user interface and interaction design. Identified finger input represents the most implicit type of identification, as users can carry on as normal, without having to change typical multi-touch interaction styles (e.g., as supported by DiamondTouch [37]). Other identification methods realize similar input granularities, which allow for precise direct manipulations, for example by using a stylus [44]. Identified tokens as user proxies placed on the surface (e.g., tangibles [113] or mobile phones [167]) can be moved to arbitrary locations on the surface, but are arguably less suited for typical direct manipulation tasks (e.g., drag-and-drop). Therefore, they require complementary GUI concepts for personalized interaction, for example by dynamically opening up personal areas. The same also applies to methods that rely on touch input without tokens, but that do not identify atomic touch interactions, such as the knowledge-based authentication methods proposed by Kim et al. [79] or multi-touch gestures [135]. Finally, several of the reviewed methods do not afford direct integration with touch-based interaction at all. For example, BlueBoard

33

requires users to swipe a badge using an external RFID reader [131], which is addressed by automatically showing a virtual representation of the user on the surface.

From a user's perspective, the identified agent of control has the largest impact on user-aware interaction. Methods that identify individual finger touches (either directly or via another entity) seamlessly blend in with familiar multi-touch styles. Such implicit identification, however, does not allow for controlling the identification scope: All input is automatically associated to the user in question, which may not be desirable in all application scenarios (e.g., due to privacy concerns). Further, requiring additional devices for identification is likely to also impact the user experience. Such devices need to be available, and users have to either wear them or use them directly for input. While they might be perceived cumbersome, additional devices also widen the interaction space. For example, users may prefer to write with a stylus rather than using the finger, or may appreciate capabilities available on their mobile phone (e.g., instant transfer of personal data).

Despite the variety of enabling methods for user identification, so far only few works have considered personalized interaction going beyond brief usage scenarios. Typically, each method is demonstrated with an interaction or application example for demonstration purposes, but is not applied to further explore personalized interaction independent of concrete applications.

Detection Characteristics

Related works demonstrated different strategies to determine a user's identity and associate it with touch input for identified interaction. One class of methods uses the same sensor to detect both identifying information and touch input. For example, DiamondTouch employs capacitive coupling to simultaneously detect a finger's location and the transmitted identifier [37]. Similarly, the IR Ring system uses the same camera for detecting identifying light pulses and finger touches, but associates them based on proximity in a second step [130]. Another class of methods relies on distributed detection and multiple independent input streams that—when taken together—enable touch identification. Typically, the surface detects touches of all users (e.g., based on computer vision). Additionally, each user provides an individual input stream, and the different devices communicate over a wireless channel. For example, a phone may detect touches based on acceleration [138]. As both shared and individual channels sense the same physical touch events, these events can be correlated to associate touch locations (provided by the surface) with user identity (provided by the mobile phone); other methods continuously observe motion rather than discrete events (e.g., [128]).

Different identification methods come with different user requirements. For some methods, users need to be instrumented (e.g., wearing gloves [86] or being physically connected to the surface [37]). Other methods demand using additional devices for interaction (e.g., mobile phones [70]). In contrast, inherence-based methods typically do not require users to do either. Relying on additional devices increases system complexity, costs, and maintenance efforts. In general, hardware requirements amongst the different methods vary largely, ranging from off-the-shelf surfaces (e.g., [86]), to requiring supplementary off-the-shelf (e.g., [70]) or custom-built (e.g., [130]) devices, to instrumenting the environment with stationary sensors (e.g., [128]), to specialized interactive surface systems (e.g., [37]).

2.4 Summary

In this chapter, we analyzed enabling techniques for multi-touch detection on interactive surfaces, focusing on vision-based approaches, and further highlighted techniques for personalized output. This served as background for a survey of existing user differentiation and identification methods in surface computing, which we compared in a discussion. In contrast to conventional SDG, surface computing allows for direct, unrestricted, and rich touch input of multiple concurrent users sharing the same interface. We showed that this interaction style comes with new challenges for user identification. While the previously used individual input devices allowed the association of input events to users by means of separate channels, users of direct-touch interfaces share a single input channel. Related works proposed various methods to identify users on interactive surfaces, which come with different identification and detection characteristics and impact hardware requirements as well as the implicitness of identified interaction. Note that several of these methods have emerged in parallel to the present thesis work (e.g., [70, 130]), and thus bear some overlap with the methods we are about to introduce in the next chapter.

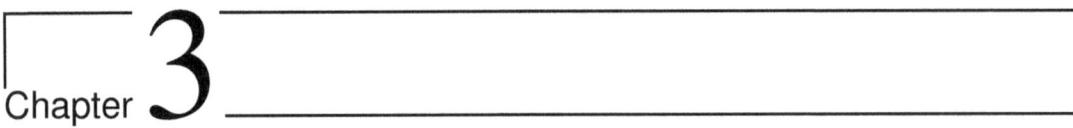

Chapter 3

Enabling User Identification

State-of-the-art multi-touch surfaces do not support identification of users. In this chapter, we contribute three novel methods for instantaneous user identification on interactive surfaces: IdWristbands, HandsDown, and PhoneTouch. The three methods integrate with typical multi-touch interaction and facilitate spontaneous identification on vision-based systems, but follow different strategies. IdWristbands identifies finger touches by associating them with LED-equipped wristbands worn by users, HandsDown is a biometric method that analyzes a user's hand placed on the surface for immediate identification, and PhoneTouch integrates personal mobile devices for user-aware stylus-like input. We demonstrate the feasibility of each method with a proof-of-concept implementation and an evaluation of its identification performance.

3.1   Introduction

Compared to prior single display groupware (SDG), surface computing supports more immediate collaboration as users share a single input channel for direct-touch input. Input without intermediate devices such as mice, however, trades off directness for user-awareness. Regaining user-awareness for interactive surfaces is desirable as it enables applications to respond to individual users and thus personalize interaction.

In this chapter, we introduce three novel methods for user identification on interactive surfaces—IdWristbands, HandsDown, and PhoneTouch—which are outlined in Figure 3.1. We designed these methods to meet the following three requirements in order to facilitate personalized interaction:

1. Instantaneous and immediately available user identification to support spontaneous interaction that integrates with ongoing workflows.

2. Direct integration of user identification with typical multi-touch interaction styles that supports independent identification of concurrent users.

3. Feasibility for vision-based interactive surface systems to support scalability and ease application.

The three methods approach user identification from different angles: IdWristbands employs wearable tokens that allow for assigning individual finger touches to a user,

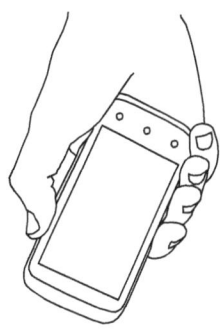

(a) *IdWristbands* associates a user's identity to individual finger touches using a wristband that continuously emits identifiers in the infrared spectrum.

(b) *HandsDown* is a biometric method that analyzes a user's hand contour placed on the surface for instantaneous and uninstrumented identification.

(c) *PhoneTouch* integrates personal mobile devices to be used in a stylus-like fashion for direct-touch interaction, thus serving as proxies for their users.

Figure 3.1: IdWristbands, HandsDown, and PhoneTouch—three novel methods of instantaneous and integrated user identification on interactive surfaces

HandsDown is a biometric approach based on hand-contour analysis, and PhoneTouch uses mobile phones for direct touch interactions much like a stylus. For each method, we present underlying functional principles, describe a proof-of-concept implementation by covering hardware and software components, and evaluate the identification performance. We conclude with comparing characteristics of the three methods in section 3.5.

3.2 IdWristbands

To enable identification based on IdWristbands, users wear one or two wristbands (i.e., for bimanual interaction) which constantly transmit unique identifiers using infrared light pulses. IdWristbands is based on a one-way communication channel from wristbands to the surface device. The vision-based surface system detects, decodes, and associates identifiers to nearby finger touch input of the same user, as illustrated in Figure 3.2. Any finger touch that stems from a hand with a wristband is identified while other touches remain anonymous. IdWristbands provides implicit and transparent user identification for arbitrary finger touches, without requiring users to change their interaction style. While wearing a wristband, touches are immediately associated to the corresponding user, who can perform familiar multi-touch input.

3.2.1 Hardware

IdWristbands is designed for vision-based multi-touch surfaces that employ infrared light for touch detection. The specific interactive surface we used for development and evaluation is a custom-built rear-projection table based on frustrated total internal reflection (FTIR), as described in detail in section A.2.1. Its camera has a resolution of 640 pixel × 480 pixel and samples at 120 Hz. We require wristbands to independently transmit two controllable narrow-angle infrared signals that are visible to the surface device. In our implementation, we use common textile sports wristbands and attach a LilyPad Arduino board, together with a LiPower board, a 3.7 V/110 mA lithium ion

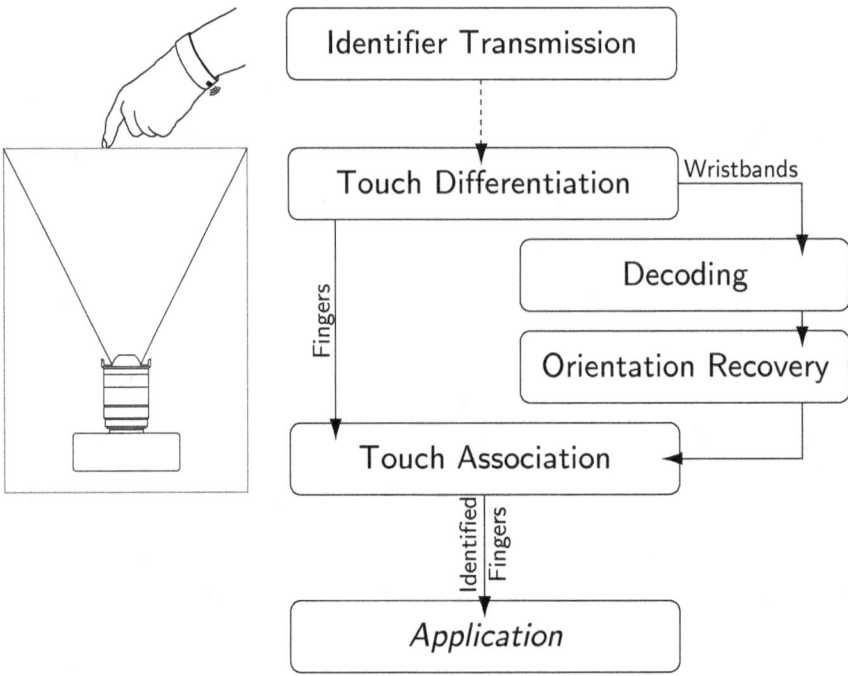

Figure 3.2: Prototype system architecture for IdWristbands: The surface detects both fingers and wristbands. It decodes wristbands and associates them to close-by fingers.

battery, and a board holding two wide-angle (24°) 870 nm infrared light-emitting diodes (LED) (Figure 3.3). The LEDs are connected using two 390 Ω resistors to the Arduino board (Figure 3.4).

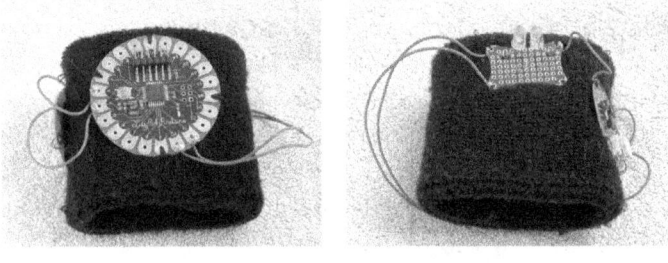

(a) LilyPad Arduino board with connections to power and LED boards

(b) Two 870 nm with 390 Ω resistors; LiPower board is mounted on the side

Figure 3.3: IdWristbands prototype: All components are mounted onto a common textile sports wristband.

3.2.2 Software

As outlined in Figure 3.2, wristbands encode and transmit identifiers, which are detected by the surface together with finger touches. The system distinguishes one from another, and decodes wristbands to then assign them to corresponding finger touches based on proximity. We implemented this entire processing chain in C#.

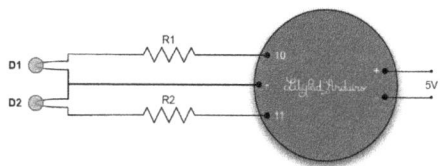

Figure 3.4: IdWristbands circuit diagram: LEDs D1/D2 are connected via resistors R1/R2 to pins 10/11 of the Lilypad Arduino board.

Identifier Transmission

We assign a unique number as identifier to each wristband. By means of toggling LEDs, the wristband continuously transmits a bit sequence that represents its identifier. We use pulse-width modulation (PWM) to encode bit sequences as follows. A short on-cycle represents a 0-bit, a long on-cycle a 1-bit. Single bits are delimited by short off-cycles, code words (i.e., identifiers) by long off-cycles. For instance, Figure 3.5 (top-row) depicts the encoding of the number '5'.

The camera's frame rate determines the minimum length of such on/off-cycles to be still detectable. Our setup uses a 120 Hz camera, which results in single frame durations of 8.3 ms (the camera's shutter stays open for the whole duration of a frame). As shown in Table 3.1, we choose on-periods of 8 ms to represent a short cycle (0-bit), and on-periods of 24 ms to represent a long cycle (1-bit). This guarantees that a short on-cycle is visible for 1–2 frames, a long on-cycle for 3–4 frames (the exact number of frames a LED is visible depends on the current timing offset between wristband and camera). To reliably detect off-cycles, we must ensure that no light falls onto the camera's sensor for a distinguishable amount of time. Therefore, we choose off-periods of 18 ms (2 × [8 ms + 1 ms buffer]) to represent a bit delimiter, and off-periods of 36 ms (4 × [8 ms + 1 ms buffer]) to represent a word delimiter. Short and long off-cycles are accordingly *not* visible for 1–2 and 3–4 frames, respectively. Using multiples of 8 ms (rather than 8.3 ms) while introducing buffer periods of 1 ms per frame has shown to increase detection robustness in practice.

Code Type	LED Timing (ms)	Resulting Visibility (frames)
0-bit	8 (on)	1–2
1-bit	24 (on)	3–4
Bit delimiter	18 (off)	1–2
Word delimiter	36 (off)	3–4

Table 3.1: Bit sequences are encoded using PWM (values for a 120 Hz camera).

With this setup, a three-bit word sufficient to distinguish eight users is transmitted in 96 ms to 142 ms (depending on the number of 0- and 1-bits it contains). This roughly corresponds to a data rate between 21 bit/s to 31 bit/s, without accounting for errors. Note that camera and wristband clocks are not synchronized.

Touch Differentiation and Decoding

The same camera detects both finger touches and wristband LEDs simultaneously. To differentiate one from another, we leverage that PWM inserts off-cycles (i.e., it switches off LEDs) between every transmitted bit. Consequently, a blob that remains visible for

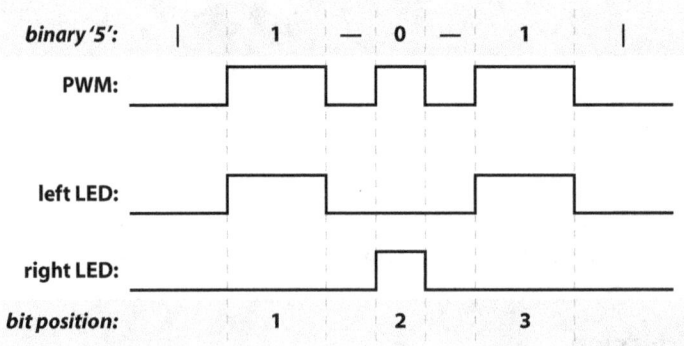

Figure 3.5: Encoding of '5' using PWM. '—' denotes a bit, '|' a word delimiter.

longer than the maximum LED on-cycle length (here, 24 ms) must be a finger touch. Alternatively distinguishing wristbands and fingers based on their shapes has proven to be less robust during our initial experiments. In particular, the constantly changing distances and angles between LEDs and the surface resulted in largely varying blob shapes.

To estimate blob positions in absence of actual observations, we added a Kalman filter to our tracking algorithms. This allows for a robust tracking of LEDs, which are not visible during off-cycles. Secondly, we keep a visibility history for each blob, which records the number of frames a blob was, or was not, visible. This history is used to distinguish between fingers and LEDs as described before, and to decode wristband identifiers. Note that the Kalman prediction is not used for blobs that have been classified as fingers. Therefore, a disappeared finger blob is instantly removed, allowing for quicker response times.

If a blob is not classified as finger, and its history holds enough data (i.e., a series sufficiently long to contain an identifier), we initiate decoding for this blob. In doing so, we initially locate word delimiters (i.e., long off-cycles). We then classify on-cycles in between as either 0-bit (i.e., short on-cycle) or 1-bit (i.e., long on-cycle). This directly translates to an identifier, with the last bit being the least significant. If evidently incorrect lengths of on- or off-cycles are encountered (i.e., cycles shorter or longer than those permitted by definition), the current word is ignored. Such errors could result from fast movement or reflections, for example.

Orientation Recovery and Touch Association

Association of finger touches and decoded wristbands is based on proximity (see Listing 3.1). The naïve approach is to define a circular area around a wristband's center and associate all touches within this area (Figure 3.6(a)). To include all valid touches, however, the resulting circle must also comprise large areas where users cannot possibly put their fingers (e.g., below the arm). This potentially increases the rate of incorrectly associated fingers, as other users are more likely to touch within such large areas. In addition, multiple wristbands are more likely to overlap.

Therefore, we determine a wristband's orientation to constrain the area within which fingers are associated. Drawing a line through the two LEDs centers allows for partly determining a wristband's orientation, but still leaves two possible orientations. To

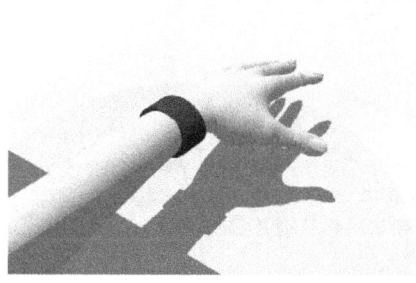

(a) Naïve approach without knowledge of orientation (b) Knowing the orientation downsizes the area to a cone

Figure 3.6: Narrowing down the area around a wristband for associating corresponding finger touches

resolve this ambiguity, we alternate between LEDs when transmitting codes, assigning specific bit positions within an identifier word to either of the two LEDs. Bits at odd positions are always transmitted by the left LED, bits at even positions by the right LED (Figure 3.5, bottom rows). Therefore, a wristband's orientation can be recovered after decoding. Using this orientation, the association area is restricted to a cone, which better matches natural finger positions while reducing chances for incorrect associations (Figure 3.6(b)). We experimentally determined a cone radius of 25 cm to be large enough not to miss any corresponding finger touches.

```
1 for every finger
2        if finger already assigned to wristband
3                continue
4        end
5        if finger is in circle around only one wristband
6                remember wristband
7                remember user of wristband
8        else
9                if finger is in circles around wristbands of only one
                    user
10                       remember user
11               end
12               if finger is in cone of only one wristband
13                       remember wristband
14                       remember user of wristband
15               else
16                       if finger is in cones of wristbands of only one
                            user
17                               remember user
18                       end
19               end
20       end
21       if wristband is not same as last run
22               reset wristband counter for finger
23       end
24       if remembered wristband
```

```
25                  increase counter for finger and wristband
26                  if counter for finger and wristband is over threshold
27                          assign finger to wristband
28                  end
29          end
30          if user is not same as last run
31                  reset user counter for finger
32          end
33          if remembered user
34                  increase counter for finger and user
35                  if counter for finger and user is over threshold
36                          assign finger to user
37                  end
38          end
39 end
```

Listing 3.1: Associating fingers to wristbands

As identifiers are transmitted by alternating LEDs, only one LED is visible at a time. This implies that, if a wristband was moved quick enough, the approach just described would produce incorrect orientation estimates. In particular, a line would be drawn through the visible LED's current position, but the invisible LED's last recorded (not updated) position. To address this, we continuously determine a wristband's current motion (using the visible LED) to estimate the invisible LED's actual position.

3.2.3 Evaluation

Goal of this system evaluation is to verify that the proposed approach allows for, first, distinguishing wristbands from finger touches, secondly, decoding the transmitted wristband identifiers, and thirdly, associating wristbands to corresponding finger touches. In addition, we were interested in qualitative feedback on wearing wristbands during interaction. To single out possible sources of error, we studied three tasks with increasing complexity.

To this end, we recruited 18 participants (eight female, aged between 18 and 51 years, $M = 23, SD = 8.5$) from the local campus and compensated with £8 for their time. Participants received two wristbands, one for each hand, to interact on the table, which had an active area of 91 cm × 57 cm. The experimenter introduced the concept of multi-touch interaction on the table and participants could try out the system freely until they felt comfortable using it. We logged all detected system input, recorded videos of the interactions with an overhead camera, and asked participants to complete a questionnaire at the end of a study session (see Figure B.1 on page 168).

Tasks

All participants performed the following three tasks, which took approximately one hour. The first task was performed individually, but all other tasks in groups of two.

- *Single.* Forty-eight circles appeared one after another on the surface (Figure 3.7(a)). Participants were asked to touch and hold those circles labeled "R" with their right, and those labeled "L" with their left hand, until they disappeared after 3 s and the next circle showed up. We used a set of pre-calculated locations in order to spread circles out and cover the entire surface area.

- *Opposite.* This task differs from the previous one in that two participants interacted simultaneously, but used only one hand each. Further, each participant was assigned a distinct color that indicated the circles to touch (Figure 3.7(b)). Twelve circles were shown per participant.

- *Sorting Game.* In this competitive game, participants were asked to sort small squares by dragging them into buckets of the same color (Figure 3.7(c)). Each participant was assigned three colors and had to take care of 15 squares; this was repeated three times. The participants were standing next to each other at the table's longer side.

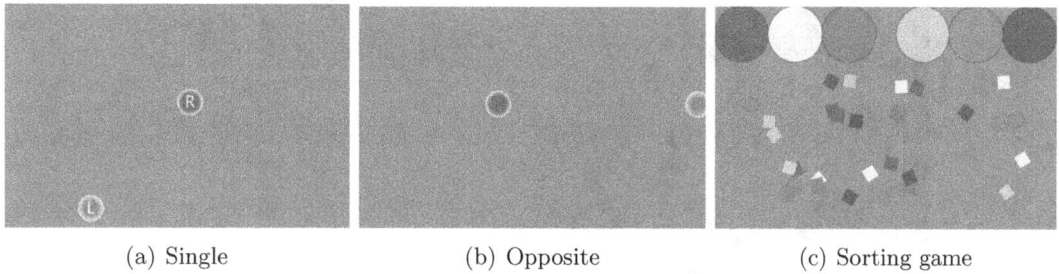

| (a) Single | (b) Opposite | (c) Sorting game |

Figure 3.7: Tasks used to evaluate the identification performance of IdWristbands

Results

To analyze the system's identification performance, we annotated the recorded data manually, using the tool shown in Figure 3.8. For this purpose, recordings of the table's internal touch detection camera were synchronized with recordings of the overhead interaction camera. This facilitated visually identifying and annotating the expected identification outcome, and hence provided the required ground truth for the following off-line analysis.

In the current prototype implementation, wristbands are not visible for finger touches close to the table's edges. This is due to the the user's hand being located outside the table's surface in such situations. Therefore, we restricted the active identification area. We experimentally determined that introducing surrounding margins of about 8 cm ensures that wristbands are visible for any finger touch, which translates to 50 pixel (left and right) and 100 pixel (top and bottom). The difference in margin width stems from different aspect ratios of camera (4:3) and projected output (16:10). Note that our system still detects finger input within these margins, but it does not attempt to identify users (i.e., to associate finger touches and wristbands).

Wristband Detection. In total, the collected data set contains 2394 finger touches and 2727 wristband sightings. Detecting and decoding wristbands inherently precedes identifying finger touches. As shown in Table 3.2, overall 99.88 % of wristbands were successfully detected, and 97.33 % correctly identified. It took 0.3 s on average to identify a wristband. Note that 90.48 % of those wristbands that were not detected or incorrectly identified were visible for less than 2 s.

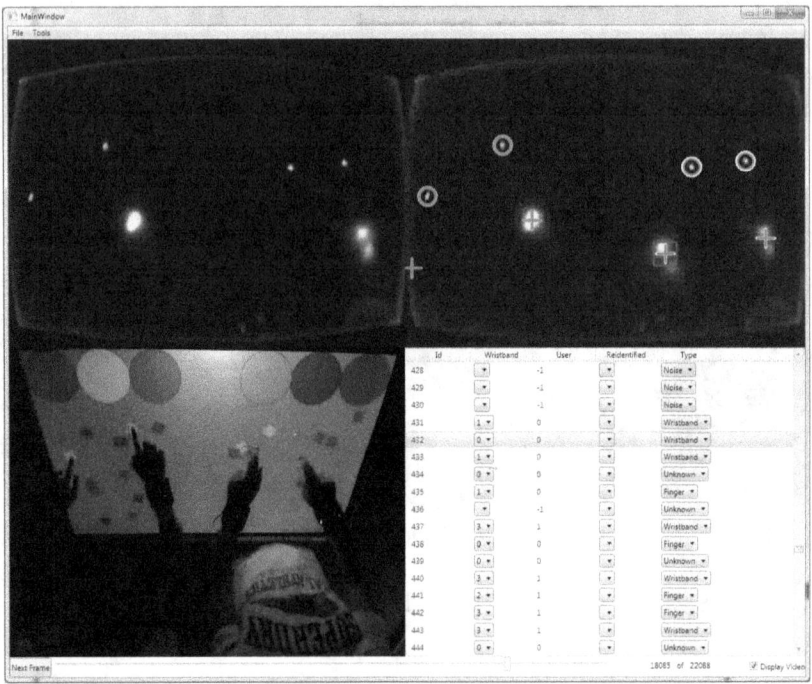

Figure 3.8: IdWristbands annotation tool (showing the sorting game), from upper left to bottom right: Internal table camera image, same image with annotations, overhead interaction camera image, list of detected blobs

		Overall (%)	Single (%)	Opposite (%)	Sorting (%)
Detected	M	99.88	99.73	100.00	99.90
	SD	0.50	0.82	0.00	0.29
Correctly decoded	M	97.33	97.71	96.53	97.76
	SD	4.56	4.48	6.16	2.89

Table 3.2: Wristband detection results

Touch Identification. Here, we use the term *identified* fingers for finger touches that were detected and correctly associated to a user. Finger touches that were not detected, not associated, or incorrectly associated are referred to as *non-identified* fingers. In the following, we excluded data from one group as we observed that they used two fingers in parallel for single touch interaction, while applying very little pressure. This lead to a high number of quickly fluctuating touch observations and unreliable detection. As shown in Table 3.3, overall 97.3 % of finger touches were successfully detected, and 85.48 % identified; 0.71 % were associated to the incorrect user. Due to the less restricted nature of the sorting game, detection rates are lower for this task. Further, we observed that 93.1 % of non-identified fingers were visible for less than 1 s. When only fingers that were visible for more than 1 s are considered, 95.16 % were successfully identified.

		Overall (%)	Single (%)	Opposite (%)	Sorting (%)
Detected	M	97.30	97.32	99.22	95.37
	SD	3.41	3.74	2.21	3.29
Identified	M	85.48	92.95	90.11	73.38
	SD	11.87	6.01	11.62	6.01
Incorrect. associated	M	0.71	0.00	0.74	1.38
	SD	1.51	0.00	2.08	1.45

Table 3.3:   Finger touch identification results

Qualitative Results. Questionnaire results, comments, and observations indicate that participants perceived wearing the wristbands as comfortable and were not constrained in their interactions. Some participants had worries that cables could become loose, which can be addressed by embedding cables into the wristbands for further revisions. Additional insights concerning the user experience are presented in Chapter 5.

Discussion of Study

As described before, our current prototype limits the active identification area, as wristbands close to the table's edges are not visible to the internal camera. Finger touches within the inactive margins, however, are still detected for anonymous interaction. Future implementations may apply additional means of tracking (e.g., overhead cameras) or use heuristics for assigning touches in question to corresponding users.

Note that we intentionally chose two concurrent users for this initial evaluation; this is not an inherent restriction of our system. While more code bits are required to identify additional users, the length of identification sequences grows logarithmically. In general, the identification performance is likely to be influenced by the number of concurrent users, the surface size, and the nature of applications. The farther away touch interactions of different users take place, the easier the wristband association turns out to be.

While we achieved identification rates of more than 95 % for finger touches that lasted at least 1 s, touches of arbitrary duration (i.e., including touches shorter than 1 s) were identified with a success rate of still over 85 %. This can be addressed on the hardware level by using a faster camera to speed up the identification and association process. Further, providing appropriate feedback on the user interface level to indicate progress and outcome of identification attempts assists users in comprehending system states.

For example, interactions that require identification could display an error message if activated by an unidentified touch.

3.2.4 Summary

IdWristbands enable implicit and untethered user identification on vision-based interactive surfaces by continuously associating finger touches with user identities. Users wearing wristbands can interact in parallel with unequipped users, whose touches remain consequently anonymous. Further, the wrist is a widely used spot for wearing common accessories, and the presented user study confirms that participants were comfortable wearing our wristbands. As the same components detect wristbands and finger touches, existing vision-based surfaces can integrate our method for user identification without hardware alterations, while the actual wristbands are inexpensive and straightforward to build.

3.3 HandsDown

HandsDown is a biometric method that analysis hand contours for user identification. Hand geometry was successfully used for authentication purposes in prior work, but its application to interactive multi-user settings is new. Particularly the low sensor and computational requirements suggest its suitability for user identification on interactive surfaces. Identifying with the bare hand does not require users to be instrumented or to use additional devices.

3.3.1 Scenario

To illustrate the user experience of HandsDown, we provide the following application example: Bob wishes to show a set of pictures he took on a hiking trip over the weekend to his colleague, Amanda. He already selected the most compelling motifs and uploaded them to an online photo platform. Now, he is standing with Amanda at the shared interactive tabletop in their office. To identify, he puts down his hand flat onto the surface, the fingers spread clearly apart (Figure 3.9(a)). His personal picture collection is automatically retrieved and displayed in the table area in front of him. Leveraging hand geometry information, the pictures are automatically oriented towards him (Figure 3.9(b)). HandsDown seamlessly extends conventional multi-touch on interactive surfaces: Bob can manipulate elements using common multi-touch gestures, such as pinching to resize (Figure 3.9(c)). Hand gestures and finger input can be used simultaneously: In Figure 3.9(d), while Bob is scrolling through his photos using conventional finger interactions, Amanda opens up her photo collection at the same time by placing her hand on the surface for identification. Both can now exchange photos by dragging them from one collection to the other (Figure 3.9(e)). If an unregistered user attempts to identify, appropriate feedback is displayed (in our prototype, a red shadow: Figure 3.9(f)).

3.3.2 Related Work

Authentication systems based on hand geometry have been used since the 1970s [74], for example to control systems access, monitor time and attendance, or to support point of

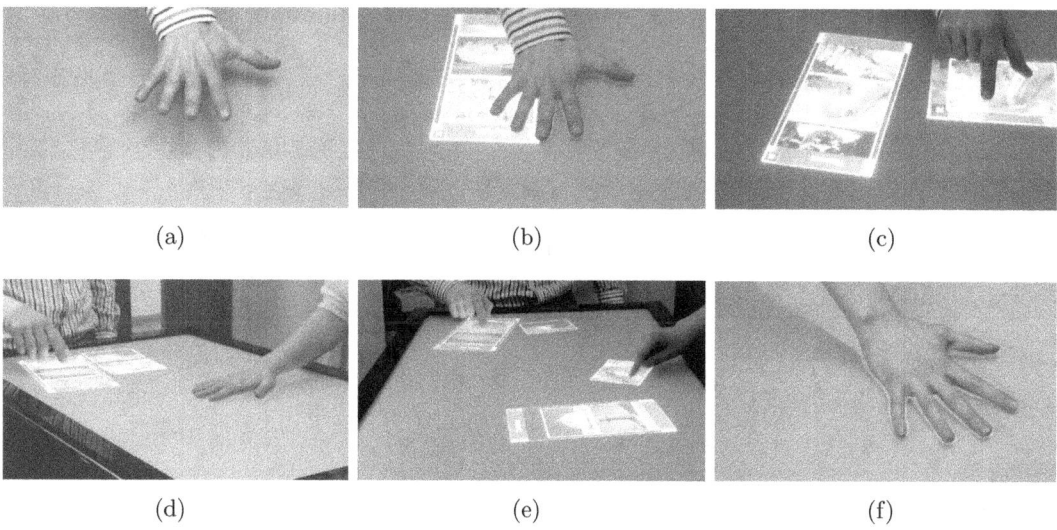

Figure 3.9: Using HandsDown to identify users and access personal picture collections. (a) A hand can be put down at an arbitrary location on the surface. (b) Once identified, a personal picture collection is displayed, automatically oriented towards the user. (c) Multi-touch manipulation is possible using finger interactions. (d) HandsDown and finger input can be used simultaneously. (e) Users can exchange pictures by dragging them between their collections. (f) Appropriate feedback is displayed if a user cannot be identified.

sales applications [171]. The authentication step, however, is isolated and occurs on a dedicated device. Placing the hand on such a device serves the sole purpose of providing one-time authentication for a connected system, which is fundamentally different from multi-user interaction on direct-touch surfaces. Previous approaches use a scanning device to acquire hand contour data, while some pose additional requirements with respect to hand alignment. Sanchez-Reillo et. al propose the extraction of finger lengths and widths, among others, for user identification and evaluate four different pattern recognition techniques [137]. Their approach, however, requires the hand to be aligned on a special platform to take top and side view pictures with a camera. While Boreki et. al's approach does not impose restrictions on the hand alignment, a flatbed scanner is used for acquiring an image of the isolated hand [23]. They present a curvature-based approach for feature extraction and use mean values of finger lengths and widths in conjunction with a distance-based classifier for system access authentication in a static context. Likewise, Yörük et. al describe a method for hand-based person identification for unconstrained hand poses [169]. In their experiment, they used a flatbed scanner to acquire images and showed a robust performance for groups of about 500 users.

3.3.3 System Design

To identify, users place their hand flat on the surface as shown in Figure 3.10(a). A snapshot of the hand is then taken to analyze its contour. The system extracts distinctive hand contour features (Figure 3.10(b)), and matches them against a database of registered users (Figure 3.10(c)). If a match is found the user is successfully identified, or otherwise rejected as unknown. Identification using HandsDown is instantaneous and takes place directly on the surface, where multiple users can identify simultaneously. Any interactive surface that can detect arbitrary object shapes in addition to finger contacts is suitable for HandsDown.

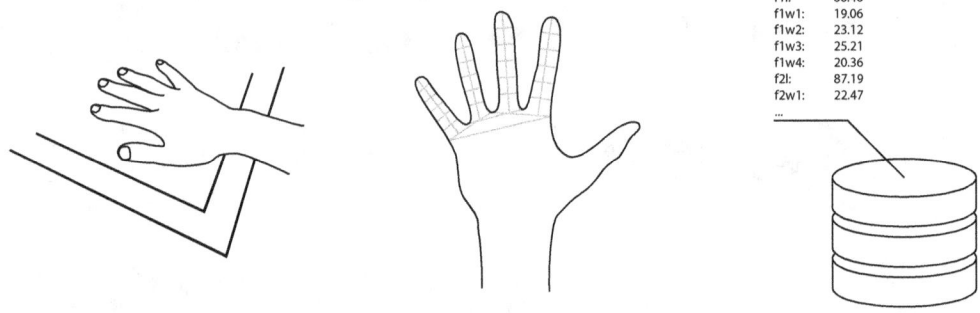

(a) Users place their hand on the surface to identify.

(b) The system analyzes hand contours and extracts features.

(c) Extracted features are compared against a user database.

Figure 3.10:   User identification procedure of HandsDown

3.3.4 Hardware

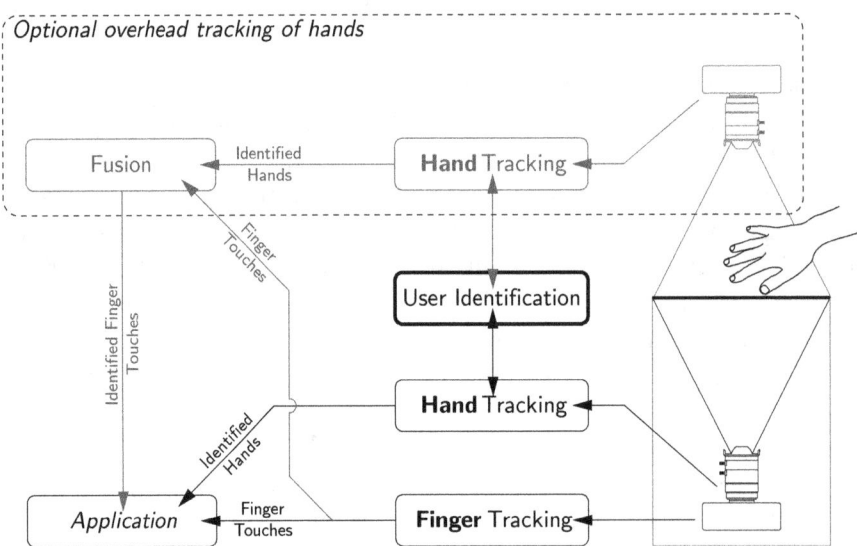

Figure 3.11:   Prototype system architecture for HandsDown: Hand contours are either detected by the integrated touch camera or by an additional overhead camera, which allows for continously tracking hands.

Our prototype is based on a custom-built tabletop using the diffused screen illumination (DSI) sensing principle, which allows for detecting arbitrary shapes, as detailed in section A.2.1. The surface has an active area of 91 cm × 57 cm. In our initial setup, two cameras are pointed at the surface, one from below (i.e., integrated into the table) and one from above (i.e., ceiling-mounted) as shown in Figure 3.11. The lower camera detects only objects close to the surface as they reflect the emitted infrared light (i.e., they appear brighter than the background as shown in Figure 3.12(a)); its range of sight is limited by a diffuser. The upper camera detects objects at arbitrary distances above the surface as they block light (i.e., they appear as dark shadow as shown in Figure 3.12(b)). Note that in case of objects touching the surface, both cameras capture similar shapes. Objects at a distance, however, are only detected by the upper camera, as the diffuser prevents the lower camera from seeing further behind the surface.

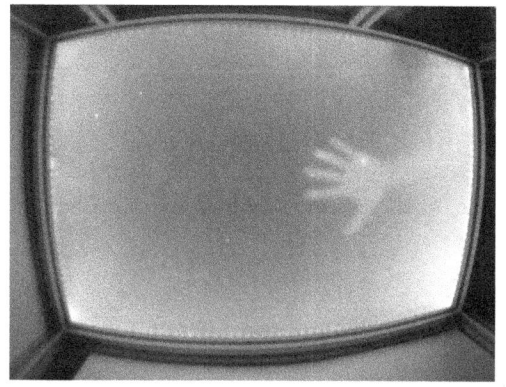
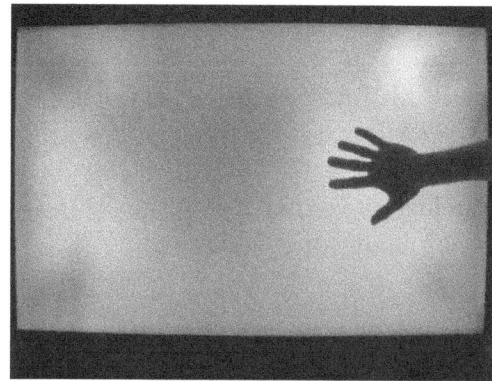

(a) Lower camera: hand reflects light   (b) Upper camera: hand appears as shadow

Figure 3.12:   Different camera sources for hand contour capturing

Adding an overhead camera was motivated by the possibility of continuous hand tracking. If hands are continuously tracked above the surface, any finger touch can be associated to a hand and its user after a single initial identification. During informal user feedback sessions, however, we found that in practice users frequently leave the tracked surface area without noticing, for example to relax their hands or to point at something in the room. Although users expect to be still identified in such cases, a hand that leaves and re-enters the surface area appears as new and yet unidentified to the system. Loosing track of hands hence may lead to confusion, as users do not anticipate having to re-identify repeatedly; Figure 3.13 illustrates this problem. Therefore, we decided to focus on interactions that do not require continuous hand tracking, using a single-camera setup, which is self-contained and more common.

3.3.5 Software

To enable hand-based user identification, our software implementation has to extract contours out of the camera images first, to then detect those contours that represent hands performing a HandsDown gesture (i.e., hands with the fingers kept apart). The next step is to localize hand extremities to take measurements of finger lengths and widths, which serve as features for the subsequent identification process. We provide details for all required steps in the following subsections, focusing on a system setup with a single camera mounted underneath the surface. The software tools to capture camera images and extract hand contours are written in C++ using the computer vision library OpenCV [26]. All evaluation scripts are written in MATLAB [87], using LIBSVM [30] as support vector machines (SVM) implementation. For later explorations of HandsDown interaction techniques (see section 4.2), we integrated hand detection and extraction, contour analysis, feature extraction, and SVM-based user identification in C#.

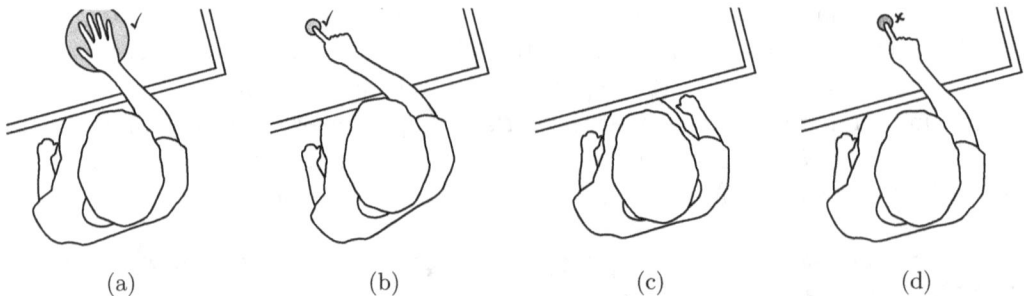

(a)   (b)   (c)   (d)

Figure 3.13: Enabling persistent identification by hand tracking above the surface easily fails: (a) After the user has identified, (b) any touch is associated to the hand and hence the user. (c) Leaving the surface area, however, results in the hand being treated as new and unidentified after re-entering. (d) Therefore, subsequent touches are not identified, although users expect otherwise.

Contour Extraction

In our DSI setup, any object placed on the surface reflects the emitted infrared light and is therefore clearly visible to the integrated camera. The camera's infrared bandpass filter removes the projected image to prevent interferences with the touch detection. We subtract the image background (i.e., the empty surface) and apply binary thresholding filters to remove unwanted noise. In doing so, we apply two image filter chains to extract finger touches and hand contours in parallel out of the same image source. They use different binarization thresholds to facilitate extraction of either finger touches or hands. In particular, finger touches appear brighter than hand contours, as they promote the effect of FTIR due to the uniformly applied pressure across their relatively small contact size. Therefore, a higher threshold can be used for touch detection to bring out fingers while suppressing hands. Using a lower threshold enables us to capture hands as a whole, including any finger touch lying underneath. We use the chain code contour method to eventually extract contours out of the binarized image. Figure 3.14 illustrates this process, albeit using an example captured with the overhead camera.

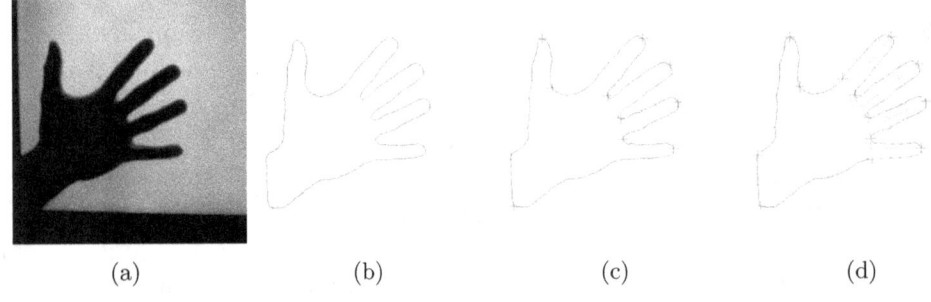

(a)   (b)   (c)   (d)

Figure 3.14:   Extraction steps using overhead camera: (a) raw camera image, (b) extracted contours, (c) high curvature points, and (d) extracted hand features

Hand Detection

The following steps are only initiated once users put down their hand flat onto the surface. We detect this particular situation by inspecting the contact areas underneath it. When placing the hand on the surface, the lower part of the hand clearly shows up in a similar intensity as the finger tips. Therefore, we can apply a heuristic that makes use of the number of contacts reported by the finger touch detection. Once six contacts are found within potential hand boundaries, this contour is considered for further processing. In doing so, we avoid unnecessary computations. More importantly though, by ensuring that a hand is completely put down onto the surface before identification, the distance between hand and camera is constant. Consistent measurements are required for biometric hand identification as the whole process is based on the hand's geometry.

Contour Analysis

To localize hand extremities (i.e., finger tips and the valleys between any two fingers) in a rotation and translation invariant manner, we analyze the contour's curvature profile, as described by Boreki et al. [23]. The profile is extracted using the difference of slope technique (see Listing 3.2). As points with high curvature correspond to changes in contour direction, we apply a threshold filter to select them. The intervals' respective center points are selected as hand extremity candidates (indicated by red crosses in Figure 3.14(c)). In contrast to previous hand contour systems for single user access control, we have to take into account that the whole surface is captured rather than an isolated area. Therefore, we do not only encounter multiple hands, but also have to deal with a variety of different shapes since parts of the arms might be visible, depending on how far users have to lean over the surface to reach a point (see Figure 3.15(b)).

```
1   /// <param name="contour">Contour points coordinates</param>
2   /// <param name="distances">Euclidean distances between neighboring
        contour points (pre-computed)</param>
3   /// <param name="distance">Distance between two points for curvature
        approximation</param>
4   /// <returns>Curvature approximations</returns>
5   public static double[] GetCurvature(Contour<Point> contour, double[]
        distances, double distance)
6   {
7     for (int i = 1; i < contour.Total - 1; i++)
8     {
9       // find point on contour before current
10      PointF p1 =
11        GetPointAtDistance(contour, i, distances, distance, Direction.
            CounterClockwise).Point;
12      // find point on contour after current
13      PointF p2 =
14        GetPointAtDistance(contour, i, distances, distance, Direction.
            Clockwise).Point;
15      // vector from previous point to current
16      Vector2D v1 = new Vector2D(
17        contour[i].X - p1.X,
18        contour[i].Y - p1.Y).Normalized;
19      // vector from next point to current
20      Vector2D v2 = new Vector2D(
21        contour[i].X - p2.X,
```

```
22        contour[i].Y - p2.Y).Normalized;
23        // angle between these two vectors
24        curvature[i] = Math.Acos(Vector2D.Dot(v1, v2));
25    }
26      return curvature;
27  }
```

Listing 3.2: HandsDown contour curvature approximation

Consequently, these non-hand parts have to be ignored. We identify valid hand parts by searching for a pattern of alternations in contour direction that is characteristic to the five spread fingers. In the same way, unsuitable hand postures and objects other than hands that triggered the identification procedure can be excluded from further processing. The outer points of little and index finger are reconstructed in a post-processing step, as they cannot be reliably detected due to their low curvature. They are placed at the same distance from the respective finger tip as the already identified valley points on the other side.

Feature Extraction

The lines connecting finger tips and center points between two adjacent finger valleys are extracted as the fingers' main axis and divided into six equally sized partitions (Figure 3.14(d)). For each finger, we select the following features: length of main axis, widths at five equidistant points, and mean width. In addition, we include the palm width as well as three distances between different finger valley points. Note that the thumb is not included as its detection proved to be unreliable. The angles between fingers turned out to vary greatly between identification attempts, and are hence not considered as identification features.

3.3.6 Evaluation

The purpose of this evaluation is to demonstrate the feasibility and evaluate the identification performance of hand-based user identification in the new context of interactive surfaces.

Methodology

User identification based on hand geometry is a classification problem. Faced with the hand of a user wishing to identify, a suitable classifier must decide which of the enrolled users matches. This decision is based on similarities between the presented hand and the stored hand samples of enrolled users. The similarity in turn is evaluated based on the extracted hand features, such as finger lengths and widths. In particular, the classifier determines the user whose stored hand features are most similar to the now presented hand's features. Alternatively, if no close match can be found, the candidate will be rejected as unknown. If the best match falls below a certain similarity threshold the user will be rejected.

We use receiver operating characteristics (ROC) curves [47] for classification evaluation as they provide a performance measure independent of class skew (i.e., unequal occurrence of individual classes) and classification threshold. Note that it is the combined performance, or the interplay, of feature extraction and classifier that is evaluated here. ROC curves plot true positive (or genuine acceptance) and false positive (or false acceptance) rates as a function of the classifier's threshold. This threshold can be chosen depending on application requirements to achieve suitable trade-offs between security (e.g., low false acceptance rates) and recognition performance (e.g., high genuine acceptance rates). The area under curve (AUC) in turn reduces the ROC performance to a single scalar value for comparison while preserving its advantages. Extending ROC to our multi-class problem, we generate a curve for each user, with the corresponding user as the positive class and all other registered users as the negative class. The AUC is calculated for each curve separately and then averaged.

Data Collection

In total, we collected 544 hand images of 17 different participants. As this data was collected before considering interaction implications (see Figure 3.13), we used the camera mounted above the surface. Since it is identical to the lower camera and the processing steps remain the same, we expect the results to be applicable also to a single-camera setup. The targeted hand locations and orientations on the surface were briefly explained and demonstrated to the subjects beforehand; neither markers nor pegs were used. Thirty-two images were captured per subject as follows ($32 \times 17 = 544$): We asked them to position their right hand successively at eight different locations on the surface, close to its edge, with varying orientations; each position was recorded twice (Figure 3.15(a)). We repeated the same procedure with the hands positioned farther away from the edge, closer to the surface's center (Figure 3.15(b)). Using our feature extraction approach, we successfully extracted 533 feature sets. Eleven hands (1.02 %) could not be processed due to low capture quality.

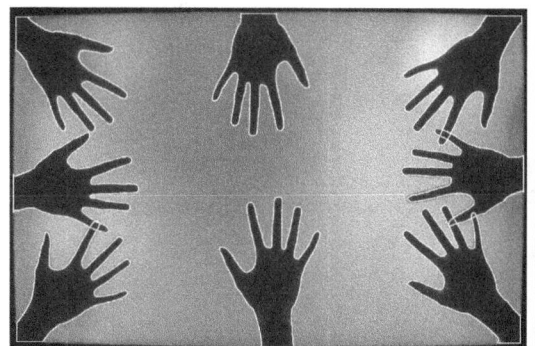 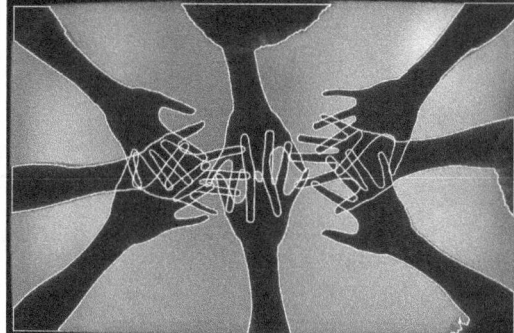

(a) Close-to-edge condition   (b) Center condition

Figure 3.15: Location and orientation of captured hand images for evaluation (superimposed camera shots; white contours added for clarity). 544 hand images of 17 different subjects were collected.

Classifier Selection

Procedure.   In a pre-study, we first compared two widely used classification approaches, naive Bayes classifier (NBC) and SVM. At the same time, we were interested in the effect of training size (i.e., number of hand samples used during enrollment) on the classification outcome.

We chose a one-against-all strategy to realize SVM multi-class support, using LIBSVM [30] with probability estimates. We trained one classifier for each user; this user provides samples for the positive class, while samples of all other users are used for the negative class. We used a similar one-against-all strategy for NBC and built one model per user, using our own NBC implementation. For both SVM and NBC, the class membership of a test sample is determined by the highest scoring classifier.

For each of the six combinations of classification method (SVM, NBC) and training samples per user (5, 17, 29), we performed a 100 trial cross validation with a stratified random selection of training samples. In each trial, we trained one classifier for each of the $n = 17$ users. For evaluation, each classifier was provided with test samples of the trained user (positive examples) and of the remaining users (negative examples). We recorded example types (positive or negative) together with the classifiers' scores, resulting in n sample sets per cross validation trial. In the end, we merged sets of the same classifier over all cross validation trials.

Results.   Table 3.16(a) shows averaged AUC for all six combinations of classification method and training size. Figure 3.16(b) depicts the ROC curves of using SVM with 5, 17, and 29 training samples, plotting the genuine acceptance rate on the vertical axis and the false acceptance rate on the horizontal axis. The optimal performance in terms of minimal combined error is indicated for each curve. For 29 samples, it is achieved at a false acceptance rate of 1.32 % and a genuine acceptance rate of 98.10 %. Due to its consistently better performance, we choose SVM as classifier and use 29 training samples per user in the following performance evaluation. As the employed camera is capable of capturing 30 images per second, enrolling a subject is quickly accomplished.

Training	AUC	
Size	SVM	NBC
5	0.943	0.884
17	0.996	0.964
29	0.999	0.969

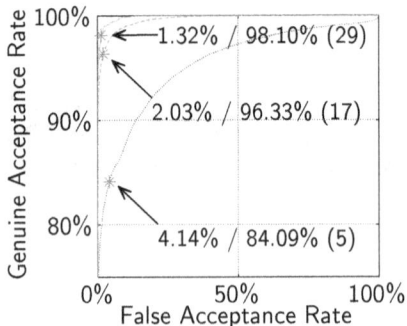

(a) AUC classification performance of SVM and NBC using 5, 17, and 29 training samples per user

(b) ROC curve for SVM, using 5, 17, and 29 training samples per user; minimal combined error rates pointed out

Figure 3.16: HandsDown classifier evaluation results

Identification Performance

Procedure. Using our database of 544 collected hand contours, we simulated six scenarios, which differed in the numbers of known and unknown users (as listed in Figure 3.17). Here, a known user is someone who has registered with the system; an unknown user is someone who has not provided any hand contour information before. Ideally, a known user is identified correctly while an unknown user is rejected. We chose these six scenarios to cover the range of known and unknown users that are possible to explore with the data samples at hand.

For each scenario, we generate 100 sets of randomly drawn known and unknown users. In turn, we perform a 100 trial cross validation with a stratified random selection of training samples for each of these sets, resulting in $100 \times 100 = 10,000$ trials per scenario of known/unknown users. In each trial, we train the classifier using only training samples of the known users. Testing samples of known and unknown users are presented to the classifier afterwards.

As discussed before, we use LIBSVM [30] with probability estimates as SVM implementation with a a one-against-all strategy in this evaluation. That is, a separate classifier is trained for each known user. This user provides samples for the positive class, while samples of the other *known* users are used for the negative class. The initially separate classifiers are then combined into a joint classifier.

During testing, the best-scoring classifier determines the result, that is the identified user. A user is rejected as unknown if the reported score is below a certain threshold. For evaluating the identification performance, the joint classifier is provided with test samples of known and unknown users. For each test sample, we record the classifier's reported score (i.e., the probability estimate of the best scoring single classifier) together with the classification result (i.e., correct or incorrect). In the end, we merge all results to create a single ROC curve and calculate the AUC value for each scenario.

Results. Figure 3.17 combines the six ROC curves into a single diagram for comparison. Table 3.4 lists the resulting AUC values for the six different scenarios of known/unknown users (higher values mean a better performance, with one being equivalent to perfect identification). The best performance is achieved for scenarios without unknown users, that are scenarios where only registered users can access the system. The performance varies only slightly for the three tested numbers of known users (5, 10, and 15). With an increasing number of unknown users the identification performance slowly decreases.

		Known Users		
		5	10	15
Unknown	0	0.999	0.999	0.998
Users	5	0.990	0.995	—
	10	0.987	—	—

Table 3.4: AUC comparison (a value of 1.0 is equivalent to a perfect identification performance); not all combinations are possible due to our limited database of 17 users

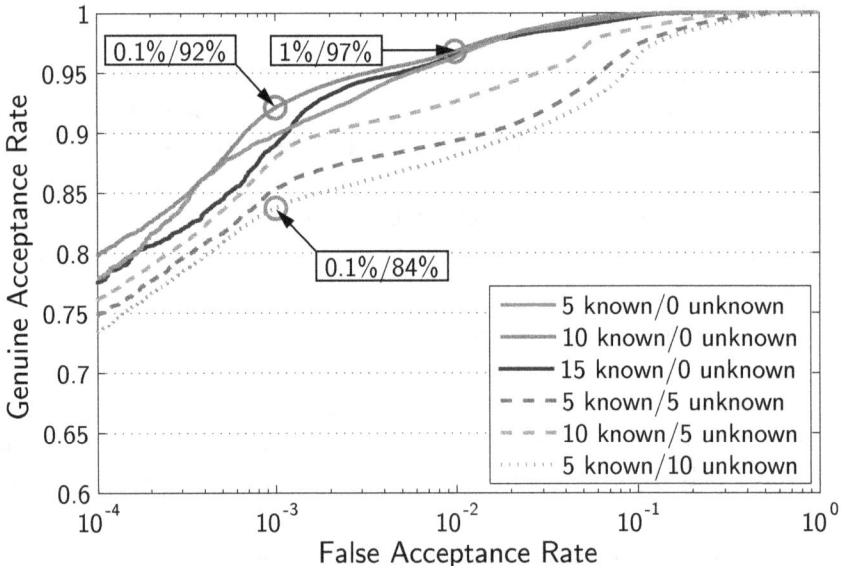

Figure 3.17: ROC comparison (trade-offs between genuine and false acceptance rates as a function of classifier threshold); three example rates are pointed out

Discussion of Study

These evaluation results suggest that HandsDown enables robust identification for small user groups. Depending on application domains, the classifier's threshold can be adjusted to meet different security requirements, or rather trade-offs between genuine and false acceptance rates. For example, for the scenario of 10 known and zero unknown users, we can achieve genuine acceptance rates of 92 % and false acceptance rates of 0.1 %, or, with a different threshold, of 97 % and 1 %. If the aim was to achieve a low false acceptance rate of 0.1 % for the scenario of five known and 10 unknown users, the expected genuine acceptance rate is 84 %, for example. Although the properties of hand contours vary greatly amongst different people, it is yet insufficient to claim that any hand contour is exclusively unique from the rest of the entire world. Instead, HandsDown is most suitable for scenarios where the size of the population is small.

3.3.7 Summary

HandsDown enables user identification based on biometric features of the users' hands without the need of extra hardware, which may be unnatural or laborious from a user's perspective. Our evaluation shows that HandsDown supports small user groups of sizes typical for interaction around surfaces. Multiple users can identify simultaneously and location-independent by placing their hands flat on the surface. Furthermore, HandsDown works with any vision-based interactive surface than can detect arbitrary object shapes.

3.4 PhoneTouch

PhoneTouch follows a token-based approach and employs personal mobile devices as proxies for their users, thereby enabling fluid and spontaneous user identification. The mobile is used like a stylus for direct and precise pointing interaction on the shared surface. Multi-touch finger and phone interactions co-exist. At the same time, finger and phone touches are distinguished, and each phone touch is associated with its user. Consequently, any phone-based input is identified, while finger touches remain anonymous. In addition, mobile phones come with expressive user interfaces and are equipped with various sensing and communication technologies. Unlike interactive surfaces, they are strictly personal devices. By exploiting a mobile's capabilities, PhoneTouch goes beyond mere user identification. In fact, it facilitates a whole new set of fluid cross-device interactions that realize synergies by bringing together complementing device characteristics, such as copying of objects from the surface to the phone and vice versa.

3.4.1 Scenario

We present a scenario that illustrates the use of PhoneTouch in the context of a photo sharing application, similar to our previous HandsDown example. Andy, Bart, and Chris meet around an interactive tabletop. One of the friends, Andy, wishes to share a collection of photos he has taken on a recent trip. He takes out his phone, starts the picture sharing application, selects the photos, and then touches the tabletop. The selected photos immediately appear on the table, spread out around the point of contact (Figure 3.18(a)). He pockets his phone and the three friends start browsing the photos, using their fingers on the multi-touch table (Figure 3.18(b)). The friends enlarge several of the photos for a closer look at them and arrange them by interest. Bart and Chris take out their phones, also start the picture application, and pick up photos they would like to take home by touching them with their phones (Figure 3.18(c)).

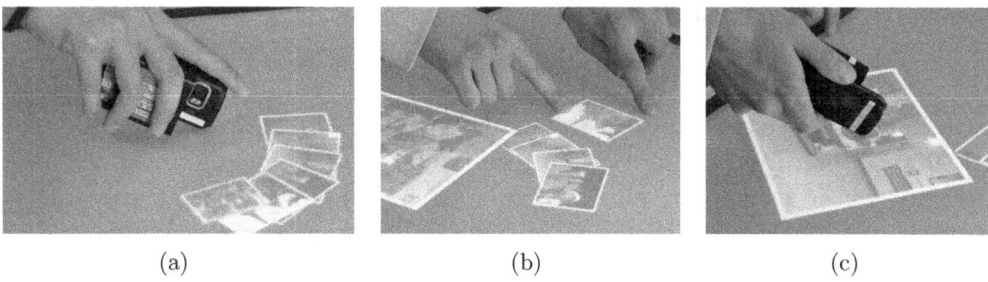

(a)   (b)   (c)

Figure 3.18: A scenario of PhoneTouch interaction: (a) Andy transfers a collection of photos onto the surface. (b) With his friends he is browsing the collection. (c) Chris copies a photo to his phone by touching it.

In summary, the user experience of PhoneTouch is defined by the following characteristics:

- The phone is used like a stylus for pointing and object selection on the surface. From a user's perspective, any interaction that can be performed with a single finger touch can in principle also be performed with a phone touch.

- The input space for finger input and phone input is identical, such that phone touches are resolved with the same level of granularity as positions on the surface.

- While the same input is possible with finger or phone, finger and phone events are distinguished, and phone events are associated with the identity of the user.

- The technique seamlessly extends conventional multi-touch on interactive surfaces. There is no restriction or compromise of established styles of tabletop interaction in order to facilitate PhoneTouch.

- PhoneTouch is also seamless in extending mobile phones. Users can move fluidly between use of their phone for touch interaction on the surface, and interaction with the phone itself as personal device.

3.4.2 Related Work

How mobile devices and larger display surfaces can be used in complementary ways was explored widely, in early visions (e.g., [48, 124]), work on combining personal digital assistants (PDAs) with SDG (e.g., [49, 107]), and recent interest in the use of phones with interactive surfaces (e.g., [70, 167]). Work was frequently driven by specific application agendas, such as working across personal and shared contexts [49], whereas our concern is to facilitate user identification and generally support symbiotic use of small personal devices and large displays.

Many of the techniques that were developed are for interaction at a distance and do not involve direct contact between mobile and surface. This includes indirect manipulation techniques, such as data synchronization through a standard user interface [49], remote cursor control by stylus [107] or key input [31] on a handheld, and mouse-like cursor control by relative motion of a mobile phone [18, 98]. Other techniques permit direct manipulation at a distance by pointing of a mobile with respect to the surface. This was first demonstrated with a PDA-mounted laser for direct pointing at a remote display, coupled with fine-grained interactions that then take place on the handheld screen, using a linked representation [108]. Recent work leveraged built-in cameras, including Point & Shoot using camera-phones as view finders for remote selection on large displays [18], related work by Pears et al. adding direct interaction on the phone's touch screen [117], and Touch projector additionally enabling multi-touch interactions [24].

A range of recent works contributed techniques that are based on contact between mobiles and surfaces, enabling initial device association in a physically grounded manner (e.g., [70, 167]). Many of these techniques were developed specifically for horizontal surfaces (tabletops), and involve placement of the mobile on the surface for the entire duration of the interaction [41, 60, 112, 167]. Moreover, mobile phones were used for touch interaction with NFC-tagged displays with a coarser-grained touch resolution due to the tag size ($4\,cm \times 4\,cm$) [54]. None of these techniques, however, focus on enabling fluid user-aware input with mobile devices on interactive surfaces, which is our primary concern.

3.4.3 System Design

The system design for PhoneTouch is illustrated in Figure 3.19. The principal idea is that all involved devices, the surface and the phones, independently detect touch events. Detected device-level events are time-stamped and communicated in real-time to a server, over a wireless link. The individual surface and phone events are matched based on their time-stamps, in order to determine PhoneTouch events. The PhoneTouch events combine complementary information contributed by surface and mobile device: location of the touch as well as identity and state of the phone. As the matching is based exclusively on synchronous timing, there is no requirement for use of specific sensors. This principle of using co-occurrence of events in abstraction of sensors has precedents in a variety of works such as Cooperative Artefacts [150] and SyncTap [123]. In other work, similarity of sensor observations was used for coupling or pairing of devices (e.g., [63, 67, 90]).

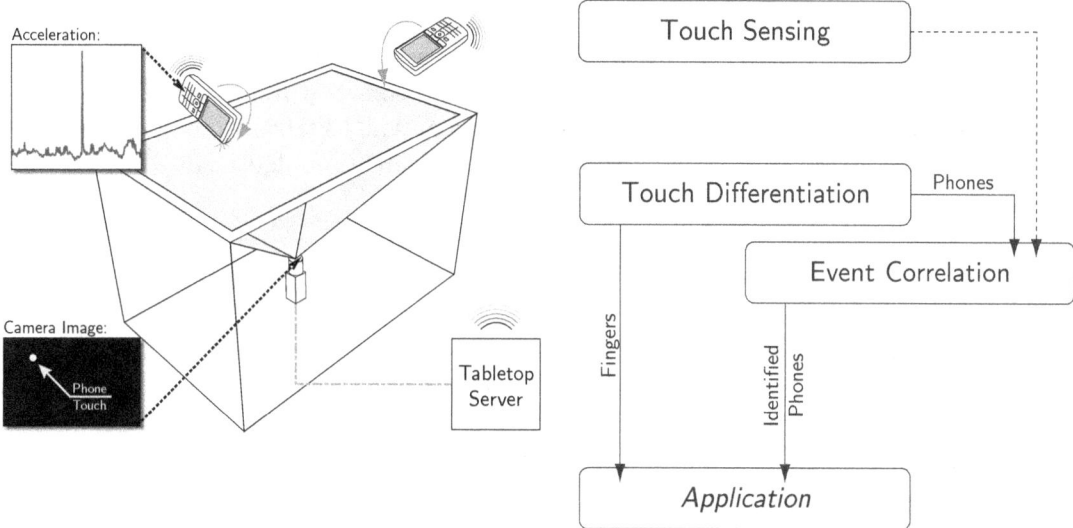

Figure 3.19: Surface and phones detect touch events independently. The device-level observations are communicated over a wireless network, correlated in time, and combined to associate a touch with both surface position and phone identity.

As the technique is based on event correlation in time, the system clocks of the surface and the phones need to be pairwise synchronized. When all participating devices already share a network, a network time protocol can be used for synchronization. For initial pairing of phones with a surface, a possible synchronization method, similar to SyncTap [123], would be to prompt the user for three successive phone touches on the surface. This would generate two relative time intervals that the devices would share to determine the offset of their clocks.

As PhoneTouch interactions are centered around the interactive surface, a natural communication topology would be to have the surface computer act as central server on which device observations are combined. For general application of the technique, the phones would not need to know the location of the touch. Depending on application needs, however, device-level events could also be shared peer-to-peer, such that phones obtain the surface location of their own touches and the phone touch of other phones.

3.4.4 Hardware

In general, any interactive surface that is capable of detecting phone touches and distinguishing them from finger touches can be used for PhoneTouch, while phones need to be able to independently detect touch events reliably. Our specific prototype is based on a custom-built interactive tabletop with an active surface area of 91 cm × 57 cm and a rear-projected screen with a resolution of 1280 pixel × 800 pixel, which is the same surface setup as also used for IdWristbands; section A.2.1 provides a detailed description of the hardware setup. Touch detection is based on computer vision in conjunction with FTIR. The employed camera has a resolution of 640 pixel × 480 pixel and captures images at 120 Hz. Any object in contact with the surface is clearly visible after applying highpass, dilate, and thresholding filters. We extract contact areas by identifying connected components.

Ronkainen et al. showed that accelerometers afford the reliable detection of tapping events on mobile devices [129]. In our initial implementation, we chose to use an externally mounted sensor unit to achieve higher sampling rates than was possible with built-in accelerometers. We attached WiTilt V3 wireless sensors to three Nokia 5800 mobile phones. The integrated three-axis accelerometer samples at 130 Hz and communicates via Bluetooth. On the phone, we run a threshold based detection algorithm that identifies narrow, sharp peaks characteristic for touches.

3.4.5 Software

Similar to IdWristbands and HandsDown, we implemented PhoneTouch in C#. Over the course of this research we changed various implementation details (e.g., switching from Bluetooth to Wifi, or using different phones). While the general processing steps remain unchanged, the specific communication and sensing details mentioned in the following reflect the status at the time of our evaluation study described in the next section.

Communication

Phones and interactive tabletop exchange synchronization messages and time-stamped events via Bluetooth, thereby operating in different piconets than the external WiTilt sensors. Pairwise synchronization between phones and tabletop is achieved by a time-stamped message exchange, described in the network time protocol [97]. Round trip times below 10 ms result in maximal clock offsets of 5 ms. Using Bluetooth, the tabletop advertises its service, which can be found by mobile devices to form an ad hoc network. Initial pairing naturally cannot be based on absolute event timing as no clock synchronization has taken place yet. Instead, users are asked to tap three times with their phones, generating relative time intervals, which are separately sensed by phones and tabletop for comparison.

Finger and Phone Discrimination

In a pilot study, we asked 12 participants (three female) recruited from our department to successively touch targets appearing on the surface at pseudo-random locations. Participants completed two rounds touching 64 targets first with a phone then with their fingers; the presentation order of interaction type was counter balanced. Our results suggest that area size is a reliable indicator for distinguishing phones and fingers. As depicted in Figure 3.20(a), a phone touch (right) results in a substantially smaller blob than finger touches (left). Testing different phone models and varying the angle while touching had very little impact on the observed contact area; even touches with the entire edge were readily distinguishable. We observed users holding phones in a variety of ways during trials.

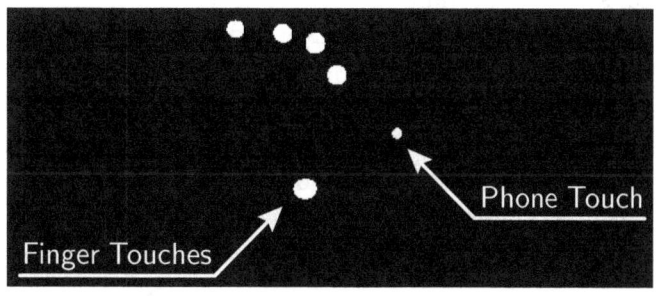

(a) Finger and phone touches yield different contact areas (table camera view)

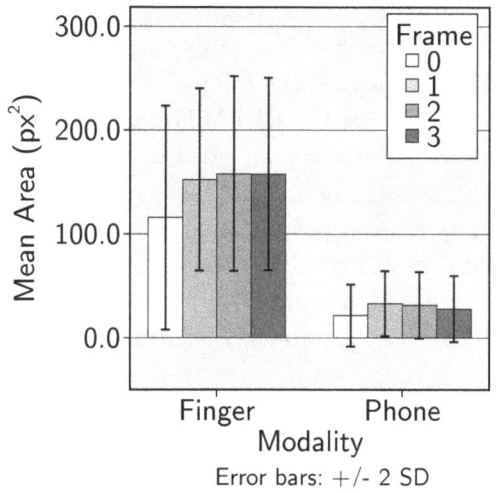

(b) Variances in contact area over the first four frames

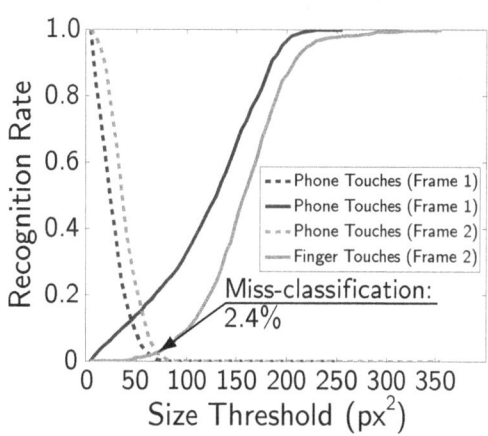

(c) Effect of size threshold on recognition rates of fingers versus phones

Figure 3.20: Finger and phone touches on the surface can reliably be distinguished by contact size.

Contact areas were analyzed over the first four frames after touch detection. We observed a high variance in the first frame, which can be explained by an approaching phase: Initially, the touch area is small and grows until full contact is made. This effect is more pronounced for soft objects like fingers. As Figure 3.20(b) indicates, there is no substantial improvement in terms of reduced variance after the second frame where mean areas of 152.35 ($SD = 43.83$) and 33.04 ($SD = 15.62$) were recorded for fingers and phones respectively. As depicted in Figure 3.20(c) the best trade-off for setting a discriminating threshold in the second frame results in a miss-classification of 2.4 %. If reliably detecting all phone touches is the aim, 9.5 % of fingers will be miss-classified. The results were observed for adults using standard phones. Phone-finger discrimination might be affected if phones are used with soft protective skins, or if users with smaller fingers (e.g., children) use the system.

Event Correlation

Conflicts arise when phone touches fall into the same recognition time frame. Ideally, a touch is instantly detected and assigned the exact time of occurrence. However, such a scenario is unrealistic due to finite sampling rates, detection latencies, and clock synchronization offsets. While sampling rate and detection algorithm cause delays, negative clock offsets possibly lead to events appearing too early.

The described prototype has a minimum recognition time frame of 25 ms (max. sample length of 8.33 ms+clock offset of 5 ms×2, rounded up to the next full sample). We designed detection algorithms for low latency but did not quantify their delay characteristics with the given prototype. It is noteworthy that conflicts are detected. Dependent on the application, suitable measures can be taken to resolve them (e.g., users can be asked to repeat their action).

3.4.6 Evaluation

The following experiment serves two purposes. First, we verified finger versus phone classification performance on the surface. Secondly, we analyzed the temporal distribution of phone touches in a multi-user task. Each user was presented with a horizontal scroll list, showing between two and three pictures at a time. Above, we printed the current search task (e.g., "Find all five pictures of cars"). Depending on this task, participants selected either a single picture out of a set of nine or multiple pictures out of a set of 14. Figure 3.21 shows the task layout. Participants could scroll by touching the arrow buttons on either side with their fingers. To generate a high number of events, we opted for repeated touching to advance the list rather than holding down a button. A picture could only be selected by phone touch.

Figure 3.21:   PhoneTouch evaluation task: The scroll buttons are activated by finger touches while phone touches select a picture.

Twelve participants (seven female), split into groups of three, were recruited from the local campus (mean age of 23.2, $SD = 5.03$) and compensated with £5 for their time. Before beginning the study task, they were given the opportunity to test the system until they felt comfortable using it. While working simultaneously but independently within their surface area, participants completed 20 search tasks each. Contacts with the surface were detected using the computer vision approach of our proof-of-concept implementation. At the end of a session, we asked participants to fill a questionnaire (see Figure B.2 on page 169).

Results

We observed a mean task completion time of 6:27 minutes. The discrimination threshold was optimized not to miss any phone events, resulting in a correct phone classification rate of 99.92 % while miss-classifying 5.66 % of fingers as phones, thus exceeding the expected performance predicted in the pilot study.

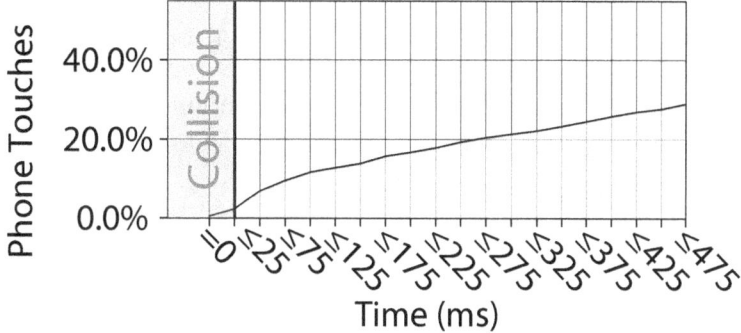

Figure 3.22: Temporal distribution of phone touches (time differences accumulated in intervals of 25 ms)

Further, we measured time differences between successive phone touches. Figure 3.22 shows the temporal distribution of phone touches, accumulated in intervals of 25 ms. With an assumed recognition time frame of 25 ms for our prototype, 97.7 % of phone events could be detected without collision, assuming no false positives. Taking into account the fraction of finger touches miss-classified as phones (competing with true phone touches) 96.3 % of phone events are still collision-free; potential false positives originating from acceleration-based recognition are not considered.

Discussion of Study

Our initial evaluation with focus on finger versus phone detection on the surface and temporal distribution of events indicates the suitability of PhoneTouch for co-located collaboration in small groups. As phones are immediately detected, PhoneTouch allows for instantaneous user identification. Any phone touch consists of a precise surface location, and is associated to a phone and its user at the same time. The presented results provide insights into the simultaneity of phone touches and requirements for sensing hardware. This evaluation, however, can only serve as an indication since touch frequencies are dependent on application and number of concurrent users.

While users might be concerned about causing damage to either their mobile or the surface, this did not appear to be an issue in our user trial sessions. Participants, however, were provided with devices and might have been concerned if they had been asked to use their own. This concern can be addressed with inexpensive bumpers or covers that are already widely used; this may, however, require to adapt detection algorithms due to different touch characteristics. We report on further insights regarding this issue in the context of a more extensive user study presented in Chapter 5.

In this study, we demonstrated PhoneTouch for a particular hardware setup. The underlying time-based matching approach, however, is independent of specific devices or sensors. In fact, for the exploration of the surrounding interaction space (Chapter 4) as well as for our study (Chapter 5), we ported PhoneTouch to different mobile platforms (i.e., Windows Phone 7 (WP7) and iOS) and interactive surfaces (i.e., Microsoft's Surface 2.0 platform [92]), using Wifi instead of Bluetooth for communication.

3.4.7 Summary

Based on a distributed sensing approach, PhoneTouch allows for fluidly identifying users through direct pointing interaction with phones, using them much like a stylus. As phones are identified, they act as proxies for their users, enabling fine-grained user-aware input in parallel with finger-based multi-touch interaction. PhoneTouch is supported by any interactive surface that can detect contacts with a mobile device. At the same time, it works with unmodified off-the-shelf mobile devices, using their built-in sensors for touch detection.

3.5 Discussion

IdWristbands, HandsDown, and PhoneTouch follow the same goals of instantaneous and direct user identification, but use distinct identification strategies. They apply different types of identifying information (e.g., biometric versus numeric identifiers) and detection methods (e.g., capturing the bare hand versus detecting events on a phone). At the same time, the three methods open up new application areas and interaction possibilities that go beyond just user identification (e.g., using a phone's screen for complementary private input). Altogether, these factors affect suitable application domains. Table 3.5 illustrates key characteristics, which we discuss in detail in the following.

3.5.1 Identification Characteristics

The proposed methods use different kinds of identifying information to determine the interacting user. While HandsDown builds on biometric identification, IdWristbands and PhoneTouch use abstract numeric identifiers connected to a token owned by the user. Both biometric and ownership factors are typically linked to a virtual representation of the user (e.g., a user account) in order to facilitate meaningful interactions. The key differences, however, are that biometric features identify an actual person, require prior enrollment, and cannot be changed at will. In contrast, users may buy a new phone or reprogram their wristband, while invalidating previously used identification tokens.

Since the users' hands represent their identities, the identification features are carried with them at all time. This is one of the benefits of using biometrics, because features are consistent even over a long time. Although this is a usability advantage, it is a security disadvantage. Once a biometric is forged, it remains stolen for life; there is no getting back to a secure state. Compared to fingerprints, hand contours are less distinguishable, and hence less appropriate to identify an arbitrary person. As a consequence, we anticipate users to be less concerned about providing hand contours to the system for enrollment and identification.

	IdWristbands	HandsDown	PhoneTouch
Identification Characteristics			
Factor	Ownership	Inherence	Ownership
Origin	Numeric identifier	Hand contour	Device identifier
Entity	Device	Person	Device
Enrollment	—	✓	—
Detection Characteristics			
Additional devices	✓	—	✓
Detection principle	Vision-based	Vision-based	Vision-based & inertial
Communication	IR (unidirectional)	—	RF (bidirectional)
Limiting factors (number of users)	Code transmission time	Hand uniqueness & surface area	Detection collisions
Anonymous input	✓	✓	✓
Identification Scope	Implicit	Controlled	Controlled

Table 3.5:   Characteristics of IdWristbands, HandsDown, and PhoneTouch

3.5.2   Detection Characteristics

Unlike HandsDown, both IdWristbands and PhoneTouch rely on additional devices. IdWristbands uses dedicated hardware (leaving aside possible future integrations with wrist watches for example) whereas PhoneTouch appropriates devices that users commonly have with them. A further difference is that IdWristbands instruments users (i.e., they wear a wristband) while PhoneTouch appropriates mobile devices like a stylus for interaction. Both wristbands and phones have in common that they must be present (i.e., they must be provided, or users must remember to bring them) and ready for interaction (e.g., their batteries must be charged)—a user's hands are readily available in general.

Relying on infrared light, both IdWristbands and HandsDown use the same sensors already in place for finger touch detection. While IdWristbands actively transmits light, HandsDown is a passive approach and relies on reflecting light off the hand. PhoneTouch additionally uses on-device sensors for distributed touch detection (e.g., accelerometers or microphones) and a separate radio channel for communication (e.g., an existing wireless network). In doing so, it facilitates bidirectional communication. IdWristbands, however, only sends information to the surface, while HandsDown does not support active transmissions at all.

Regarding the number of identifiable users, we demonstrated that HandsDown supports small groups of sizes typical for interaction around surfaces. Moreover, related work showed that hand geometries are sufficiently different for groups of about 500 people. The number of registered users for IdWristbands is theoretically unlimited, but restricted in practice by the growing transmission time (via infrared light pulses) for long identifiers. This is not an issue for PhoneTouch as it uses fast wireless networks for communication. To address potential limitations, especially for HandsDown and IdWristbands, a system may limit the number of users that are active and can be identified at the same time (e.g., by having users to activate their account before interaction). Identification by multiple simultaneous users is further limited by the available surface area. In the case of HandsDown, which uses the whole hand for identification, free space runs out faster; this may be an issue if many users wish to identify simultaneously. PhoneTouch, which relies on time-based matching, is prone to collisions if too many users attempt to identify simultaneously. Our evaluation, however, showed that this is not an issue for small groups of users despite frequent PhoneTouch interaction. Further, using higher sensor sampling rates reduces the likelihood of such collisions.

All proposed methods support the co-existence of identified and anonymous input, and hence allow for parallel interaction of users who are not enrolled or unequipped. HandsDown and PhoneTouch further give users full control over their identification scope. Therefore, any user can fluidly switch between identified and anonymous input. In contrast, IdWristbands is designed for continuous and implicit identification. Switching to anonymous input requires users to consciously turn or take off their wristbands, potentially causing interruptions.

Going beyond user identification, the different methods support a variety of additional interaction opportunities. For example, as wristbands emit light, they are already detectable while still hovering above the surface (e.g., to invoke tooltips). The distinctive HandsDown gesture provides orientation information, for instance to automatically rotate content towards the user for better readability. Finally, PhoneTouch seamlessly combines private and shared devices, for example allowing for private input on the phone's screen. We explore open questions with regard to these opportunities and the surrounding interaction spaces in Chapter 4.

At the time of development, our methods addressed existing gaps. IdWristbands made possible implicit user identification of individual fingers on vision-based surfaces, HandsDown was the first approach to integrate biometric user identification with direct-touch input on interactive surfaces, and PhoneTouch pioneered using mobile phones in a stylus-like fashion for precise, continuous, and spontaneous interactions. In parallel to our efforts, however, related work emerged pursuing similar goals. For example, the IR Ring was developed at the same time as IdWristbands and is conceptually similar, but with a focus on secure authentication rather than fluid identified interaction [130]. Hutama et al. proposed a related approach for phone-based interaction after we had introduced PhoneTouch [70].

3.5.3 Further Considerations

Considering suitable application domains, IdWristbands, to start with, requires users to wear dedicated identification devices throughout surface interaction. Such devices need to be provided or brought by the user. By identifying individual finger touches, it supports the most transparent type of user identification, but does not allow to fluidly control the identification scope (i.e., to interleave identified and anonymous input). We therefore envision IdWristbands most suitable for applications that rely on continuous identification of any touch input in environments where it is feasible and acceptable to wear a dedicated device, such as in business or control room scenarios, as well as for user studies that analyze touch interaction behaviors. In the future, identity-emitting LEDs may be integrated into wrist watches or clothing, making IdWristbands more accessible.

HandsDown requires prior enrollment and involves a quick yet explicit identification step. It lends itself to application domains that are targeted at children or the elderly, as no additional devices are required (which may be perceived unnecessary or complicated) and users can identify with a simple gesture. In general, HandsDown supports walk-up scenarios (the one-time enrollment is quickly accomplished) and applications that require frequent but not continuous identification. HandsDown is designed for low risk environments, such as home settings, as hand contours are not sufficiently unique to provide high security.

Similar to IdWristbands, PhoneTouch also relies on additional hardware, but uses devices that users commonly have with them, making this method more accessible. Like a stylus, it enables precise selection of targets on the surface. No prior enrollment is required and PhoneTouch is ready to use after installing a small application on the mobile device. Interleaving anonymous, finger-based with identified, phone-based touch interaction is straightforward. In contrast to the previous two methods, PhoneTouch allows users to interact with a surface without having to use their bare hands, which may be desirable in public settings because of hygiene factors. Further, any scenario that requires an additional private screen or the instant availability of personal data (stored on the phone) benefits from adopting PhoneTouch.

Security Considerations

Security in the context of user identification plays an important role. Thoroughly analyzing and contrasting the security afforded by our three methods, however, is beyond the scope of this thesis, which puts an emphasis on enabling technologies and interactions. We therefore confine ourselves to a high-level discussion of selected security aspects.

By virtue of the computational resources that PhoneTouch has at its disposal on both surface and mobile devices, it supports advanced encryption algorithms to secure all communication and verify identities. In general, adversaries cannot forthrightly eavesdrop on transmissions as communication takes place over an encrypted wireless link in the first place. Users may, however, attempt to trick the time-based matching approach. For example, an adversary may attempt to perform a timed PhoneTouch on a different object to coincide with a legitimate PhoneTouch on the surface. Such an attack is spatially restricted as both a clear view on the surface and wireless connectivity are required. Further, provided that all events are correctly detected, this attempt will result in a collision, which prevents a successful interaction, but does not compromise the system.

In contrast, IdWristbands uses infrared light, which is more easily observed. Therefore, a suitable camera could record the transmitted pulses at a distance to be used in a replay attack. Our basic communication protocol is particularly vulnerable. More advanced encodings, however, are straightforward to integrate and provide additional security (e.g., discussed by Roth et al. [130]). HandsDown also relies on computer vision to capture hand contours. As it does not perform a livelihood detection, our current implementation could be tricked by using a mock-up hand (e.g., a copy made of cardboard). Furthermore, hands of different users may turn out too similar for reliable differentiation. While a more strict identification threshold may be applied, this also results in an increased false negative rate.

The simple gesture of placing a hand on an interactive surface allows the user to achieve both identification and authentication. We do not recommend designers to adopt the approach for both schemes as a combine, however. The uniqueness of hand contours is not guaranteed, hence a false identification of a user's hand subsequently implies a false authentication. Further consideration of robustness between identification and authentication is recommended. Results by Yörük et al. show the performance of using hand contours for authentication is more robust than identification [169]. Each hand identification requires a search against the list of stored hands templates to find a specific identity; whilst, authentication only requires comparison between a hand input against a specified template.

3.6 Summary

We demonstrated that IdWristbands, HandsDown, and PhoneTouch all enable user identification on interactive surfaces, following the goals laid out in section 3.1: First, they allow users to instantaneously identify for spontaneous user-aware interaction. Using IdWristbands, identification implicitly extends finger touch; placing the hand on the surface for identification with HandsDown is quick and does not require preparation; PhoneTouch enables users to simply tap the surface with their phone for identified interactions. Secondly, our methods integrate with the prevailing direct-touch interaction style. Again, IdWristbands is based on typical finger touch; HandsDown gestures are a type of direct-touch as well, albeit more coarse-grained; touching with a phone is similar to using a stylus and allows for precise and direct target selection. Thirdly, they are implemented using common vision-based surface systems. While HandsDown does not require extra hardware, IdWristbands and PhoneTouch use additional devices, but integrate with common vision-based surface systems.

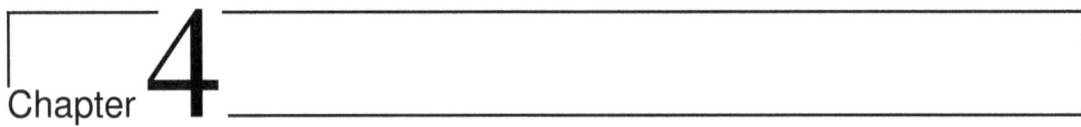

Chapter 4

Exploring Personalized Interaction

Instantaneous user identification for surface computing enables fine-grained personalization on the level of individual interactions. In this chapter, we illustrate the utility of such personalized interaction by introducing a wide range of user-aware interaction techniques that address typically encountered issues in surface computing. At the same time, we demonstrate how HandsDown and PhoneTouch, two user identification methods based on hand biometrics and mobile devices respectively, integrate with typical multi-touch input to facilitate spontaneous personalization on shared surfaces. Our exploration is preceeded by an in-depth analysis of the distinct HandsDown and PhoneTouch interaction spaces, which inform the development of the proposed interaction techniques.

4.1 Introduction

Instantaneous user identification—as enabled by IdWristbands, HandsDown, and Phone-Touch—opens up the compelling design space of personalized interaction. First of all, user identification facilitates the access to a plethora of personal information, such as account privileges, application preferences, or private documents. The instantaneous and direct availability of such information adds a new quality to surface-based interaction. Therefore, any application can dynamically personalize its responses on the level of individual interactions.

4.1.1 Personalized Interaction for Surface Computing

The concept of personalized interaction has been considered in a different context before, but its application to surface computing takes new forms. Previous work focused on personalization for either single-user interfaces (e.g., to determine a user's interest to personalize museum web sites [132]) or distributed multi-device environments. Researches concerned with the latter typically investigate infrastructures and software architectures for user preference management (e.g., [33, 110]). In contrast, we focus on personalized interaction for a single and shared interface with multiple users interacting simultaneously; our vision comprises personal information on the level of individual interactions.

Uses of Personal Information

Identifying the user who provided input allows for personalizing corresponding interactions to various extents. Type and volume of available personal information (e.g., ranging from just the user's identity to detailed application preferences) determine the degree of possible personalization. To illustrate this, we group personalized interactions with similar information demands into three categories—ranging from low to high demands, and consequently from low to high degrees of personalization. The more personal information involved, the deeper the integration with the corresponding application is. Although presented as discrete categories for the sake of clarity, the information requirements and extents of personalization rather shift on a continuous spectrum (Figure 4.1). Further, we do not intend to present an exhaustive list of applications but aim at providing a general framework for personalized interaction.

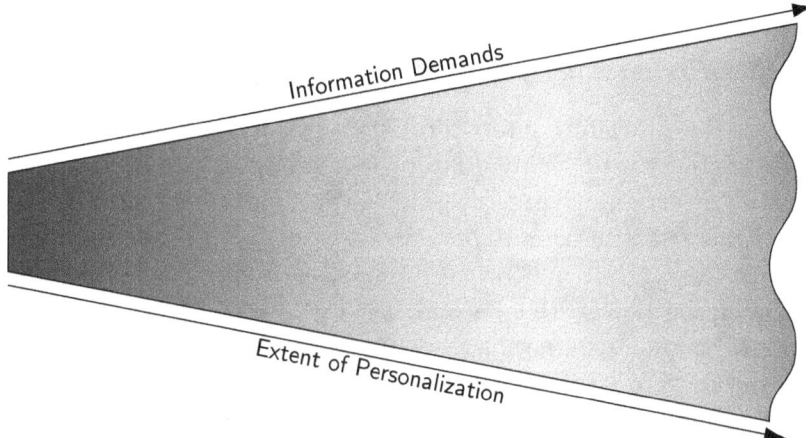

Figure 4.1: The type and volume of available personal information determines the extent of possible personalization.

- *Basic User Identity.* User identity on its own (i.e., basic identifiers such as unique names) already open up a wide range of possibilities for tailoring interactions to the user in question. For instance, to implement privileged access, user identity serves as key to unlock otherwise restricted functions. Similarly, it facilitates applications that require their users to cast votes. Generally, keeping track of different user identities allows for logging and auditing interactions, for example to analyze user behavior on a multi-touch surface. Further, users may wish to attach their identity to various objects, such as to tag their occurrence in a photo or to claim ownership of documents. The presented examples have in common that they do not require additional personal information besides the users' identities.

- *Accessing Personal Data.* User identification facilitates instantaneous access to personal files such as documents or photos. This is particularly relevant for collaborative scenarios, which typically benefit from users contributing individual documents as basis for subsequent teamwork. Similarly, users often wish to obtain a personal copy of the meeting's outcome. This kind of personalized interaction requires more information than just a user's identity. In particular, it utilizes user identity to provide direct and convenient access to personal storages in a shared environment. Here, personalization is limited to accessing such data, however, and does not involve further customization.

- *Personalized Behavior.* Knowing a user's preferences allows for powerful personalization concepts to customize interaction to a great extent. For instance, to implement a multi-user undo function, an application needs to keep track of individual actions on a per-user base. Further, providing custom lists or menus, such as a personal collection of bookmarks, calls for access to corresponding information, which is enabled through user identification. Finally, independent input sequences, which consist of first selecting a tool to later apply it, require an application to be aware of such selections for each user separately. Depending on the application, the underlying user-specific knowledge may already be available and provided up-front (e.g., by means of an existing user account) or may be created and collected during the course of interaction (e.g., by logging and interpreting a user's input and selections).

Immediate Access to Personal Information

To blend in with the prevailing interaction style of surface computing and to enable personalization on the level of individual interactions, suitable identification methods have to make user identity immediately available when and where needed. The directness of input enables interactive surfaces to provide users with equal and unrestricted access to a shared interface. As a result, such input, originating from multiple users, is interwoven to a large extent. In particular, there are neither clear spatial boundaries (e.g., windows) nor clear temporal boundaries (e.g., well-defined user sessions). Instead, users interact anywhere on a surface while swiftly changing locations. Therefore, surface computing calls for fine-grained personalization on the level of individual interactions. User identification has to be tightly integrated with typical touch input, turning identity into an input parameter alongside others, such as touch location.

4.1.2   Exploring the Design Space

We explore the design space of personalized interaction for surface computing by contributing a wide range of concrete interaction techniques. Our techniques simplify existing, or enable new types, of interaction, thereby addressing a set of typically encountered issues in surface computing (e.g., providing privileged access). They apply personal information to various extents while remaining generic and hence applicable to a larger spectrum of applications.

As shown in the previous chapter, IdWristbands, HandsDown, and PhoneTouch allow for instantaneous and location-specific identification. Their particular identification strategies, however, impact the corresponding interaction flows differently. As summarized in Table 4.1, the varying agents of control (i.e., fingers, hands, and phones) impact different dimensions of input, such as transparency of identification, input granularity, and available degrees of freedom.

- *IdWristbands* identifies individual finger contacts and therefore seamlessly extends typical multi-touch input. The resulting identification is implicit as the common finger-based interaction style and its granularity are unaltered. In addition, all five fingers of a wristband-equipped hand are transparently identified, which allows for

	IdWristbands	HandsDown	PhoneTouch
Agent of control	Finger	Hand	Phone
Identification	Implicit	Explicit	Implicit*
Interaction style	Finger multi-touch	Distinctive gesture	Stylus single-touch
Number of contacts	5	1	1
Granularity	Fingertip	Hand	Device corner

Table 4.1: The different agents of control used by IdWristbands, HandsDown, and PhoneTouch impact interactions differently. All characteristics shown refer to *identified* input.
*once phone is in hand

performing identified multi-touch gestures. Enabling bimanual identified input is as easy as wearing a second wristband.

- *PhoneTouch* offers a comparable input granularity by providing identification for stylus-like input with a handheld device. Using such a mediator for control, however, reduces the available number of identified contacts for a hand to one (i.e., the contact provided by the phone's corner). While identification is implicit as long as users interact continuously with the phone, it becomes explicit for sporadic phone usage. Note that PhoneTouch lends itself to mixed bimanual input with one hand holding the phone for identified interaction while the other performs finger-based input.

- *HandsDown* is based on performing a distinct identification gesture with the hand. This agent of control occupies a substantially larger surface area compared to a fingertip or a phone corner. Therefore, designing interactions for HandsDown will follow different strategies to provide precise target selections. We envision asymmetric bimanual interaction that uses the non-dominant hand for identification, thereby setting a coarse frame of reference. At the same time, fingers of the dominant hand perform dexterous input; the analogy would be holding and moving a paper with one hand while writing with the other.

In contrast to IdWristbands, both HandsDown and PhoneTouch identify entities other than fingers, the primarily used agent of control on direct-touch surfaces, which results in both challenges and new opportunities for personalized interaction at the same time. On the one hand, HandsDown and PhoneTouch require additional attention to seamless integration with conventional multi-touch interaction. On the other hand, they empower users to take control over the identification scope, allowing them to fluidly switch between identified and anonymous input. Further, in the case of PhoneTouch, personal mobile devices offer private input and output spaces that can complement the shared surface. We therefore focus on personalized interaction techniques based on HandsDown and PhoneTouch in the following. For each method, we initially analyze the interaction space to then develop and demonstrate a range of novel interaction techniques.

4.2 HandsDown

Personalized interaction based on HandsDown is characterized by placing a hand flat on the surface for instantaneous identification. Compared to typical finger touch, a hand touch occupies a substantially larger surface area, which makes precise selection more challenging. Therefore, our exploration of the HandsDown interaction space in this section focuses on the issue of target selection. Based on this analysis, we introduce a versatile and application-independent interaction technique, IdLenses, which we illustrate with a series of usage scenarios. IdLenses employs asymmetric bimanual interaction to facilitate personalized interaction.

4.2.1 Interaction Space

HandsDown has distinct advantages with the potential to ease instantaneous user identification and personalization on shared surfaces. Besides prior enrollment, there are no further requirements on the user side. In particular, users do not have to carry devices or tokens, and do not have to remember passwords. The identification procedure built on hand contour analysis is quick. It consists of merely placing a hand flat on the surface. Users can do so at arbitrary locations on the surface, and multiple users can identify at the same time. The distinctive hand gesture is easy to remember and to carry out. The on-demand characteristic of HandsDown puts users in full control of the identification scope.

Although HandsDown is a form of direct-touch input, it differs from conventional finger touch in various aspects. Above all, the hand occupies a substantially larger area on the surface compared to a fingertip. This naturally results in a reduced input granularity. Therefore, target selection demands particular attention, especially with multiple potential targets in close proximity. A flat hand is also less dexterous and provides fewer degrees of freedom compared to a finger. Gestures (e.g., pinching to resize) are not possible and common interactions (e.g., drag-and-drop) become arguably more cumbersome. In addition, we need to consider the occlusion caused by a hand when integrating HandsDown into a user interface.

While HandsDown enables users to fluidly identify on demand directly on an interactive surface, it is clearly not a substitute for conventional finger touch. HandsDown does not aim at implicit user identification that would comprise all touch interaction, but assumes a complementary role instead. The unique advantages of HandsDown are accompanied by the challenges with respect to its particular interaction characteristics. In the remainder of this section, we explore the question of how to integrate HandsDown into surface applications to enable personalized interaction. We devise and analyze concrete target selection strategies that embed user identification with HandsDown into direct multi-touch interaction.

Target Selection

Personalized interaction takes place in the context of particular targets, which utilize the provided identification information in order to react in a customized way. Depending on the application, identification targets may vary greatly in type and size. For example, text fields for password entry are typically smaller than documents scattered on the surface. Both are, however, potential targets for identified interactions. As a matter of fact, multiple targets may be in close proximity or even overlap. Beyond that, a target does not need to be a concrete and visible object. For example, a personalized start menu may appear wherever a HandsDown gesture is performed, independent of what is underneath the hand.

Integrating HandsDown with typical surface interaction requires effortless target selection. Figure 4.2 provides an overview of possible selection strategies. On the topmost level, we distinguish between *autonomous* (i.e., a single HandsDown interaction completes the target selection) and *integrated* strategies (i.e., the target selection requires supplemental finger touch interactions).

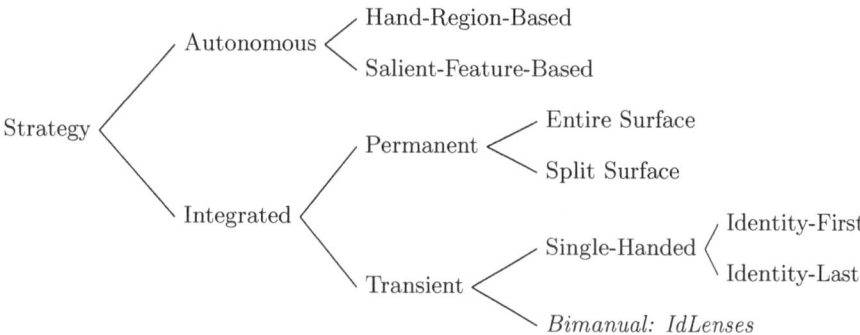

Figure 4.2: Different strategies for target selection using HandsDown come with different interaction characteristics.

Autonomous Strategies. We discuss the two autonomous strategies, *hand-region-based* and *salient-feature-based*, only briefly as we do not consider them being suitable for general purpose target selection. Hand-region-based selection, using the HandsDown gesture for direct selection, is only unambiguous in the case of a single target located underneath the hand (Figure 4.3(a)–(b)). This, however, is arguably the exception rather than the norm. Salient-feature-based selection, for example using a fingertip as reference point, could be used for fine-grained selection. Yet, such an approach is problematic for targets located in corners or close to surface edges. In particular, users may have to awkwardly twist their hands or change location around the surface in order to reach the target in question (Figure 4.3(c)–(d)). Therefore, we focus on integrated strategies, which we discuss in the following.

Integrated Strategies. Integrated strategies combine HandsDown with additional finger touch interaction. We are particularly interested in *transient* approaches that allow for fluid and spontaneous user identification. *Permanent* approaches, however, are not considered in greater detail as they do not align with our idea of personalized interaction for surface computing.

- Applying a permanent approach, users can claim a particular surface area by performing a HandsDown gesture. Within this area all touches are treated as belonging to the initiating user. For example, using HandsDown to take over the *entire surface* as exclusive workspace is limited to single-user applications. In contrast, claiming dedicated parts (i.e., resulting in *splitting* the available space)

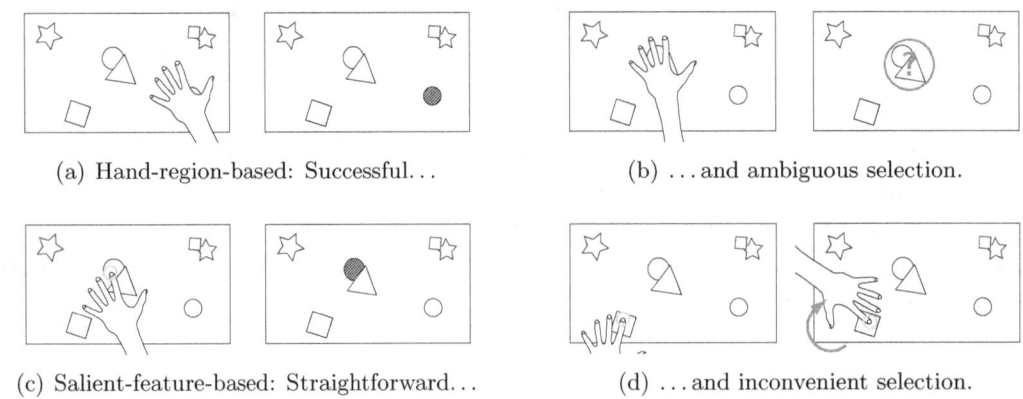

(a) Hand-region-based: Successful...   (b) ...and ambiguous selection.

(c) Salient-feature-based: Straightforward...   (d) ...and inconvenient selection.

Figure 4.3: Autonomous selection strategies: (a)–(b) Hand-region-based: Selection in a single step using HandsDown is only possible if potential targets are sparsely distributed. (c)–(d) Salient-feature-based: Targets close to corners or edges may require users to twist their hand or change location around the surface before a selection is possible.

does not scale with a growing number of users that might only sporadically interact and identify. Further, areas equally accessible by all users are commonly used in table-based interaction to jointly complete tasks [140]. Interactions within such group territories may also benefit from user-aware interactions, which is not compatible with permanent strategies.

- Amongst transient approaches, we differentiate between *single-handed* and *bimanual* selection.

(a) Identity-first: The intended target is selected in a refinement step after performing a HandsDown gesture.

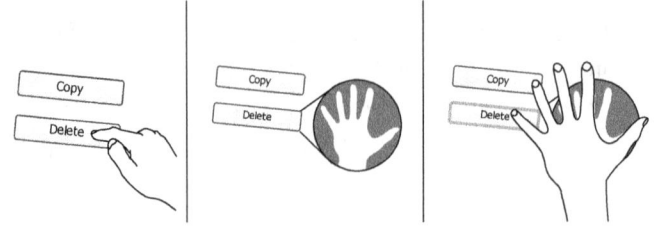

(b) Identity-last: After selecting a target using finger touch, the user is prompted to provide identification in a second step.

Figure 4.4: Integrated, transient, single-handed selection strategies

– Using a single-hand strategy, users identify performing a HandsDown gesture before making a supplemental refinement selection by means of finger touch, or vice versa. Although these two selection strategies comprise the same steps (albeit in the opposite order), they differ in the underlying concepts. Identifying first implies that users are aware of the requirement for user identity (Figure 4.4(a)). In contrast, first selecting a target that requires identification using finger touch will result in a prompt for subsequent identification and is hence of a more disruptive nature (Figure 4.4(b)). Of course, these two approaches are not mutually exclusive and can be implemented side by side within the same application. Further note that users can perform single-hand strategies using different hands for identification and refinement. Conceptually, however, only a single hand is required.

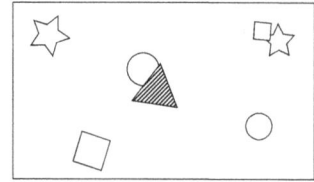

Figure 4.5: Integrated, transient, bimanual selection strategies: The non-dominant hand performs a HandsDown gesture to define the scope of identification. Within this frame of reference the dominant hand performs finger touch input associated to the user's identity.

– Bimanual strategies are characterized by using one hand for identification and the other for simultaneous fine-grained selection (Figure 4.5). In particular, the non-dominant hand performs the HandsDown gesture and stays on the surface for the duration of personalized interaction. It thereby sets a frame of reference for accompanying dexterous finger touches with the dominant hand. Finger touches in close proximity to the non-dominant hand are associated to the same user; applications may visualize this area in which finger touches are associated (i.e., the identification scope). The resulting asynchronous bimanual interaction resembles real-world tasks [51]. For example, when composing a letter, the non-dominant hand holds and guides the paper while the dominant hand writes.

Table 4.2 compares HandsDown target selection strategies based on the characteristics "multiple selection" (i.e., does a single identification gesture allow for multiple subsequent interactions?), "unrestricted selection" (i.e., does a strategy allow for selecting arbitrary targets?), and "transient scope" (i.e., is the identification transient, as opposed to permanent?). A transient identification scope and allowing for unrestricted selections are fundamental requirements for the type of personalized interaction that we envision, whereas the ability to select multiple targets with a single identification gesture is not as such. However, if target selection strategies require more than one step—as it is the case for most, including both identity-first and -last—not being able to select multiple items is at odds with the aimed at immediacy of identified interaction. We therefore focus on exploring a bimanual strategy for HandsDown, which allows for unrestricted, multiple target selection in the context of a transient identification scope.

Strategy	Multiple Selection	Unrestricted Selection	Transient Scope
Hand-Region-Based	—	—	✓
Salient-Feature-Based	—	—	✓
Identity-First	—	✓	✓
Identity-Last	—	✓	✓
Bimanual: IdLenses	✓	✓	✓
Entire Surface	✓	✓	—
Split Surface	✓	✓	—

Table 4.2: Characteristics of HandsDown target selection strategies

4.2.2 IdLenses

Informed by the above analysis, we introduce IdLenses, a bimanual interaction concept that facilitates personalized interaction and builds on previous magic lens concepts (e.g., [22, 73, 147]). It provides each user with their own personal lens in a shared environment. A lens is summoned by a HandsDown gesture that simultaneously provides user identity. The user's identity is always attached to a lens in order to dynamically personalize input and output. Figure 4.6 illustrates the user experience of IdLenses. The ability to create a lens instantaneously anywhere on the surface, and to move it around freely, enables users to fluidly control which part of their input is identifiable, and which shall remain anonymous. IdLenses facilitates a wide range of personalized interaction techniques, which we introduce in the remainder of this section, informed by the following discussion of general design considerations.

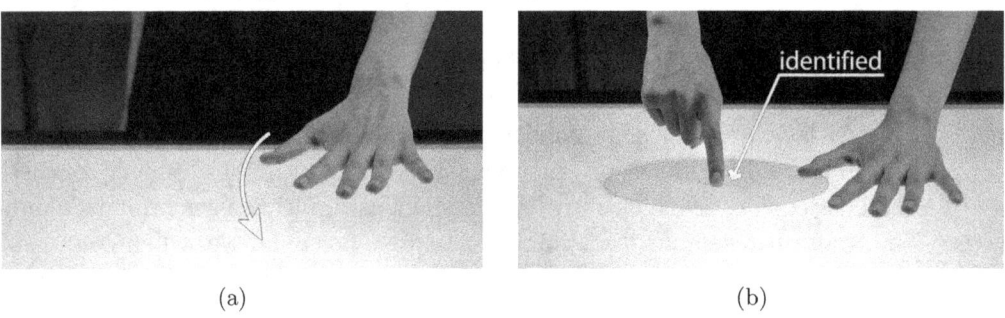

(a)   (b)

Figure 4.6: (a) IdLenses can be accessed anywhere on the surface, using the distinctive HandsDown gesture. (b) All touches through the lens are identified.

Design Considerations

Conceptually, an IdLens is a virtual layer overlaying above the application layer. In surface computing, this virtual layer can be used for both input and output of information flow between users and applications. By attaching user identity to the virtual layer, any information that flows through the layer can be personalized. In other words, any input made through the personal lens is attached with a user identity, while any input made outside the lens is anonymous. Similarly, display output can be personalized through the IdLens as well.

The position of the IdLens should avoid causing any obstructions. For instance, if a left hand is used to activate an IdLens, the lens should appear on the right side of the hand. If not, the user needs to cross arms to interact with the lens, which may result in an obstruction. An alternative solution is allowing the user to define the lens' position, for example by drawing its outline with the dominant hand. Of course, this flexibility comes at the cost of an extra user interaction each time an IdLens is called.

The appearance of IdLenses can be determined by the system or the users. Although our examples use an elliptical shape to resemble a real lens, the shape can vary according to the application needs. Alternatively, as just mentioned, the lens can be drawn by users. Also, to resize an IdLens, we can adopt existing objects resizing gestures. For example, using a dedicated button or a slide-bar, dragging the frame of the lens towards or away from its center, or using multi-touch gestures like pinch-to-zoom.

We introduced IdLenses as transient identification concept; a lens is hidden as soon as the user's hand is lifted. This prevents an IdLens to be left active while its owner is away, but it limits the use of the registered hand since it must linger on the surface to keep the lens active. While it is possible to leave a lens active even the user's hand is lifted, we focus on transient identification scopes. In this case, the non-dominant hand coarsely positions the lens, setting the frame of reference for dexterous interactions with the dominant hand for asymmetrical bimanual interactions.

In a collaborative scenario where multiple IdLenses are opened, some of the lenses may overlap. The overlapping denotes a metaphor of users sharing a private group space. Hence, any action performed on the intersected area has all the IdLenses' identities attached. Nevertheless, this may cause conflicts; designers can avoid such situations by forbidding overlapping of IdLenses.

Interaction Techniques

After these general design considerations, we now turn our attention to interaction techniques based on IdLenses. In particular, IdLenses facilitates personalized interaction on three levels: The first level ("touch identification") is concerned with general uses of personal information, while the remaining two levels ("personalized magic lens" and "personalized toolglass") appropriate particular lens-characteristics to further tailor input and output to the corresponding user. Note that for the sake of clarity, we chose drawings rather than actual photos to illustrate most of the presented techniques.

Touch Identification.   On the input side, an identity is attached to every finger touch made through a lens, thus allowing for fine-grained selection in this extended identification scope. In doing so, underlying applications and interface elements can attribute interactions to a user. This allows for several user-aware concepts, following the three uses of personal information as outlined in section 4.1.1.

- *Basic User Identity.* As all input through a lens can be attributed to a user, the attached identity can serve as primary input. In particular, certain functionalities may only be available to a privileged subgroup of users; a button related to such a function can only be activated through the lens of an authorized user. For example in a crisis management scenario, any user could inspect the map while only authorized personnel would be allowed to issue commands to units in this interface.

Further, users can attach their identity to documents or parts thereof, for example to claim ownership or tag themselves in a photo, by touching through the lens.

- *Accessing Personal Data.* IdLenses can facilitate access to personal data by opening corresponding folders if activated through a lens. In doing so, any user can transfer personal files to the shared surface by invoking a lens and selecting the file in question. Conversely, users can copy shared files to their personal storage by selecting them through the lens.

- *Personalized Behavior.* Essentially the same function is performed but with a different behavior, depending on the user. For instance, the button "My Bookmarks"—appearing the same to all users—would retrieve a different list depending on who touches it (through their IdLens). Furthermore, a start button could display the user's favorite applications, and even provide applications with the user's identity (e.g., enabling an email client to start up instantly presenting the personal inbox).

Personalized Toolglass.   So far, touch input through a lens is simply given the additional parameter of user identity. Going further by applying the Toolglass [22] concept, we can add click-through elements (such as buttons) onto the lens, thus enabling extended functions (e.g., assigning a color to a shape). Now, users can directly activate a variety of functions, which otherwise might be difficult to access on a tabletop (e.g., menus might be out of reach). While the general concept of having a set of tools readily at hand anywhere on the surface is compelling as such, we focus on functions that are used in conjunction with user identity.

- *Custom Set of Functions.* Users can customize the set of functions to be shown in the lens. This way, multiple users can work in parallel with different sets of tools and easily access their preferred configuration.

- *User-Dependent Functions.* Functions that inherently rely on user identity to be useful in a collaborative scenario are candidates for being added to an IdLens. For example, a clipboard function allows users to maintain a personal clipboard and hence work independently on a shared surface (Figure 4.7). We used a similar implementation for our user study in Chapter 5.

- *Alternative to Modal Input Sequences.* Selecting a tool or property to perform a related action (e.g., selecting a color to draw a line) is not straightforward to realize in shared applications [109]. IdLenses provides a convenient alternative as these selections can be made through functions available on a lens.

Personalized Magic Lens.   In addition to input customization, IdLenses can also customize output. Acting as a personalization filter, the appearance of elements underneath a lens is modified.

- *Personalized Preview.* As discussed before, the IdLenses concept allows the behavior of functions to be personalized. In this context, it makes sense to provide visual feedback to indicate that a personalized behavior is available. For example, moving a lens over the login area of a web page fills out user name and password fields to indicate that personalized credentials are used when clicking on the login button (Figure 4.8).

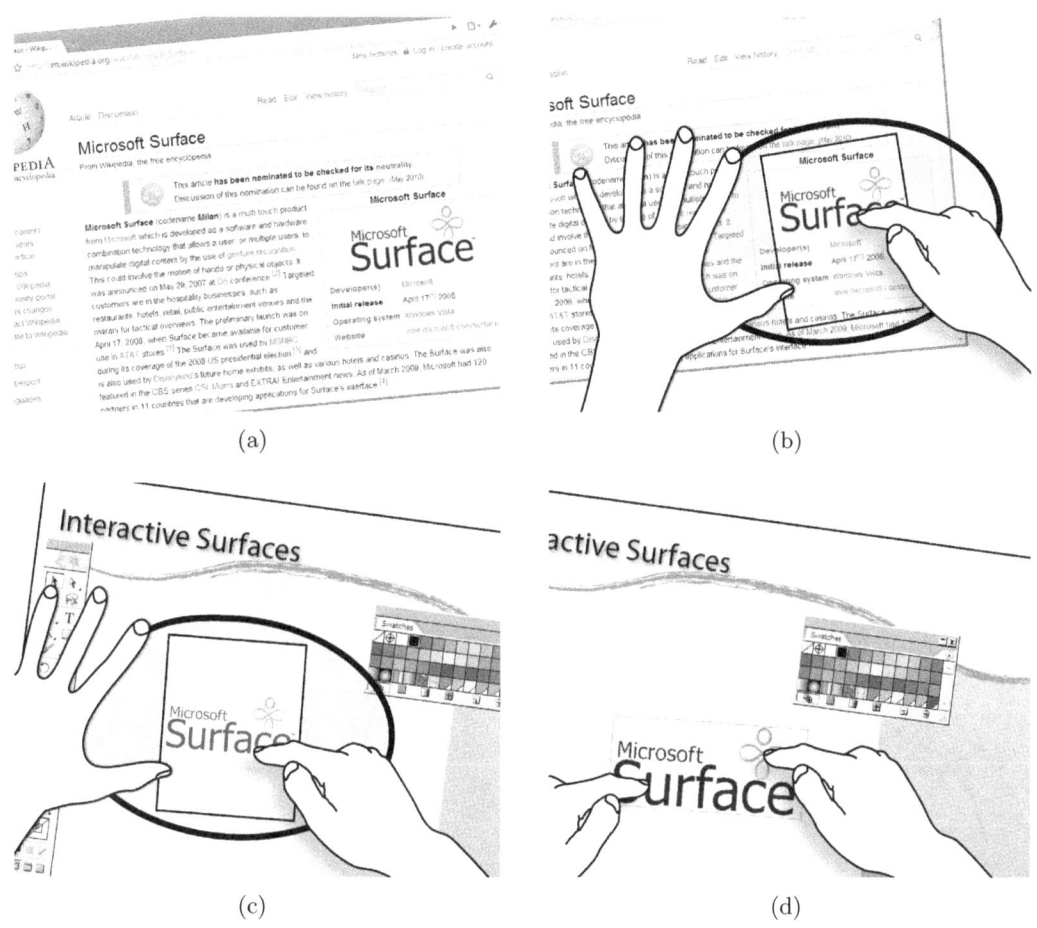

Figure 4.7: Individual clipboards as example of a personalized Toolglass: (a) The user browses a web page to find an image of interest. (b) Selecting the image through the lens puts it into the user's clipboard. (c) The lens is invoked over the target document where the image is to be pasted. (d) It is now part of the document and can be edited.

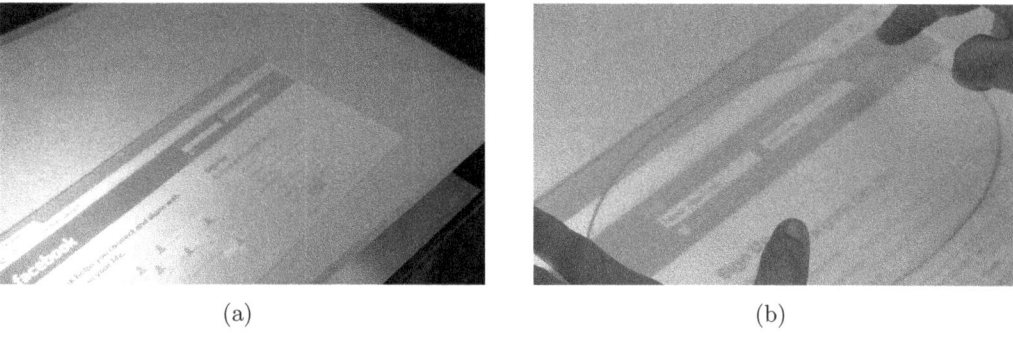

Figure 4.8: Example of personalized behavior (with preview): (a) A protected web page requiring login. (b) Moving the lens over the login area automatically fills in credentials and enables login by simple touch.

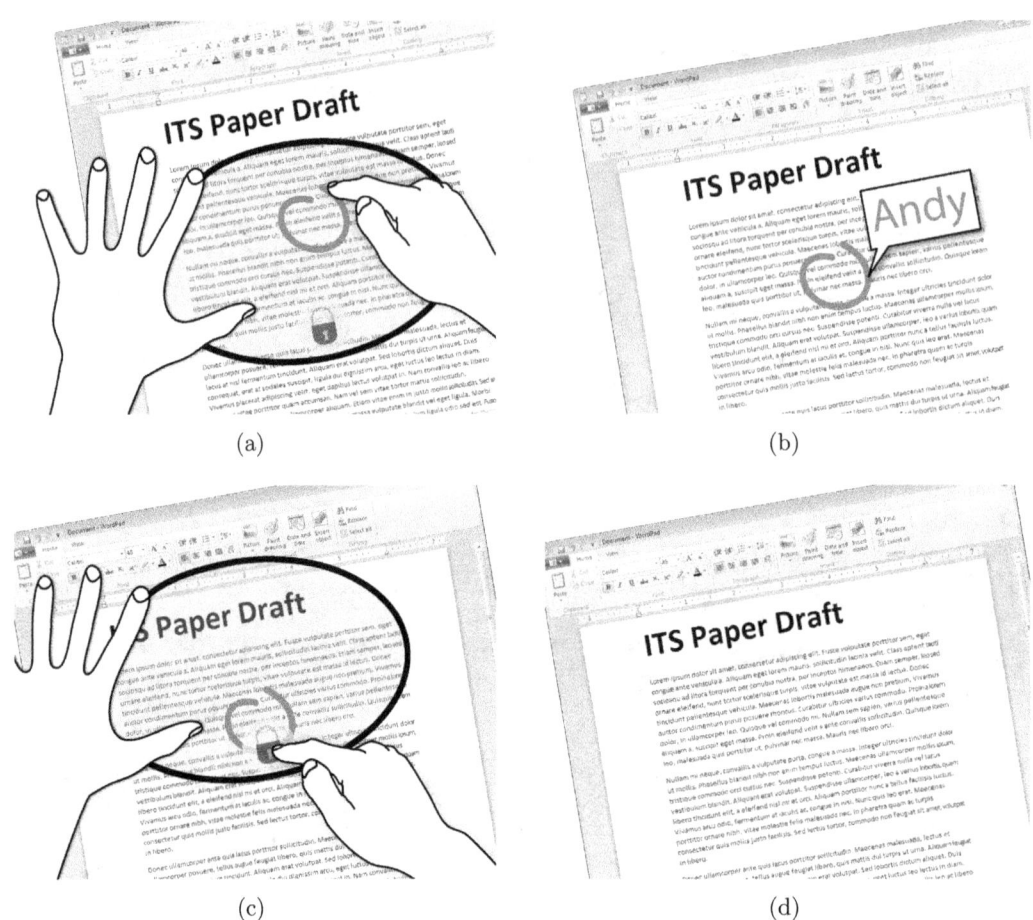

Figure 4.9: Personal annotations example: (a) Adding an annotation to a document. (b) As entered through the IdLens, the annotation's author is known. (c) To make it private, the annotation is selected through a lock button. (d) Only the author can now see the annotation through his lens.

- *Appearance.* Users may specify personal preferences, such as language, which are then applied when viewing the surface through a lens. For example, multiple users can explore a shared application in parallel in their respective language in a museum or exhibition setting. In another example users may adjust color schemes or contrast for easier readability.

- *Selective Output.* Moving the lens over a private or hidden piece of information makes it visible to an authorized user. For example, personal annotations are revealed when the corresponding user places the lens above it (Figure 4.9).

4.2.3 Summary

In this section, we demonstrated the feasibility of HandsDown for personalized interaction on interactive surfaces by introducing IdLenses, a flexible and versatile interaction concept. To inform the design of interaction techniques based on HandsDown, we first discussed issues of hand-based input granularity and analyzed possible strategies for precise target selection. Based on this analysis, we introduced IdLenses, which demonstrates the seamless integration of HandsDown with typical multi-touch interaction for spontaneous identification directly on the surface. IdLenses facilitates dexterous finger-touch input with the dominant hand, while providing full control over the identification scope. Input inside a lens, however, is not restricted to legitimate users by default; anyone in physical reach can perform such input. Therefore, we expect social protocols to be in place. Finally, we introduced a range of interaction techniques based on IdLenses, which illustrate that HandsDown can provide spontaneous personalization for various types of surface applications.

4.3 PhoneTouch

Following the same structure as for HandsDown, we first analyze the interaction space of PhoneTouch before introducing novel personalized interaction techniques. Our interaction space exploration takes into account the phone as complementary device with a user interface and storage capabilities in its own right. Informed by this analysis, we introduce 13 novel interaction techniques. We address six issues typically encountered in surface computing and demonstrate synergistic use of phones and surface. We further present four applications that integrate multiple of our proposed interaction techniques and report on initial user feedback.

4.3.1 Interaction Space

PhoneTouch enables spontaneous user identification and personalization for interactive surfaces, using mobiles as proxies for their users. The essence of PhoneTouch is that a mobile device is used for precise selection of targets on a surface by direct-touch, much like a stylus, creating touch events that are associated with a position on the surface and the identity of the user.

Moreover, PhoneTouch serves as a generic platform for synergistic interaction with mobiles and surfaces. There are compelling reasons for combined use of mobiles and surfaces, and for seamless interaction across the two. Mobiles are great for carrying data and media while surfaces offer better scale for interaction with content. Mobiles provide user control over personal data while surfaces make it easy to share. Surfaces can be used by multiple users in the same way while mobiles can be used in highly personalized ways. Surfaces can be interacted upon in parallel while mobiles have more degrees of freedom in input. PhoneTouch naturally lends itself for fusion with other interactions that users can perform with either the mobile or the touch surface.

In the following, we identify the fundamental input, output, and contextual attributes that define the building blocks for personalized mobile-surface interaction techniques and characterize the proposed interaction style. The sequence in which we present the attributes does not imply any dependence. Each attribute stands by itself, and attributes can be combined in a variety of ways, as we will illustrate in subsequent sections (see Table 4.5).

Input Space

The user action at the heart of the PhoneTouch style is a touch performed with a mobile on a surface. Table 4.3 describes the basic input attributes associated with this action: the identity of the mobile device, the location of the touch point on the surface, and the relative orientation of the mobile device during the touch. Table 4.4 captures additional input attributes that are available as a result of fusing the basic touch action with information on the mobile, input on the mobile, and input on the surface.

Output Space

The output space for our interaction style is made up of the surface area under the touch, and output on the mobile. In contrast to feedback on the surface, output produced on the mobile can provide localized or private feedback. Visual, haptic, or audio responses

Source, Type	Input Attribute
Mobile, fixed value	**Identifier:** The mobile's identifier allows different mobiles to be distinguished. Therefore, each mobile touch can be associated to a corresponding mobile and consequently its user. Note that the identifier is fixed for a particular device.
Surface, 2D position	**Location:** The touch location is detected at the same granularity and within the same input space as finger touches. Note that finger and mobile touches are distinguished.
Mobile, 3D rotation	**Orientation:** The mobile's orientation determines the device part that is in contact with the surface (e.g., allowing different functions to be bound to each corner of the mobile). In addition, orientation can provide a stream of continuous input through rotation of the mobile around its axis while it touches the surface.

Table 4.3: Basic input attributes associated with the touch of a mobile device on a surface

Source	Input Attribute
Mobile	**Data Context:** Mobiles (e.g., phones) hold a great amount of personal information, which can provide useful data in the context of a touch action. For example, touching the recipient field in an email application on the surface could automatically fill in a selection of known contacts, using the address book on the mobile as source.
Mobile	**Selection:** Users may explicitly select options to parameterize a touch. For example, they might first choose a command (e.g., "delete") from a UI shown on the mobile, and then touch targets on the surface to apply it. Likewise, they could specify photos to transfer from mobile to surface. Input on the mobile during a touch could also trigger events to realize additional input states, similar to mouse clicks [28].
Surface	**Multi-touch:** On the surface, a natural relationship between the touch with a mobile and finger touches from the user's other hand is established based on proximity. This can be used for bimanual interactions. In particular, finger touches close to a mobile device touch point can be associated to the mobile and by extension to its user.

Table 4.4: Additional input attributes, which attach contextual information to a touch

may be given in the context of a touch by using output components commonly available on mobile devices, such as displays, vibrators, or speakers (Figure 4.10). For example, audio feedback can be localized using the mobile's speaker, or delivered in private using a connected headset. Vibration can be used for unobtrusive feedback or alerts, and visual feedback on the mobile might provide tooltips or personalized information related to a touch.

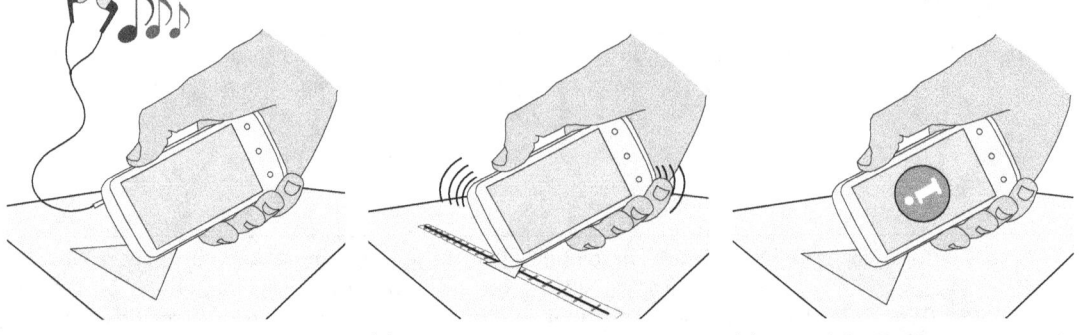

(a) Audio feedback can be local-   (b) Haptic feedback may indicate   (c) Visual feedback is given with-
ized or private (via headsets).   slider ticks, for example.   out occupying surface space.

Figure 4.10:   Output on the phone provides localized or private feedback.

4.3.2 Interaction Techniques

Our development of personalized interaction techniques based on PhoneTouch is framed by six issues in the use of multi-touch surfaces that we identified and that can be addressed in novel ways by symbiotic use of phone and surface. The first four issues correspond to the possible uses of personal information that we have discussed in section 4.1.1 while the remaining two focus on integrating capabilities additionally offered by the mobile device.

- *Data Transfer.* Phones store personal information that are a rich data source for surface applications, and surfaces are natural for viewing of personal media [167].

- *Instantaneous Personalization.* As their user's proxy, phones can be used for personalization in shared interfaces to enable novel interactions that are otherwise not possible [133].

- *User Interface Composition.* Command menus and tool palettes present challenges with respect to orientation, reachability, and clutter [142], which can be addressed by moving such interface elements from the surface to a mobile.

- *Authentication.* The inherently private process of authentication is a design challenge in shared interfaces [79], which can be addressed by integrating personal devices.

- *Localized & Private Feedback* Individual feedback can be beneficial in collaboration around shared surfaces [104, 53], for which phones can provide suitable channels.

- *Input Expressiveness.* Interactive surfaces enable natural input on a two-dimensional plane, but additional degrees of freedom can benefit certain tasks [17].

Issue	Technique	Identifier	Location	Orientation	Data Context	Selection	Multi-touch	Local Output*
Data Transfer	**1 PhonePick&Drop** facilitates bidirectional data transfer between phones and surface.	✓	✓			✓		
	2 PhoneCopy&Paste employs phones as personal clipboards for surface applications.	✓	✓			✓		
	3 PhonePeer2Peer[†] uses the surface as context to initiate data transfers between phones.	✓	✓			✓		
Instantaneous Personalization	**4 PhoneFill** makes existing personal information from phones available on the surface.	✓	✓		✓			
	5 PhoneLenses provide flexible ad hoc personalization of any surface content.	✓	✓				✓	
User Interface Composition	**6 PhonePalettes** move tool palettes and menus from surface to phone.	✓	✓			✓		
	7 PhoneFaçades afford fluid interface customization.	✓	✓			✓		
Authentication	**8 PhoneKey** enables fine-grained ad hoc authentication on the surface.	✓	✓		✓			
	9 PhonePass[†] allows users entering passwords unobserved on their phone.	✓	✓			✓		
Localized & Private Feedback	**10 PhoneSpeaker** provides localized or private audio feedback.	✓	✓					✓
	11 PhoneZone[†] opens continuous private spaces spanning surface and phone.	✓	✓			✓	✓	✓
Input Expressiveness	**12 PhoneHandle** allows for direct manipulation of scalar controls.	✓	✓	✓				
	13 PhoneGestures enables motion-based gestural input.	✓	✓	✓				

Table 4.5: PhoneTouch interaction techniques, the addressed issue, and input or output attributes that they use

*Local output indicates that audio, haptic, visual, or any combination of these three is conceptually required.

† PhonePeer2Peer, PhoneZone, and PhoneGestures were developed conceptually; all other techniques are fully implemented.

Table 4.5 provides an overview of the 13 techniques we have conceived to address the above issues. For each technique we show how it leverages attributes of the input and output space for mobile-surface interaction. All techniques exploit mobile device identity and touchpoint location as core feature, as well as selected other attributes. All techniques are fully implemented with the exception of numbers 3, 11, and 13, which represent more speculative ideas that we chose to only develop conceptually at this stage. Unlike our proof-of-concept implementation introduced in section 3.4, we use mobile phones based on Windows Phone 7 (WP7) to implement the following techniques. This allows for rapid prototyping and a coherent user interface as both mobile and surface development is based on the same framework.

Data Transfer

Data transfer across devices is naturally desirable around shared surfaces, for users to be able to bring personal data into a shared context and to collect data for personal use. We contribute three techniques to support this in a fast and fluid manner: *PhonePick&Drop* for transfer from phone to surface and vice versa, *PhoneCopy&Paste* for temporary transfer onto the phone as personal clipboard, and *PhonePeer2Peer* for transfer between phones mediated by the surface.

① PhonePick&Drop. This technique is for intuitive transfer of data objects from phone to surface and vice versa. To transfer objects from phone to surface (drop), the user makes a selection in private on the phone (Figure 4.11(a)) and then touches the surface with the phone to initiate transfer and display at the selected location on the surface (Figure 4.11(b)). To transfer objects from the surface to the phone (pick), the user directly selects objects on the surface by phone touch to initiate their transfer (Figure 4.11(c)). The technique inherits the simplicity of Rekimoto's Pick-and-Drop [120] but is adopted for fast and intuitive data transfer between phone and surface. Users can in one step choose and transfer items to pick, and likewise select a target location and initiate a drop in one go.

PhonePick&Drop is based on a blackboard metaphor for sharing. This affords users to asynchronously interchange information from their phones via the surface, and to inspect items on the surface before picking them up onto their personal devices. In this respect, the technique is related to other work on data transfer by placement of phones on a shared surface [14, 95, 167]. In contrast to those works, our technique provides fine-grained control over which items to reveal: Users select data items in private on the phone before dropping them onto the shared display. We believe this is important, as phones are very private devices that users would not typically share. For example, while it is common that users show content on their phones to others, they typically do so without giving their phone out of their hands in our cultural area.

② PhoneCopy&Paste. This technique extends surface interaction with phones as personal clipboard. It is based on the same user actions as above for selection of objects and target locations on the surface, however with a copy-and-paste semantic. PhonePick&Drop was motivated for sharing of phone content, while PhoneCopy&Paste is designed for manipulation of surface content, with phones serving as transient storage only. This enables multiple users to each have their individual clipboards, addressing

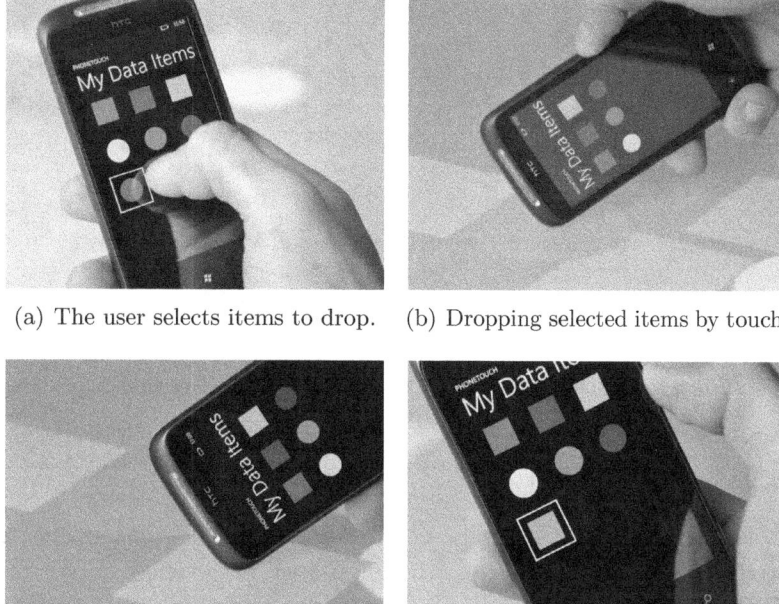

(a) The user selects items to drop.   (b) Dropping selected items by touch.

(c) Picking up items by touch.   (d) Transferred items on the phone.

Figure 4.11: *PhonePick&Drop* allows users to transfer data between phone and surface in both directions.

the problem of correctly associating copy-and-paste actions in multi-user environments, and also affords visualization and efficient access to a history of copied items without consuming surface space. We use PhoneCopy&Paste to implement personal clipboards in our user study presented in Chapter 5.

③ PhonePeer2Peer. Our third data transfer technique was designed to support synchronous data transfer between mobile phones, with the surface used in a mediating role. The concept is shown in Figure 4.12. A user wishing to send data selects the data on their phone and then touches the surface to open a transmission area on the surface (Figure 4.12(a)). Users who wish to receive the data switch their phones to receive mode and touch the surface in the transmission area. Visual feedback in the form of animated links between sender and receivers indicate ongoing activities (Figure 4.12(b)). Note the technique exists only as a mock-up at present.

PhonePeer2Peer enables users who collaborate around shared surfaces to transfer data between their personal devices, without knowledge of device names or addresses, and in a comprehensible and transparent way. In contrast to our other data transfer techniques, no content is transferred between phones and surface. The role of the surface is to provide a context through which peer-to-peer transfer between phones can be initiated and visualized. Note that the technique allows for one-to-many transfers as multiple receivers can participate.

 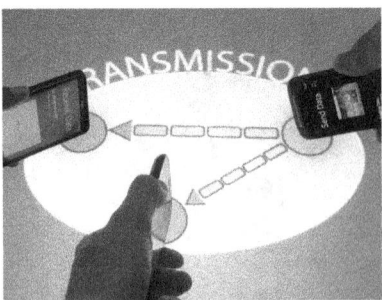

(a) Opening a transmission area.   (b) Touching the area to receive data.

Figure 4.12: *PhonePeer2Peer* supports synchronous data transfer between phones.

Instantaneous Personalization

Using phones as proxies for user-aware interaction makes available the personal data typically stored on such devices (e.g., documents or preferences). We introduce two techniques, *PhoneFill* and *PhoneLenses*, that leverage this data to facilitate dynamic and instantaneous personalization.

4 PhoneFill. Users commonly store a variety of personal collections on their phone, such as contacts, music playlists, and browser bookmarks. This information can also benefit surface applications. For example, browsing the web on the surface, users may want to access a site they have previously bookmarked on their personal device, but manual transfer of the uniform resource locator (URL) to the surface browser is tedious. To address this, we have designed the PhoneFill technique, enabling users to make existing personal information instantly available on the surface. This is illustrated in Figure 4.13: The surface object touched with the phone determines the context for PhoneFill. Based on this context, the phone identifies and provides relevant information to the surface application. In the shown example, the user phone-touches the browser's bookmark control (Figure 4.13(a)). This triggers the phone to automatically retrieve and send its bookmark collection to the surface, where it becomes instantly available. Users can then choose from their personal bookmarks directly on the surface (Figure 4.13(b)), even in collaborative scenarios where browser interaction may be shared between multiple users. In the same way, a phone can provide contact details to send email from a surface application, or automatically fill-in payment forms.

5 PhoneLenses. A phone touch can act as a proxy for user identity, but is limited to a single point of contact. To extend user identification to multi-touch, we have integrated PhoneTouch with IdLenses, the concept we introduced for HandsDown in section 4.2.2. The interactions are the same, but here we use a different source of user identity (i.e., a mobile device rather than the user's hand). A user can open a PhoneLens by performing a phone touch anywhere within an enabled surface application. The lens then defines an area in which any finger touch input is associated with the phone's user. The lens moves along with the phone and disappears once the phone is lifted off the surface. The concept allows for any form of personalization of the surface content under the lens. Figure 4.14 shows an example from one of the applications we built. A user explores the map of a

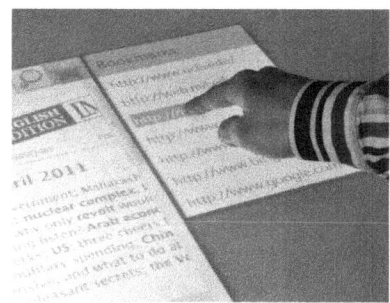

(a) Touching a web browser   (b) Transferred personal bookmarks

Figure 4.13: *PhoneFill* makes existing personal information from the phone available to surface applications.

museum with a personal lens through which content is adapted to their language, based on individual preferences automatically provided by the user's phone. In this way, a user can view content adapted to their needs, without disrupting others viewing different parts of the shared display. Users can also provide input through the lens, for example by marking a museum room on the shared map as a personal favorite.

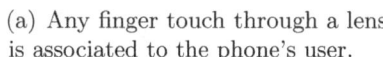

(a) Any finger touch through a lens   (b) The surface area under a lens is
is associated to the phone's user.   personalized (e.g., translated).

Figure 4.14: *PhoneLenses* can be invoked anywhere on the surface and move along with the phone.

User Interface Composition

Placement of command menus and toolbars can be problematic on shared surfaces, as it can be difficult to make them easily accessible for different users in terms of physical reach and orientation [142]. We propose two techniques that address this issue with user interface composition across surface and phones. *PhonePalettes* are for off-loading of tool palettes to the phone, and *PhoneFaçades* support ad hoc customization of the interface.

⑥ **PhonePalettes.** The principal idea is to move tool palettes from the surface onto the phone to be close to hand on whichever part of a larger surface the user is working. This is related to the concept of detached user interfaces, in which tools were moved off the main display and onto a handheld device, in analogy to a painter whose focus lies on the canvas while keeping tools handy on a palette [50, 121]. However, PhonePalettes are different as the phone itself is used to select the target of a command on the surface. For demonstration of the technique, we implemented a simplified graphics editor. In the example shown in Figure 4.15, the user selects the "Circle" command on the phone (Figure 4.15(a)) and then touches the surface to apply the command at the selected location (Figure 4.15(b)). The same command can be applied repeatedly on the surface. The commands can also be parametrized through the phone's interface, for example to choose from different colors (Figure 4.15(c)). It is possible to preselect multiple compatible commands to be executed simultaneously with the next phone touch (e.g., fill and stroke color can be applied together). Frequently applied tool settings can also be stored on the phone as personal preferences.

(a) Selecting tools and commands...   (b) ...which are applied by touch.

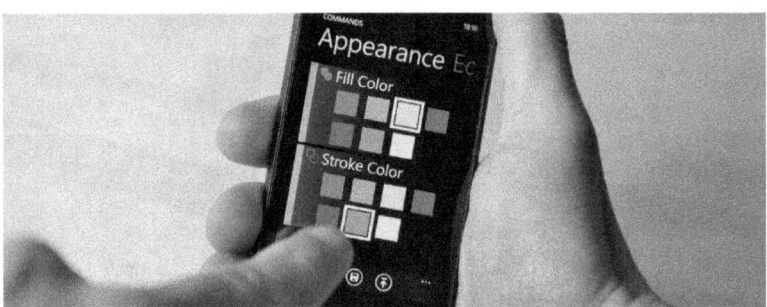

(c) *PhonePalettes* also support parameterized commands.

Figure 4.15:   *PhonePalettes* move tool palettes and menus from surface to phone.

Input sequences that require prior selection of a mode (e.g., selecting "bold" before text entry) are common in graphical user interface (GUI), but problematic on interactive surfaces that lack the ability to distinguish touches of different users [133]. A related problem is visual feedback that indicates the selected mode [45]. PhonePalettes solve this issue as commands are selected on the user's personal device, thereby enabling multiple users to work on a shared interface, each within their own mode. It is also possible to keep an audit trail based on the phone identifier, and to provide per-user undo operations.

7 PhoneFaçades.   Many tasks involve only a small set of an application's command set. The idea of PhoneFaçades, inspired by User Interface Façades [151], is to enable users to pick commands from the surface in order to assemble a customized interface on the phone. In the example shown in Figure 4.16, the user picks the application's "Square" command by selecting it with a phone touch (Figure 4.16(a)). As a result, a representation of the command is automatically added to the phone (Figure 4.16(b)). The command is now ready to be used as described above for PhonePalettes. As this shows, PhoneFaçades involve only minimal overhead for interface customization. Users can pick up and arrange commands on their phone in an ad hoc fashion, to match their workflow. Multiple users can each assemble individually customized interfaces to use in a shared surface application.

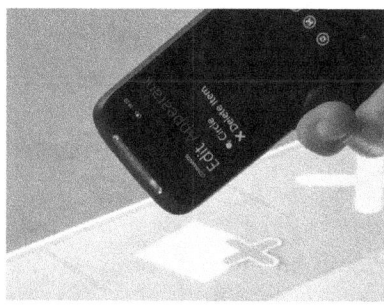 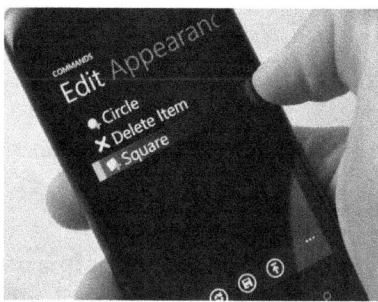

(a) Picking up surface commands   (b) Customized command set

Figure 4.16: *PhoneFaçades* lets users assemble a set of commands picked from the surface.

Authentication

Authentication is an inherently private process that presents a distinct design challenge on shared surfaces. System-wide authentication is typically not appropriate due to the multi-user context, but interaction-based authentication can be desirable, for example if users have different roles with varying levels of authority. We contribute two new techniques for authentication, *PhoneKey* for locking and unlocking of restricted content and *PhonePass* for remote and unobserved password entry.

8 PhoneKey. PhoneKey is a technique for token-based authentication. Metaphorically, the phone serves as a key to control access to items on the shared surface, for example interactive applications or restricted content. To demonstrate the PhoneKey technique, we implemented multiple personal workspaces on a shared surface. A user can lock their workspace to protect enclosed data by touching the lock button (Figure 4.17(a)). To regain access, the user unlocks the workspace with a phone touch on the lock button (Figure 4.17(b)). Authentication takes place implicitly, with the phone serving as the access token. Finger touches and other phones cannot unlock the workspace, but could for instance trigger display of an alert message.

9 PhonePass. Many existing applications, for example many web-based services, require users to enter a password to log in. This is problematic on shared services due to potential shoulder-surfing attacks [79]. PhonePass addresses this problem by enabling users to enter passwords via their phone. The user initiates this interaction by touching the password field with their phone (Figure 4.18(a)). A corresponding control appears on the phone where the password can be entered unobserved (Figure 4.18(b)). The only feedback on the surface is given in form of disguised characters, shown as asterisks. The

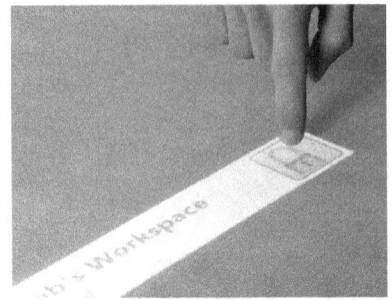

(a) Locking a workspace   (b) Access with an authorized phone

Figure 4.17: *PhoneKey* enables token-based authentication and fine-grained access control.

phone could also store a collection of passwords in an internal vault. A phone touch on a password field would then automatically retrieve and fill-in the matching password, similar to a PhoneFill interaction. In contrast to other proposed surface authentication approaches [79], PhonePass integrates readily with existing applications. Closely related is PocketPIN [35], but PhonePass affords a simpler method of associating phone and password field.

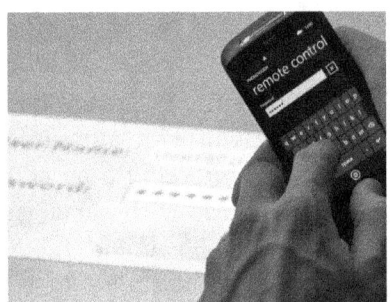

(a) The user touches a password field   (b) ... and enters the password unob-
on the surface to select it...   served via the phone.

Figure 4.18: *PhonePass* enables users to enter passwords unobserved on their phone.

Localized & Private Feedback

Output on large displays and shared surfaces is public by default. However it has been argued that private feedback can be beneficial [104]. We contribute two new feedback techniques: *PhoneSpeaker* provides a personal audio channel and *PhoneZone* an output zone that is shielded from the view of other users.

10 PhoneSpeaker.   This technique implements audio feedback for PhoneTouch events. Localized feedback is given through the phone's internal speaker, and private feedback when headphones are connected. For example, localized feedback of affirmative or negative sound has been shown to raise user-awareness of input errors [53]. Private audio feedback can be useful to access audio content on surfaces while avoiding interference among multiple users. In an example application we implemented, multiple users can browse a music collection on a shared surface and preview tracks individually by touching them with their phones (Figure 4.19(a)).

(a) Using *PhoneSpeaker* for private audio feedback

(b) *PhoneZone* creates a private space across phone and surface

Figure 4.19: Localized and private feedback

⑪ PhoneZone. The idea of PhoneZone, developed as concept but not yet implemented, is to provide the user with a visual output area that is not overlooked by other users. As shown in Figure 4.19(b), the concept is for users to place their phone sideways on the surface in order to open a private space that combines display space on the phone with display space on the surface, "in the shadow of the phone". Like the horizontal hand gesture proposed by Wu et. al [168], the phone shields parts of the surface, thereby blocking it from other users' view. The combined display space of a PhoneZone could also be exploited for direct manipulations, such as sliding content off the phone down onto the surface.

Input Expressiveness

Input on interactive surfaces is inherently two-dimensional. We contribute two new techniques that exploit the phone as a device that we use for planar interaction on the surface but that offers additional degrees of freedom (in similar ways as the Rockin' Mouse [17]). *PhoneHandle* uses device motion to manipulate scalar controls, and *PhoneGestures* enables discrete gestures performed with the phone.

⑫ PhoneHandle. The idea of this technique is to manipulate scalar controls that are selected by a phone touch on the surface. As the phone is held like a stylus with a contact point on the surface, it can be manipulated naturally in terms of varying pitch (forward-backward tilt), yaw (left-right tilt), or roll (rotation around the z-axis). The range of device motions is constrained by the way a phone is held, and limitations of arm and wrist movement, but this can be accommodated in the design of the control. Figure 4.20(a) shows an example of a slider control that we implemented as PhoneHandle. The slider on the surface is selected by a phone touch, and the user manipulates its value by tilting the phone forward and backward, using a rate control mapping. A second example, in Figure 4.20(b), shows rotation of a phone to control a knob displayed on the surface.

(a) Slider control by tilting   (b) Knob control by rotation

Figure 4.20: *PhoneHandle* allows users to directly manipulate scalar controls through device motion.

13 PhoneGestures. PhoneGestures are based on the same device motions used in PhoneHandle, but afford discrete gestures instead of direct motion-to-control mapping. We did not include PhoneGestures in our current implementation, but conceptually we foresee two types of gestures. The first type are counter-intuitive movements of a phone in extension of a phone touch, as a safety catch to avoid accidental activation of critical functions. For example, in order to delete items on the surface permanently, a user could be required to not only select the delete button but to also perform a rotation of the phone while the button is selected. The interaction metaphor here is that of a launch key. Such a gesture can be designed to be unlikely performed accidentally but to be easily integrated into the touch interaction flow.

The second type of gesture we propose is metaphorical. For example, a PhoneTouch could be combined with screwdriver motion, for fastening or unfastening of an object on the surface. It could also be combined with a pumping motion, to lift or lower an object selected on the surface. This allows for additional forms of expression that may build on metaphors that are intuitive in particular application contexts, or that provide for playful interaction in games and entertainment.

Applications

We implemented a number of applications to further illustrate mobile-surface interaction. The applications make use of a variety of the interaction techniques and demonstrate them in realistic flows to show benefits of personalized interaction. They also highlight the fluidity of the interaction style in terms of seamlessly moving between interactions on the phone and on the surface.

Word Game. This application is a clone of the Scrabble board game. It makes use of PhonePick&Drop and illustrates use of the mobile device for private display and interaction fluidly interwoven with shared interaction on the surface. Between two and four players individually form words to then place them into a shared grid like a crossword. In our implementation, players receive a set of letters on their phone to arrange them in private (Figure 4.21(a)). Once it is a player's turn, the word is dropped by a phone touch on the surface, simultaneously specifying the target cells on the displayed game board (Figure 4.21(b)). Players can also pick up and rearrange letters using PhoneCopy&Paste if their initial choice of word does not fit as planned.

 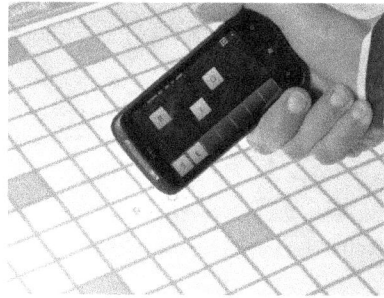

(a) Users arrange words in private on   (b) ...drop them onto the shared
their phone to then...   word game board.

Figure 4.21: *Word game* seamlessly integrates private and shared interactions.

Collage Designer. This is an application for multiple users to bring their photos to
the surface, and to creatively arrange them into a combined collage, making use of
PhonePalettes in addition to the techniques demonstrated in the word game. Users can
freely move, rotate, and scale photos with multi-touch, and they can use editing tools,
for instance to choose from different picture frames, to add captions, or to delete photos.
Editing options were integrated in two ways, on PhonePalettes as shown in Figure 4.22,
and alternatively via context menus on the surface. This provides users with choices in
their workflow.

Figure 4.22: *Collage designer* lets users arrange photos with editing tools on both the
phone and the surface.

Music Store. The music store application allows users to browse through different
albums using common multi-touch interaction on a shared surface (Figure 4.23(a)). To
preview a song we apply PhoneSpeaker, providing individual audio over headphones. In
doing so, multiple users can listen to songs without disturbing each other. Users can
directly buy songs by touching them with their phone, thus using the phone not only to
transfer the music to, but also for authenticating the purchase (Figure 4.23(b)).

Calendar. Personal calendars are a standard application on mobile phones. However,
scheduling or sharing events amongst multiple co-located users is not readily supported,
as each user has access to their own calendar only. We address this with a calendar
sharing application that we built on our platform. The application lets users drop their
personal calendar onto a surface by tapping the surface while the application is open

(a) Browsing music using multi-touch   (b) Using the phone to purchase

Figure 4.23:   *Music store* lets users browse music and integrates a phone for transactions.

on the phone (Figure 4.24(a)). The calendar becomes shared in a privacy-sensitive way, initially only showing the blocked times but without event details. This allows users to jointly look for free slots. The owner of the calendar can also selectively unlock individual entries in the calendar using PhoneKey. This makes the event detail visible, and allows other users to copy the event to their own calendars, using PhonePick&Drop (Figure 4.24(b)).

 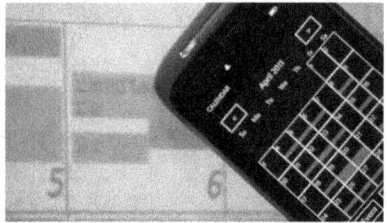

(a) Dropping a calendar for sharing   (b) Unlocking event detail

Figure 4.24:   *Calendar* lets users share their personal calendars with fine-grained privacy control.

Informal User Feedback.   We asked six test users to try the implemented interaction techniques and applications in order to learn about their perceived usefulness. We gathered feedback by observing interactions and conducting informal interviews. Users found the style of interaction natural. One of them suggested that others might be concerned about using expensive phones for input by impact on a surface, but none of the users showed any hesitation in applying the PhoneTouch techniques. Of all techniques, PhonePass and PhoneFill appealed most to the test users as they address problems that users found familiar and important, beyond the setting of interactive tabletops that was used in the trial session. In the multi-user part of the trial, users engaged quickly with the word game as its board game variant is well-known. Without having been prompted to do so, they intuitively used the phone as a private screen, and naturally moved back and forth between interaction on the phone and on the surface. The collage designer presented a more artificial task but it prompted users to comment on the distinct ease by which photos stored on the phone can be shared for joint viewing on a larger screen, a process that is clearly perceived as cumbersome with state of the art camera phones and digital cameras.

4.3.3 Summary

In this section, we analyzed the interaction space of PhoneTouch, particularly highlighting additional input and output attributes relevant to the symbiotic use of mobiles and surfaces. Based on this analysis, we introduced 13 personalized interaction techniques (summarized in Table 4.5). This exploration shows that PhoneTouch facilitates personalized interaction on shared surfaces by employing mobile devices as proxies for their users. At the same time, it offers a wide range of compelling opportunities for fluid cross-device interaction with the phone as a complementary device. Using the phone like a stylus facilitates instantaneous user identification, thus allowing for precise and identified interactions. As a direct manipulation style, PhoneTouch is well suited for interactions that take place in the context of specific elements or objects on an interactive surface, where fine-grained selection is key. It further lends itself to applications that involve a combination of interaction on mobiles and interaction on surfaces, where people need to easily switch between the devices. Finally, we integrated several of our techniques into applications to illustrate their interaction flow and to gather informal user feedback.

4.4 Discussion

By means of introducing a wide range of user-aware interaction techniques, we showed that HandsDown and PhoneTouch are both viable solutions for enabling personalized interaction on interactive surfaces—despite their different identification strategies. Either method enables instantaneous user identification through direct-touch interaction. Therefore, multiple users can independently and spontaneously identify on a shared interface, while specifying intended targets at the same time. Further, both methods allow for simultaneous conventional multi-touch input, providing full and flexible control over which interactions are identified versus remain anonymous.

Since HandsDown and PhoneTouch base user identification on different entities (i.e., hand and phone), the resulting interaction styles and techniques vary greatly. While HandsDown appropriates a simple and distinctive hand gesture for identification, PhoneTouch uses mobile devices in a stylus-like fashion. Consequently, PhoneTouch facilitates identifying individual touches for precise selection, while HandsDown relies on supplementary finger touch input. To this end, we proposed IdLenses, a bimanual interaction concept, which opens up a transient identification scope attached to the HandsDown gesture for dexterous input with the other hand. In doing so, IdLenses relies on social protocols to prevent other users from intruding.

We do not intend to provide an exhaustive list of personalized interaction techniques, but aim at demonstrating the utility of such techniques by addressing various existing issues in surface computing, such as fluid integration of personal data or instantaneous authentication, to name but a few. Despite using HandsDown and PhoneTouch as particular identification methods, the resulting breadth of interaction techniques suggests that personalized interaction can indeed address such issues. While several of the proposed techniques rely on method-specific capabilities, others are adaptable to different user identification methods. For example, we applied the IdLenses concept, originally developed for HandsDown, as PhoneLenses to PhoneTouch. Many of the PhoneTouch techniques use particular capabilities provided by the mobile device (e.g., instantaneous data transfer or integrated inertial sensors), which highlights the potential of synergies that can be realized by integrating shared surfaces with personal handhelds.

The presented exploration is mainly conceptual. Therefore, several questions remain unanswered, which can only be addressed through experimental evaluation (see Chapter 5). For example, it is not clear how interleaving phone and finger touches will impact the resulting interaction flow. Further, users might find it less natural to use a mobile as a stylus, and they might be concerned about causing damage to either their mobile or the surface, as both represent expensive devices. Regarding HandsDown, it is not clear to what extent the relatively large space occupied by hand plus lens will impact multi-user interaction.

4.5 Summary

We set out by framing the concept of personalized interaction for surface computing, and discussed the defining characteristics of such interaction as well as various uses of personal information. For both HandsDown and PhoneTouch, we analyzed the corresponding interaction space to inform the design and implementation of concrete personalized interaction techniques. Due to their particular characteristics, we focused on different aspects, specifically considering precise target selection strategies for HandsDown while attending to synergistic usage of personal devices with shared surfaces for PhoneTouch. Our main contribution in this chapter is two-fold: First, we explored the design space of personalized interaction by populating it with a wide range of novel techniques. Secondly, we demonstrated the suitability of HandsDown and PhoneTouch as enabling approaches for personalized interaction.

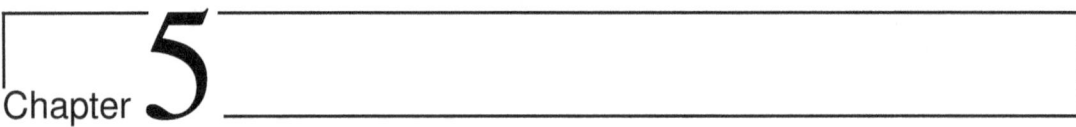

Chapter 5

Evaluating User Experience

Clipboards are widely used in desktop and mobile computing to conveniently transfer data across applications or to provide temporary storage via copy-and-paste. In a qualitative user study, we show that instantaneous user identification allows for carrying over the well-proven clipboard concept to surface computing. Using either IdWristbands, HandsDown, or PhoneTouch, multiple simultaneous users can independently access their personal clipboards for individual copy-and-paste activities on a shared interactive surface. We implemented personal clipboards for each of our three identification methods in order to shed light on interaction particularities and to guide the design of user-aware applications.

5.1 Introduction

Instantaneous user identification for surface computing enables personalized interaction that is difficult or impossible to realize otherwise. Using the example of individual clipboards, we demonstrate how IdWristbands, HandsDown, and PhoneTouch allow for applying a proven and tested interface technique to interactive surfaces. Clipboards are widely used in desktop and mobile computing, and supported by all major operating systems. They enable cross-application data transfer (e.g., users can look up information in a web browser to later insert it into a presentation) and facilitate work flows by providing means to duplicate, temporarily store, and rearrange information junks (e.g., to move entire text passages within the same document).

It is not obvious, however, how this clipboard concept translates to shared surfaces and co-located collaboration. Existing work in ubiquitous settings focuses on copy-and-paste across devices (e.g., [149]). On the other hand, related approaches that have been proposed for surface computing primarily support the organization of items through visible control elements (e.g., [139, 118]). Clipboards, in contrast, keep stored items in the background, do not occupy screen space permanently, and provide persistence across context switches (i.e., the copied content is available after switching to another application).

We exploit instantaneous user identification to enable personalized clipboards on shared surfaces, which allow each user to individually copy, cut, and paste without interfering with others. In a qualitative user study, we compare and evaluate IdWristbands, HandsDown, and PhoneTouch as enabling methods for personalized clipboards to demonstrate their feasibility for such fine-grained personalized interaction. At the same time, we investigate particularities that arise from method-specific interaction characteristics to inform the design of user-aware applications.

5.2 Experimental Design

We recruited 18 participants from our local campus through posters and mailing lists. Participants could sign up in groups of two, or were randomly assigned a group member by the experimenter otherwise. They received £8 each for their participation.

5.2.1 Apparatus

We implemented IdWristbands, HandsDown, and PhoneTouch for the Samsung SUR40 device (i.e., Microsoft's Surface 2.0) in order to provide participants with the same interactive table for all methods. The SUR40 has a height of 73 cm and a surface diagonal of 120 cm at a resolution of 1920 pixel × 1080 pixel. It uses PixelSense to detect finger touches and objects. For IdWristbands we used the bracelets described in section 3.2, and for PhoneTouch we used iPhone 3GS devices. In each condition, participants sat at the longer table sides opposite each other (Figure 5.1). We implemented surface-based applications in C# using Microsoft's .NET framework, Windows Presentation Foundation (WPF), and the Surface 2.0 software development kit (SDK).

Figure 5.1:   Participants during the study

5.2.2 Task

The experiment consists of a copy and a paste task. The tasks are interdependent and based on the same concept of personal clipboards, but individually adapted to leverage IdWristbands, HandsDown, and PhoneTouch. Items to be copied and pasted differed in three features (Table 5.1): color (×2), pattern (×4), and shape (×4). The task order was strictly sequential (i.e., the copy task had to be completed before proceeding to the paste task).

In the copy task, we used each unique feature combination twice on the surface, resulting in 64 items. To start with, participants had to select a color and then search

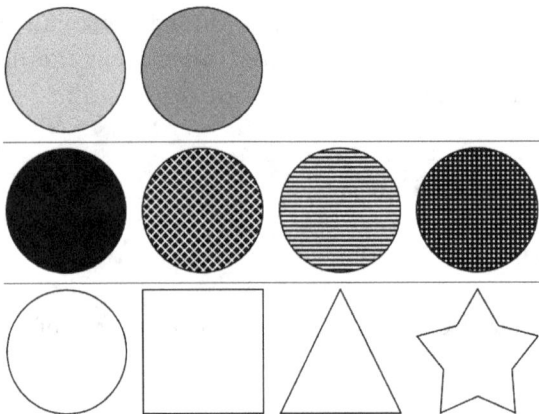

Table 5.1: Items differ in color (×2), pattern (×4), and shape (×4).

for and copy multiple items to their individual clipboards; they were instructed to find all 16 unique combinations of shape and pattern (of the chosen color). As shown in Figure 5.2(a), the items were randomly arranged and could be moved, rotated, and resized using typical multi-touch interactions. It was not possible to copy duplicate items (i.e., items of the same color, pattern, and shape). Copying an item was acknowledged by flashing it, and a copy error (i.e., the attempt to copy a duplicate) was indicated with a shaking animation. To remove an item from the clipboard, participants had to tap and hold it (on the surface in the case of IdWristbands and HandsDown, and on the phone in the case of PhoneTouch).

After switching to a second screen, participants were asked to collaboratively paste a selection of the items they had copied into nine target locations (Figure 5.2(b)). We asked them to select and arrange items in pairs that differ in both color and pattern, but have the same shape as suggested by the dotted outlines. In contrast to the copy task, participants closely collaborated during the paste task. Participants had to contribute one item each for every target location. In addition, they had to coordinate to ensure they selected items of the same shape but of different pattern.

(a) Copy: Randomly arranged items

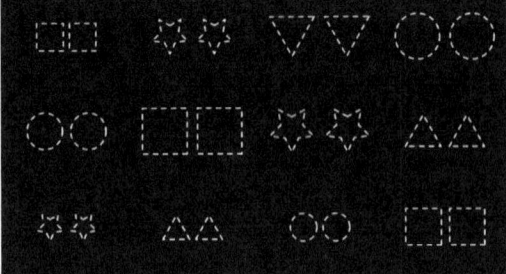

(b) Paste: Designated target locations

Figure 5.2: Copy and paste screens

In summary, the copy task comprises an individual search for multiple items that fulfill certain criteria, while the paste task requires participants to work together in selecting a subset of copied items to then arrange them. We decided for this abstract experiment design, without reverting to a specific application domain, to reduce side effects due to increased mental load and task comprehension problems. A corresponding real-world task could be to individually search for a set of photos first, and then select some of them to create a presentation while working together in a team, each member contributing their share.

5.2.3 Conditions

We provided the same functionality for personal clipboards based on IdWristbands, HandsDown, and PhoneTouch, but adapted user interfaces to method-specific characteristics. Our goal was not to unify clipboard designs across methods, but to emphasize their particular advantages (e.g., using the phone's screen to display clipboards).

IdWristbands

Using IdWristbands, user identity is available for any finger touch. To enable convenient location-independent access to copy-and-paste functions without occupying permanent space on the surface, we provided personal context menus. Users can invoke context menus via the default Windows 7 press-and-tap gesture, which is performed as follows [96]: "Press the item with one finger, then quickly tap with another finger, while continuing to press the item with the first finger."

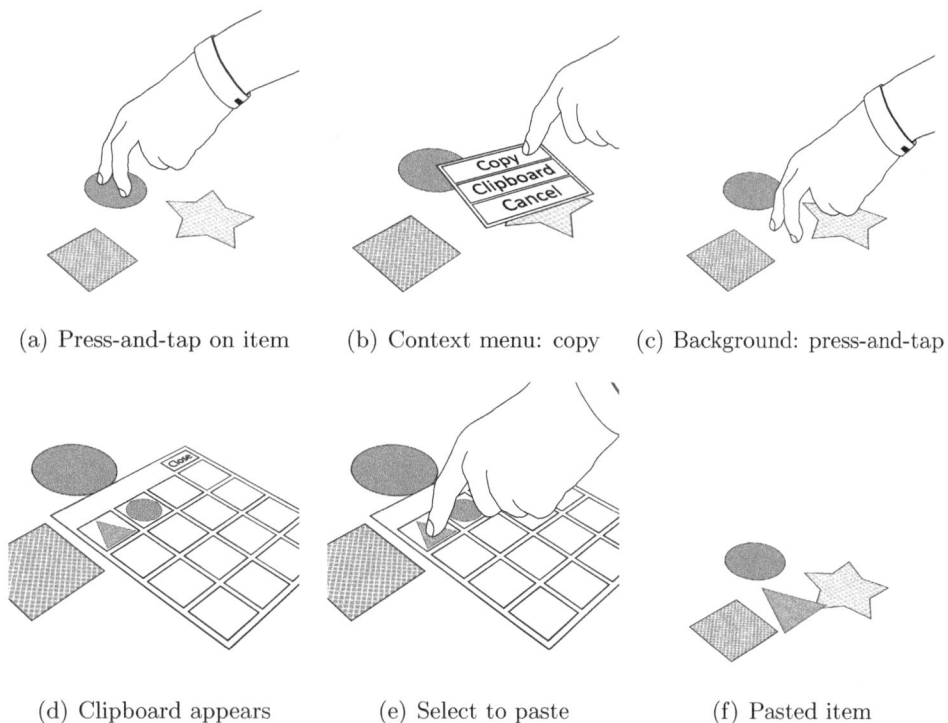

(a) Press-and-tap on item   (b) Context menu: copy   (c) Background: press-and-tap

(d) Clipboard appears   (e) Select to paste   (f) Pasted item

Figure 5.3: Copying and pasting items with IdWristbands

To copy, participants performed this gesture (with the instrumented hand) on top of an item (Figure 5.3(a)) and selected "Copy" from the appearing menu (Figure 5.3(b)); the menu then closed automatically and the item flashed as confirmation. As only menu invocations required user identification, participants could perform the subsequent selection with either hand. The remaining two context menu options were "Clipboard" (to inspect already copied items) and "Cancel" (to close the menu). Performing press-and-tap on the background (Figure 5.3(c)) or on top of an already copied item brought up the clipboard right away (Figure 5.3(d)), which could be moved freely. Participants could select any of the contained items for pasting by touching them (Figure 5.3(e)); items were inserted directly underneath the finger (Figure 5.3(f)). The clipboard closed automatically after pasting.

HandsDown

HandsDown provides instantaneous user identification on the surface, but does not lend itself to precise target selection per se. Therefore, we based our personal clipboard implementation on IdLenses (see section 4.2.2) to allow for individual copy-and-paste actions. To copy, participants had to perform a HandsDown gesture next to the items they intended to copy. A dotted rectangle visualized the identification scope. Any item inside this scope was highlighted with a border (its color indicating the current user), and could be copied by simply touching it, using the other hand (Figure 5.4(a)). Participants could move items inside the identification scope (Figure 5.4(b)); likewise, they could move items out (e.g., to reduce clutter). The "C" button brought up the clipboard (Figure 5.4(c)), the "X" button switched back to copy mode; note that participants could not copy items while the clipboard was shown. Lenses could not be moved as pre-studies had shown that sliding the entire hand on the surface was not desirable due to friction. Lifting the hand off the surfaces closed the identification scope (or clipboard) immediately. To paste, participants first identified, bringing up the clipboard, and then tapped the item to paste (Figure 5.4(e)), which was inserted right in place (Figure 5.4(f)). The clipboard stayed open as long as the HandsDown gesture was active, allowing to paste multiple items in a row.

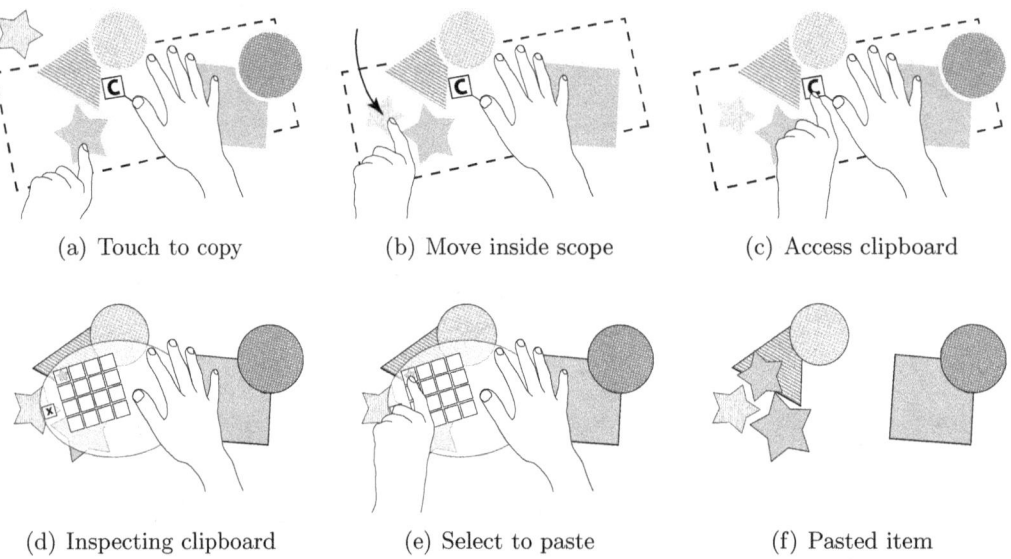

(a) Touch to copy	(b) Move inside scope	(c) Access clipboard
(d) Inspecting clipboard	(e) Select to paste	(f) Pasted item

Figure 5.4: Copying and pasting items with HandsDown

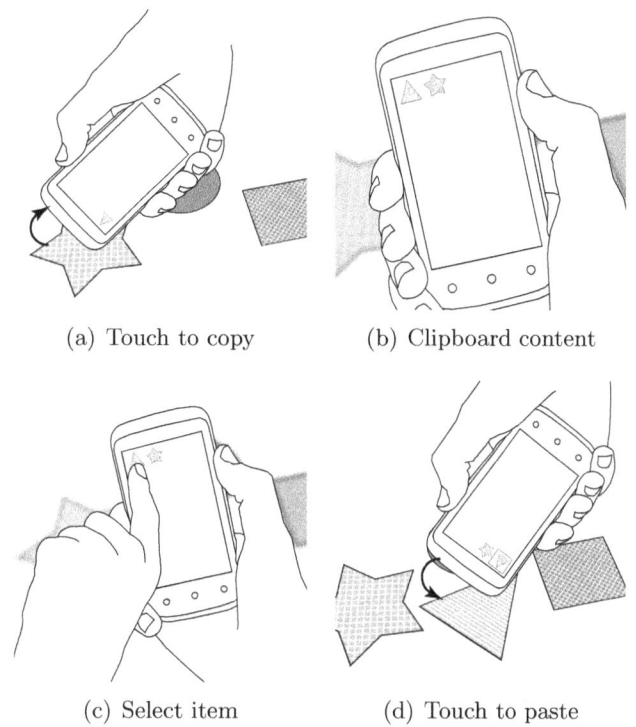

(a) Touch to copy   (b) Clipboard content

(c) Select item   (d) Touch to paste

Figure 5.5:   Copying and pasting items with PhoneTouch

PhoneTouch

PhoneTouch allows for precise user-aware selection, providing a second modality in addition to finger touches. We therefore enabled copy-and-paste actions directly through phone touches, while using the additional interaction space offered by the phone's screen for clipboard visualization and item selection. We adapted PhoneCopy&Paste for copying multiple items (see section 4.3.2). Participants had to touch an item with the phone to copy it, using either of the phone's two top corners (Figure 5.5(a)). The copied item instantly appeared in the clipboard, which was permanently shown on the phone (Figure 5.5(b)). To paste, participants first selected one or multiple items on the phone screen (Figure 5.5(c)), and then performed a phone touch on the surface; so pasted items appeared in place (Figure 5.5(d)). Moving, resizing, or rotating items on the surface (e.g., to bring them closer or align them in the paste task) called for finger input; phone touches were reserved for copy-and-paste interaction.

5.2.4   Procedure

We used a within-subject repeated-measures design with the independent variable identification method (IdWristbands, HandsDown, or PhoneTouch). Participants performed copy and paste tasks for all identification methods; the presentation of methods was counter balanced.

Figure 5.6 outlines the study procedure. After completing research consent forms, the experimenter introduced participants to the copy and paste tasks. Participants were seated opposite each other for the duration of the study (see Figure 5.1). Before

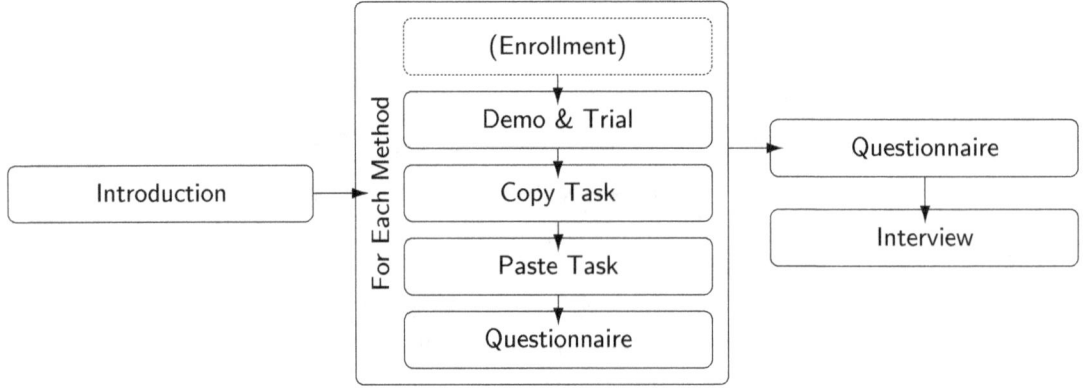

Figure 5.6: Study procedure

each condition, the experimenter demonstrated the identification method and how to perform copy-and-paste interactions; participants then could test the method until they felt comfortable using it. In the case of HandsDown, we further asked participants to enroll beforehand by placing their hands repeatedly on the surface. The copy task was completed once both participants had collected 16 different items of their color; the paste task was completed once both participants had pasted and arranged items matching the indicated target locations. Task completion was not automatically registered but determined by the experimenter.

Throughout the task, we observed participants and took notes. In addition, we video-taped all sessions for detailed post-hoc analysis using an open coding approach [156] and ChronoViz to facilitate annotations [163]. Our field notes provided a starting point for initial coding categories. All coding was perfromed by the author, and consisted of multiple iterations over all recorded sessions for refinement.

After completing each method, participants filled in a questionnaire (see Figure B.3 on page 170). We asked them to state their agreement with eight items selected from the *IBM Computer Usability Satisfaction* questionnaire[1] on a seven-point Likert scale ranging from "strongly agree" to "strongly disagree" [84]. Using three items from the *NASA Task Load Index* [58], participants were further asked to rate the amount of mental demand required to fulfill the task as well as their frustration level, and to give a self-assessment of their performance. We were also interested in comments on advantages and limitations of the method they had tested.

After completing all three methods, we asked participants in a separate questionnaire to rank the methods according to several criteria, including general preference as well as their perception regarding execution time, efficiency, enjoyment, learnability, and responsiveness (see Figure B.4 on page 171). We further gathered basic demographic data and information about experiences with computers and touch interfaces. Finally, we conducted an open-ended interview to gain additional insights into particular interaction patterns we had observed.

---

[1]Statements 2, 4, 5, 6, 7, 9, 17, and 19 of the *Post-Study System Usability Questionnaire* were selected as applicable to the test system.

5.3 Results

The age of recruited participants ranged from 19 to 29 years ($M = 22.35, SD = 3$), eight of them were female (44 %), and all were students (from various backgrounds). Participants of five groups (56 %) were acquaintances and had signed up together for the study. The others did not know each other beforehand and were randomly assigned to groups by the experimenter. Two groups were mixed-gender. Further, all but one participant reported to be right-handed. When asked for their experience with computers in general and with touch interfaces in particular, in both cases participants most frequently picked "high", corresponding to 4 on a 5-point rating scale ("high" was picked 13 times for computer, and eight times for touch interface experience). Only three participants had used a large multi-touch surface before (e.g., in similar studies or during a museum visit), but many were familiar with smart phones (12) or tablets (4).

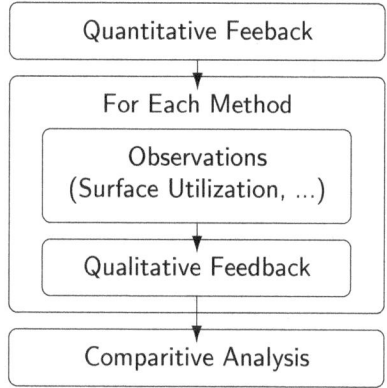

Figure 5.7:   Result presentation order

As illustrated in Figure 5.7, we first summarize the collected quantitative user feedback, which includes usability and task load ratings (based on questionnaires given out after completing each method) as well as method rankings (based on a final questionnaire). For each method, we then report on observations (made during the study and derived from post-hoc analysis of recorded videos), which are supported by a detailed system log of interactions. We further summarize qualitative user feedback (based on various questionnaires and open-ended interviews). Note that due to system malfunctions log data for pasting is missing in two, and only partially available in four cases (i.e., with a limited set of items), as pointed out below.

5.3.1 Quantitative Feedback

We analyzed usability and task load ratings (Figures 5.8 and 5.9), but did not find any significant differences (using Friedman tests). Figure 5.10 shows the result when asked to rank the three methods according to general preference and five additional dimensions.

5.3.2 IdWristbands

All but one participant choose to wear wristbands on the dominant hand. Although the other hand was available for (anonymous) touch input (e.g., to move or resize items), all but two participants limited themselves to one-handed input. One of those using both

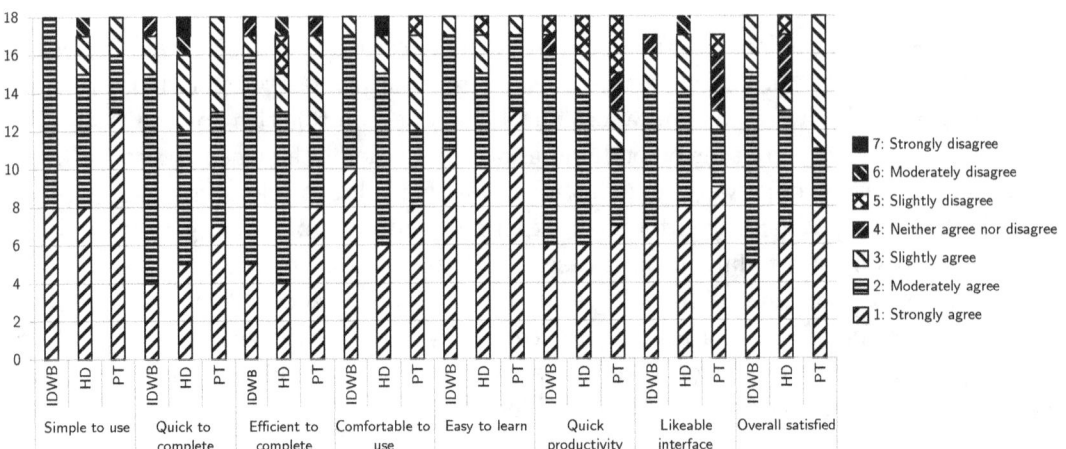

Figure 5.8: IBM Computer Usability Satisfaction results (not all participants responded to all questions)

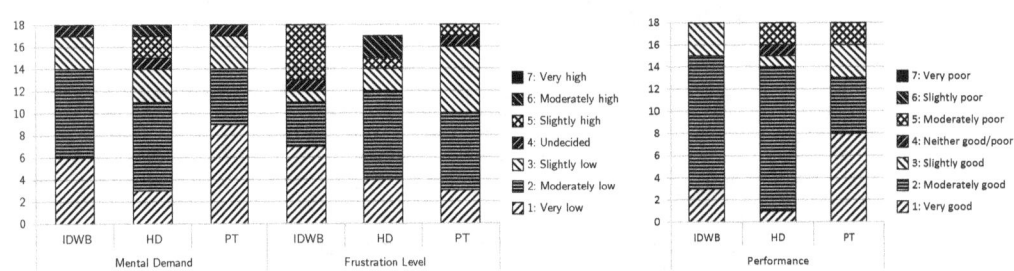

Figure 5.9: NASA Task Load Index results (not all participants responded to all questions)

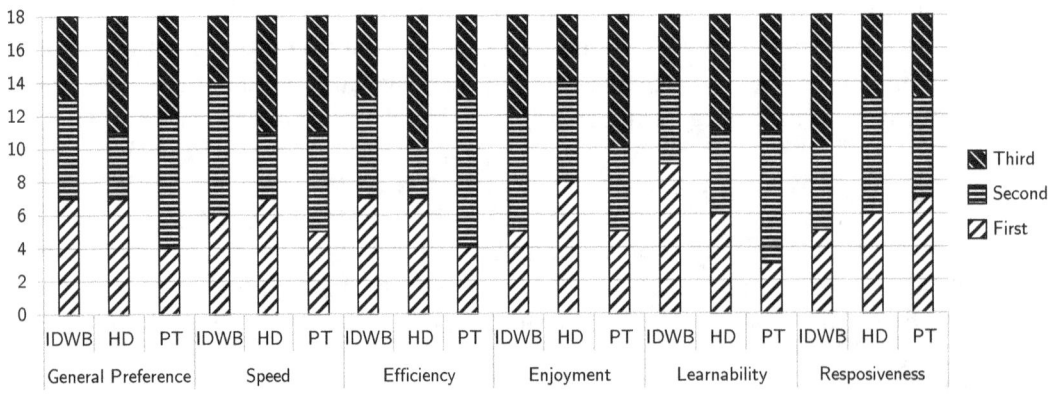

Figure 5.10: Ranking results showing the number of participants who picked a particular method as first (green), second (orange), or third choice (red).

hands did so to access the context menu and move items (Figure 5.11(a)), while the other used the non-instrumented hand only once to paste an item (Figure 5.11(b)).

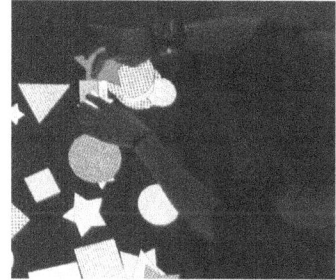 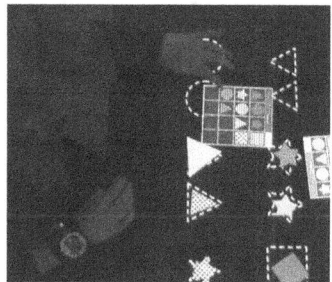

(a) Accessing context menu with two hands simultaneously

(b) Pasting an item using the non-equipped hand

Figure 5.11: Bimanual interaction observations

Before the first copy operation, three participants (17 %) sorted items according to color, moving them to the respective table sides. Two of them collaborated in doing so (Figure 5.12(a)), while one arranged items independent of the other group member. Further, roughly half of the participants (44 %) copied items following a particular order, such as picking up squares before proceeding to stars and so on (Figure 5.12(b) shows the resulting clipboard content, which is clearly ordered by shape).

 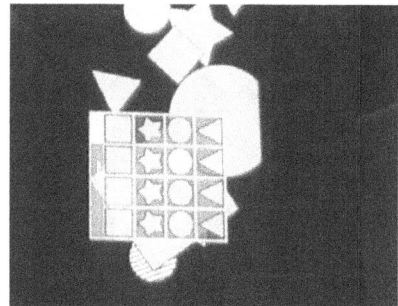

(a) Items sorted according to color   (b) Following a particular copy order

Figure 5.12: Copy strategies observations

During the copy task, participants explicitly accessed their clipboard 3.56 times on average, varying substantially between individuals ($SD = 4.18$). Those following a particular copy order did so less frequently ($M = 2.25, SD = 1.67$) compared to others ($M = 4.6, SD = 5.3$). In an extreme case, one participant (not following a particular copy order) accessed the clipboard 18 times (i.e., at least once for each copy activity).

On average, participants tried to copy duplicates (i.e., items already contained in the clipboard) 4.18 times, also varying substantially between individuals ($SD = 4.54$). (Attempting to copy a duplicate instantly brought up the clipboard to indicate that the item in question had already been copied.) Again, those following a particular copy order did so less frequently ($M = 1.88, SD = 1.89$) compared to others ($M = 6.5, SD = 5.06$). One participant tried to copy 19 duplicates, exclusively relying on the provided feedback instead of attempting to identify missing items according to the task instructions.

We observed that about half of the participants had initial problems to perform the press-and-tap gesture. It often required several trials and repeated demonstrations by the experimenter before they were able to invoke a context menu without difficulties. Most of the observed difficulties were due to coordinating independent touch interactions. For instance, five participants touched sequentially, not keeping the first finger pressed, but releasing it right before tapping with the second finger.

Surface Utilization

On average, 81 % ($SD = 13$ %) of a participant's copy activities took place within the own table half (Figure 5.13). We observed six participants (groups 4, 7, and 8) who spread out more and performed at least 25 % of copy actions within the opposite table half. In contrast, participants of group 3, who had sorted items beforehand, stayed within their respective table halves throughout. Further, we calculated the percentage of covered surface area during copying, using the convex hull of the individual copy activities, and found that on average a participant's copy activities stretched out over 34 % ($SD = 12$ %) of the available area.

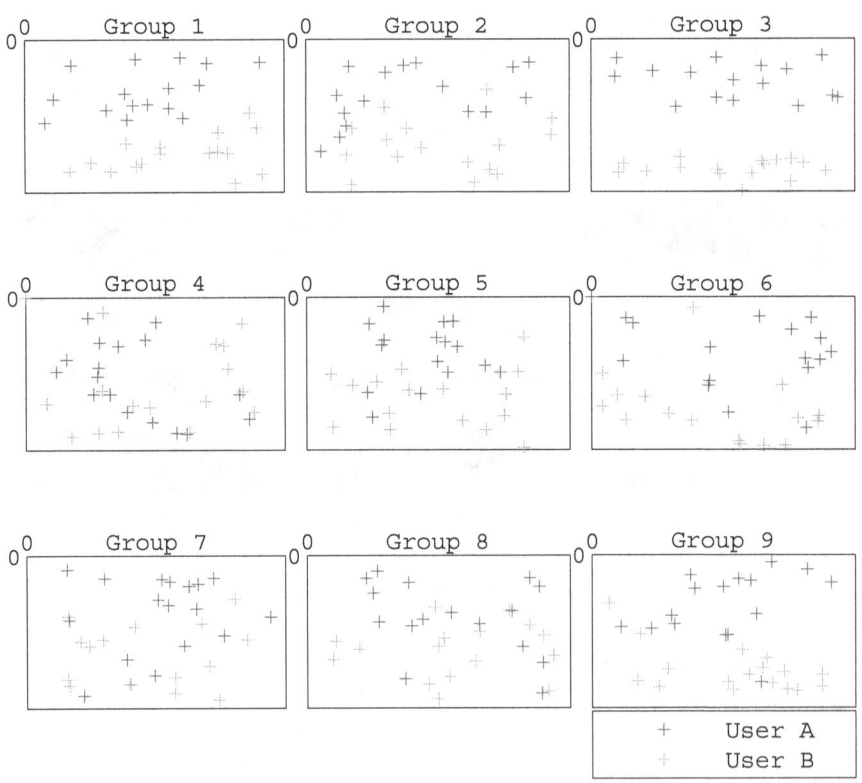

Figure 5.13:   IdWristbands: Locations at which participants copied items. Groups 4, 7, and 8 spread out their copy activities; group 3 had sorted items beforehand.

On average, participants pasted 81 % ($SD = 22$ %) of items within their own table half, while covering 20 % ($SD = 15$ %) of surface area (Figure 5.14). Nine participants (50 %) pasted most items close to the designated target locations, while the remaining half accessed clipboards at seemingly arbitrary positions, arranging items only after inserting them. Some following the latter approach, however, decided on a rough location before accessing the clipboard (e.g., after pasting all items in the left half, they accessed the clipboard in the right half). Note that participants who pasted directly at target locations had to decide on the next shape before accessing their clipboards (as targets suggested shapes), while the remaining participants often opened the clipboard to inspect available items and target locations in parallel.

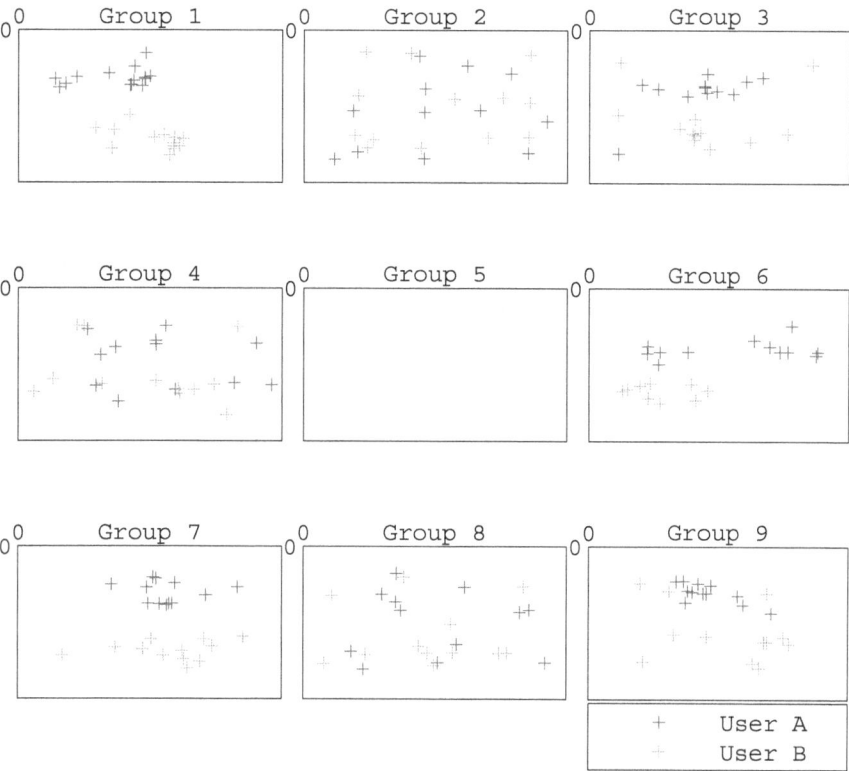

Figure 5.14: IdWristbands: Locations at which participants pasted items. The pattern of group 2 is representative for pasting items directly at target locations, while the other strategy is clearly recognizable for group 1. No log data available for group 5.

User Feedback

Nine participants explicitly mentioned that the wristbands were not perceived as being cumbersome or uncomfortable. Some compared the experience to wearing regular accessories, such as wrist watches, or perceived them as being "invisible". When the experimenter forgot to request back the wristbands after task completion for one group, the participants did not take them off on their own, but started filling out the questionnaires instead. When asked about it afterwards, they stated that they had forgotten about the wristbands. Three participants, however, raised the concern that this perception might change under different conditions, such as in warm or outdoor environments. A single participant did not like the wristbands (without giving specific reasons), and another one said that it might be uncomfortable having to wear them everytime when using the touch interface.

We received positive comments from nine participants about the implicitness and subtleness of identified interaction enabled by IdWristbands. Three emphasized the consistency with regular touch screen interaction, as familiar touch styles could be used without having to adapt for identification ("it's like normal finger motion"). Several participants made comments comparing IdWristbands to PhoneTouch. They highlighted that, with IdWristbands, both hands are free for selection, that there is no need to hold something in the hand for interaction, and that the touch interaction is more direct and potentially easier to control. One participant found the press-and-tap gesture for invoking context menus "great and easy to command". Five other participants, however, reported on difficulties with performing this gesture; one of them suggested that more practice was needed.

We also received some comments regarding potential application scenarios for IdWristbands. Two participants suggested that such a system is particularly suitable within the home context for use by the entire family, because identification is achieved with typical and familiar touch input. Another participant saw potential for IdWristbands in an educational context for young children, especially when compared to PhoneTouch, as mobile phones may not be readily available to such user groups.

5.3.3 HandsDown

Participants of three groups (33 %) collaborated in sorting items according to color before the first copy operation. Further, two participants (11 %) followed a particular copy order (e.g., collecting all items of a specific shape before proceeding to the next). On average, participants accessed the clipboard 3.39 times ($SD = 2.5$), and tried to copy duplicates 6.44 times ($SD = 5.14$); those following a particular copy order did so less frequently ($M = 1.5, SD = 2.12$) compared to others ($M = 7.06, SD = 5.09$).

Regarding pasting, most participants (72 %) pasted one or more items at a time to then arrange them before proceeding, while three participants pasted all items at once to arrange them in a separate step.

In general, participants did not seem to object placing their hand on top of items for identification. Three participants, however, explicitly made space by moving items aside before performing a HandsDown gesture. Some initially intended to copy items directly underneath their hands, but typically reverted to selecting items next to the identified hand, or to move items inside the identification scope. We observed four participants who initially expected the lens to stay after lifting the hand. For instance, they tried to touch an item inside the clipboard with the same hand used for identification, causing the lens to disappear immediately. Seven participants assumed they could directly drag items out of the clipboard onto the surface, which was not supported.

We observed a single participant who used one hand to press the other down for identification (Figure 5.15(a)), apparently to facilitate better detection as the previous attempt just had failed. Another participant seemed to be hesitant to keep down the entire hand on the surface, which resulted in loosing identification several times. In contrast, yet another participant was hesitant to lift the hand, trying to touch items partially occluded instead of repositioning the hand.

(a) Pressing down   (b) Taking item from other lens   (c) Crossing arms

Figure 5.15:   HandsDown copy observations

Surface Utilization

During copying, participants identified 7.94 times on average ($SD = 6.93$). All but two participants (participants A of groups 4 and 9 in Figure 5.16) performed HandsDown gestures exclusively within their own table half. Correspondingly, 94 % ($SD = 9\%$) of a participant's copy activities also took place within the respective half, while covering 14 % ($SD = 8\%$) of surface area.

We observed two prevalent approaches to copying with HandsDown: Nine participants (50 %) primarily dragged items towards the identified hand, keeping its position mostly unchanged, while the other half frequently varied the identification location, hence bringing the hand closer to the items in question. One participant performed the HandsDown gesture anew before copying each item, while the others copied multiple items per identification.

During pasting, participants identified 4.56 times on average ($SD = 3.31$). They did not vary identification locations much, and hence pasted items grouped together independent of target locations (Figure 5.17). They performed all HandsDown gestures and pasted 96 % ($SD = 11\%$) of items within their own table half, thereby covering 4 % ($SD = 3\%$) of surface area on average.

We found that the other group member's identification area was largely respected. Five participants, however, occasionally dragged items directly out of the other participant's lens (Figure 5.15(b)); items were consequently removed from the other participant's identification scope and added to the own scope, once sufficiently close. This was usually accepted except for once when the disadvantaged participant removed his hand from the surface, as he apparently felt the other hand coming too close.

Handedness

Participants could perform HandsDown gestures with either of their hands. Including both copy and paste tasks, we observed that 12 participants (67 %) consistently stayed with the same hand for identification (seven used the dominant and five the non-dominant hand), while the remaining six alternated at least once.

All but three participants crossed arms during the copy task, reaching over the identified hand placed on the surface to copy items on the other side (Figure 5.15(c)). This was less pronounced when pasting, as items were typically moved after closing the lens.

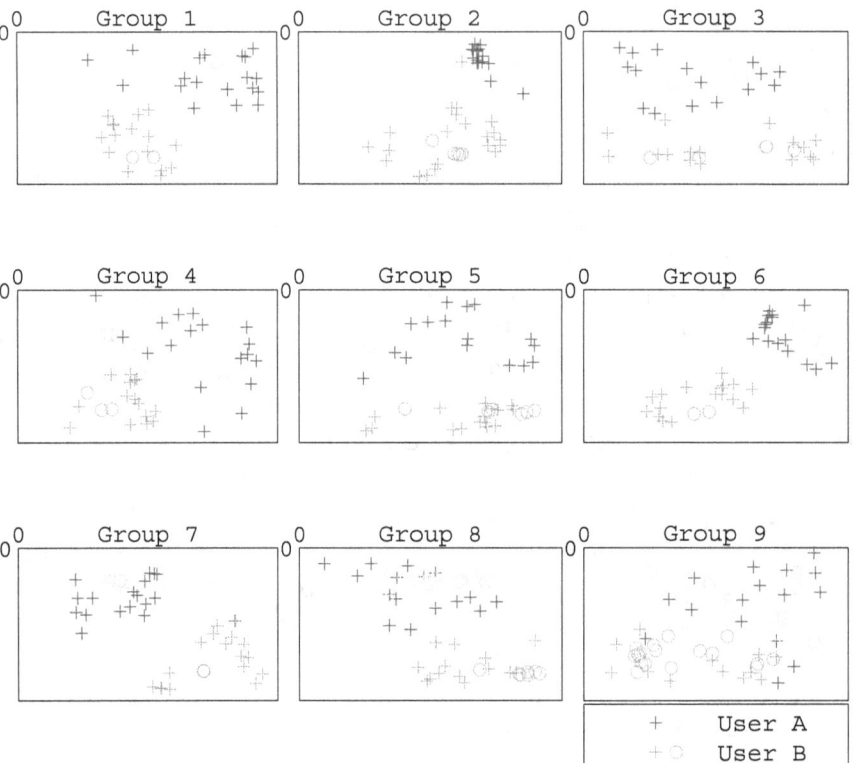

Figure 5.16: HandsDown: Locations at which participants copied items (crosses) and performed HandsDown gestures (circles).

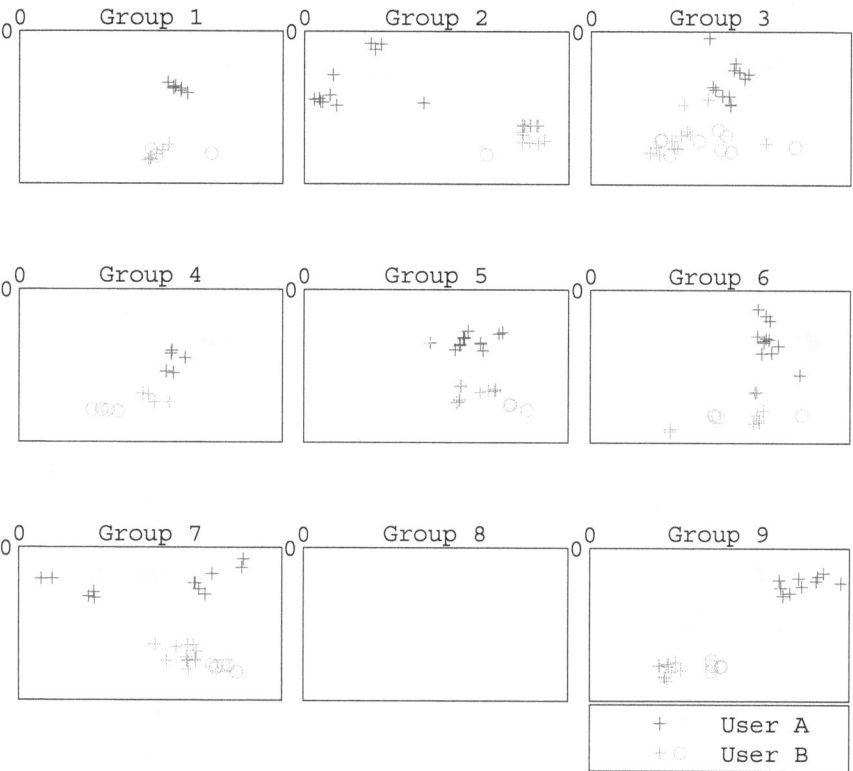

Figure 5.17: HandsDown: Locations at which participants pasted items (crosses) and performed HandsDown gestures (circles). No log data available for group 8; only limited log data available for groups 1, 4, and 6.

User Feedback

Seven participants appreciated the fact that no user instrumentation or additional devices were required for identification. Comparing the other two approaches to HandsDown, participants pointed out the "inconsistency" of using another device, which moreover relies on batteries that need to be charged (referring to PhoneTouch), others explicitly appreciated that there was "no need for extra tools", or found it more accessible in general ("you can just use it").

None of the participants brought up privacy issues with respect to using biometrics. When questioned, only one showed privacy concerns about "giving away personal information", but acknowledged that this depended on the location and environment of the surface device. Similarly, another participant mentioned during the interview potential concerns if the interaction took place in a public setting, while a third stated potentially being more concerned if fingerprints instead of hand contours were used.

Two participant raised concerns about the available surface space, one of them found the overlapping of lenses "irritating". Moreover, six participants felt that the system did not recognize their hands well, while another four would like to have seen a quicker identification (identification took on average 1.34 s, $SD = 1.23$ s). One participant felt more comfortable using HandsDown compared to IdWristbands as it was possible to put the "hand down to rest" to open up an identification area, rather than having to "keeping hands up", which was considered tiring. Five other participants, however, would have preferred having both hands available, for example to "chat on the phone", or because single-handed interaction was perceived as more familiar from devices such as smartphones.

Finally, we received a few comments about potential application scenarios for HandsDown. Two participants suggested its suitability for children, while two others saw it fit for public environments, particularly as no additional devices are needed.

5.3.4 PhoneTouch

Before taking the phone into their hands, four participants (22 %) sorted items according to color. In doing so, two of them collaborated, while the other two worked on their own. Further, roughly half of the participants (44 %) copied items following a particular order.

Clipboards were permanently shown on the phone and hence readily available throughout the task. All but two participants had the phone screen usually facing them (Figure 5.18(a)). In particular, one had turned the phone around because touches with a specific corner were not detected reliably. Nevertheless, this participant often tilted the screen to catch a glimpse of its content. We also observed that participants frequently had a closer look at their phone to inspect copied items. Besides, one participant held up the phone to show the clipboard content to the other participant.

Participants attempted to copy 3.44 duplicates on average ($SD = 4.38$). Those following a particular order did so less frequently ($M = 1, SD = 1.51$) than others ($M = 5.4, SD = 4.99$).

Two participants pasted most items in batches to arrange them together, but the majority interleaved paste and (finger-based) arrange interactions. In general, having the clipboard on a separate screen allowed participants to inspect both remaining items on the phone and targets to fill on the surface at the same time, without occluding the shared work space (Figure 5.18(b)).

   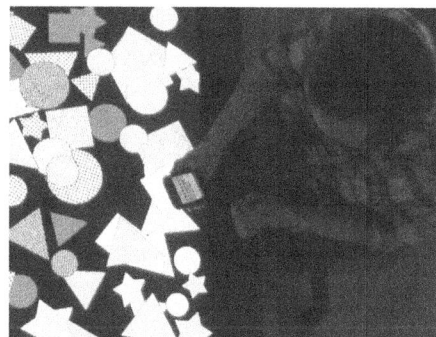

(a) Watching phone during interaction   (b) Inspecting both surface and phone

Figure 5.18:   PhoneTouch screen usage observations

Surface Utilization

On average, 63 % ($SD = 21$ %) of a participant's copy activities took place within the own table half, thereby covering 40 % ($SD = 15$ %) of surface area (Figure 5.19).

All but the two participants who pasted in batches (89 %) choose to directly insert items at the intended target locations, even if close to the other participant, resulting in a clearly visible pattern (Figure 5.20). About half of the paste locations were located within the own table half ($M = 54$ %, $SD = 11$ %), while covering 44 % of surface area ($SD = 12$ %).

Touch Interleaving

All but one participant set out using the dominant hand to hold the phone and copy items. During the copy task, six participants switched hands, for example to delete an item they had copied by mistake, to better reach the opposite table side, or to use the hand for a finger-based interaction on the surface.

During copying, participants seldom used finger touch input on the surface. In fact, six participants (33 %) exclusively relied on phone touches. (By design, the copy task could be completed without finger input.) Even if items were partially occluded, participants could copy them directly by touching visible parts with the phone corner.

Unlike copying, pasting required combined finger and phone interaction to align items with target locations. Further, participants had to regularly select items on the phone's touch screen before pasting. These different interaction types (i.e., on the surface: phone touch to paste and finger touch to align; on the phone: finger touch to select) resulted in participants alternating hands for holding the phone more frequently.

Depending on the hand used for phone touches on the surface and the preferred hand for phone screen interactions, participants had to switch hands. For example, participants holding the phone in the right hand (for touching the surface) had to take it into the left hand if they wanted to make selections on the phone screen with the right hand as well. Only three participants (17 %) selected items on the phone with the hand also holding it (e.g., using the thumb). Likewise, switching hands was also required if participants preferred performing both finger and phone touches on the surface with the same hand. For example, a person holding the phone in the right hand for touching the surface (and

120

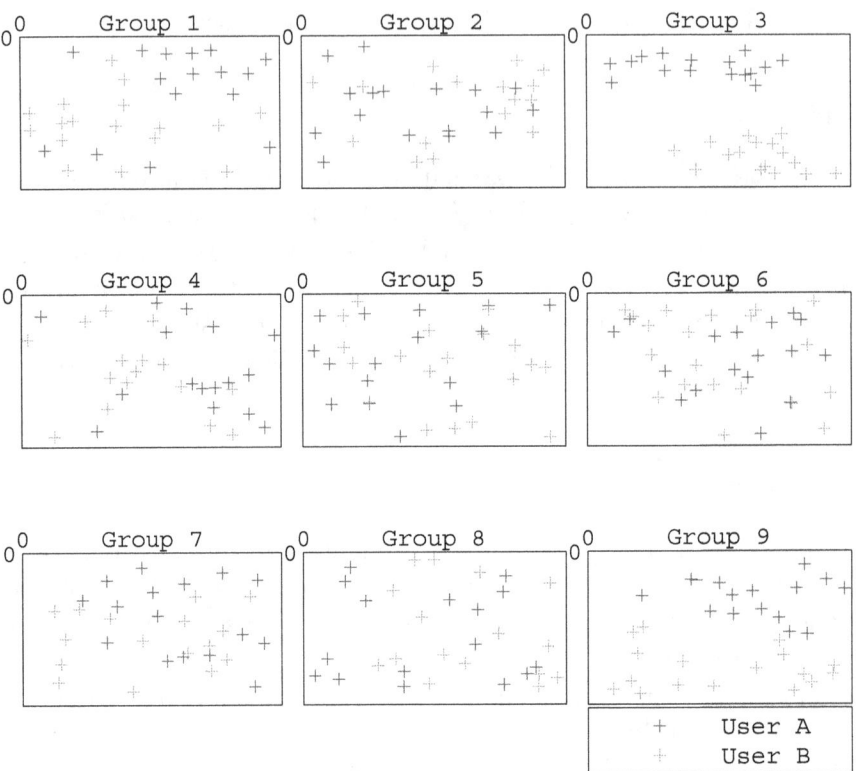

Figure 5.19: PhoneTouch: Locations at which participants copied items. Participants 1A, 9B, and group 3 had sorted items beforehand.

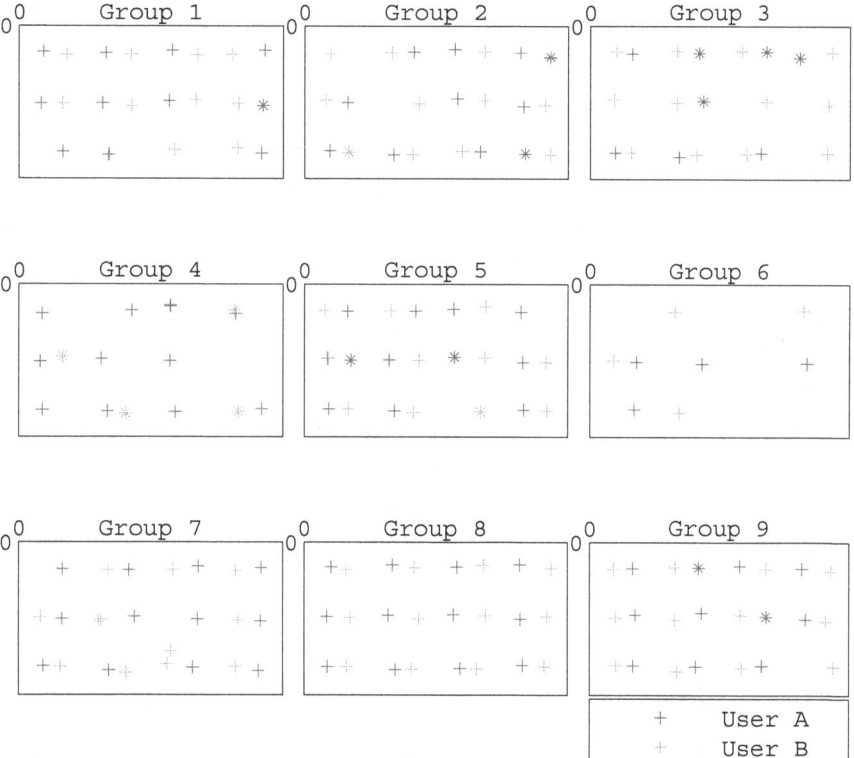

Figure 5.20: PhoneTouch: Locations at which participants pasted items. Participants 3A and 4B pasted multiple items at once (denoted by asterisks). Limited log data available for group 6.

pasting items) had to take the phone into the left hand before being able to arrange items on the surface with the right hand (using finger touches).

We observed various approaches with regard to hand preferences and alternating hands for the different interaction types. Seven participants (39 %) kept the phone in one hand throughout. For six of them, this was the dominant hand, but one used the non-dominant hand for phone-based touch interaction. Another participant changed from dominant (for copying) to non-dominant hand (for pasting). The remaining 10 participants (67 %) frequently alternated the hand holding the phone as they saw fit.

To illustrate the interaction flow, we describe the approach consistently followed by two participants (both using bimanual phone selection and the same hand for surface-based finger and phone touches): Keeping the phone in their non-dominant hand, they selected items to paste using fingers of the dominant hand (Figure 5.21(a)). Before touching the surface with the phone, they turned it over to the dominant hand (Figure 5.21(b)), pasted items (Figure 5.21(c)), and handed it immediately back to the non-dominant hand (Figure 5.21(d)) for arranging the just pasted item using finger input on the surface (Figure 5.21(e)). This sequence was repeated for the remaining items (Figure 5.21(f)). Approaches varied greatly amongst participants, however. For example, others switched hands only occasionally for finger interaction with the dominant hand on the surface, while otherwise performing such input with the non-dominant hand.

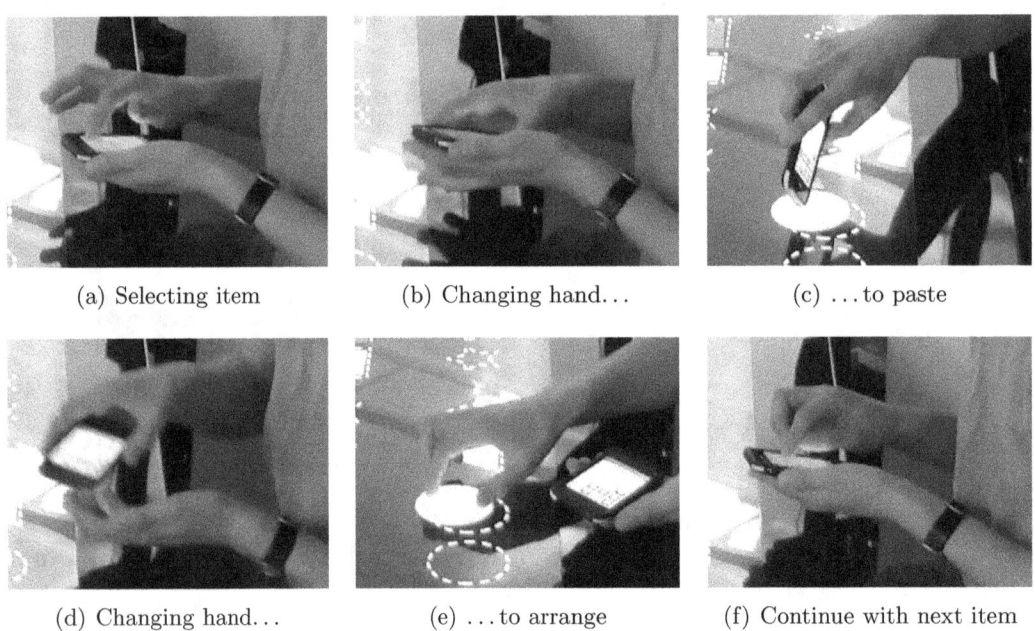

(a) Selecting item	(b) Changing hand...	(c) ...to paste
(d) Changing hand...	(e) ...to arrange	(f) Continue with next item

Figure 5.21: PhoneTouch finger and phone interleaving observations

User Feedback

Seven participants explicitly mentioned the ease of use of PhoneTouch, while we received eight complaints about the touch detection not being sensitive enough. Four participants appreciated the mobile phone as a familiar and readily available device, and two participants actually preferred interacting with the phone on the surface compared to using fingers, while another one commented that replacing finger touch entirely by phone touch was not desirable. A single participant felt that using the phone for touch interaction was not intuitive. None of the participants raised concerns with respect to potential damages of phone or screen.

One participant saw the phone as a dedicated tool and highlighted that there were "no gestures or sequences to remember"' to copy and paste. The additionally available phone screen was welcomed by 10 participants, as it allowed them to permanently see and quickly inspect what had already been copied, for example to identify what was still missing. Another participant mentioned the potential of the private screen for competitive gaming applications. One participant, however, did not like the additional screen as it diverted attention, but acknowledged that others might find it beneficial. Three participants felt critical about using the phone as it constitutes "one more tool to rely on" and one must take care that it is ready to be used (e.g., batteries need to be charged).

With respect to integrating mobile phones and surface, five participants gave positive feedback about the instantaneous transfer of data between devices ("transferring objects to the telephone was very cool"). One of them saw the potential for taking information from the shared surface back home using the phone. None of the participants commented about having to alternate hands for interaction on the surface or on the phone.

Regarding possible application scenarios, one participant suggested PhoneTouch for corporate environments for transferring documents, as smartphones are readily available in such settings.

5.3.5 Comparative Analysis

Table 5.2 shows the number of participants who sorted items according to color or followed a particular copy order, and the number of failed copies. We did not find any significant effects of method on the number of participants who pre-sorted or followed a particular copy order. Likewise, the method did not have a significant effect on the numbers of failed copies.

	IdWristbands	HandsDown	PhoneTouch
Pre-sorting	3	6	4
Copy order	8	2	8
Failed copies	4.2	6.4	3.4

Table 5.2: Number of participants following different copy strategies, and number of failed copies

Figure 5.22 summarizes completion times split by method and subtask. The used method had a significant effect on copy times ($\chi^2(2) = 12.6, p < .05$), but not on paste times. We used Wilcoxon tests to follow up on these findings and applied a Bonferroni correction, hence all effects are reported at a .017 significance level. We found copying with PhoneTouch was significantly faster compared to both IdWristbands ($T = 0, p < .017, r = -.62$) and HandsDown ($T = 1, p < .017, r = -.6$).

Figure 5.23 summarizes surface utilization for the three methods based on the percentage of copy-and-paste activities within the own surface half (*vicinity*), and the percentage of covered surface area based on the convex hull of copy-and-paste activities (*coverage*). Identified interactions typically took place closer to the corresponding participant for

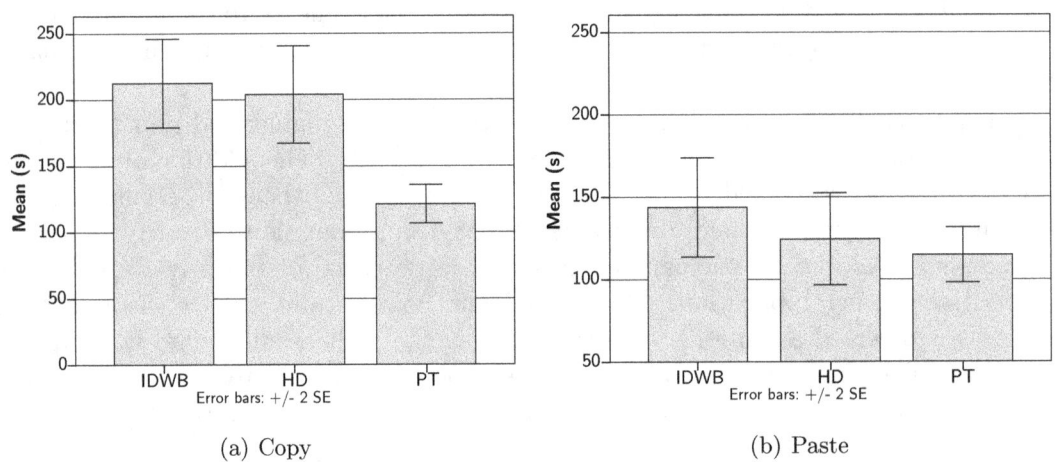

Figure 5.22:   Mean completion times of copy and paste tasks for all methods

HandsDown than for PhoneTouch; IdWristbands lies in between. Likewise, HandsDown copy-and-paste activities covered the smallest area, followed by IdWristbands and then PhoneTouch. All four measures were significantly affected by the used identification method: copy vicinity ($\chi^2(2) = 20.49, p < .05$), copy coverage ($\chi^2(2) = 16.44, p < .05$), paste vicinity ($\chi^2(2) = 17.33, p < .05$), and paste coverage ($\chi^2(2) = 22.43, p < .05$). Wilcoxon post-hoc tests revealed (Bonferroni-corrected significance level of .017) that there were no significant differences between PhoneTouch and IdWristbands for copy coverage and between between HandsDown and IdWristbands for paste vicinity; all other pairwise tests showed significant effects. Further, participants who did not know each other beforehand did not differ from those who were acquainted with respect to their surface space utilization.

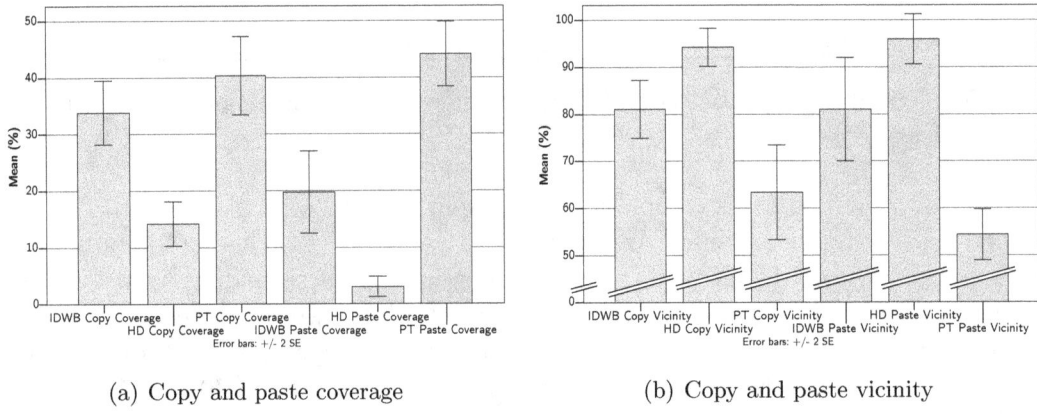

Figure 5.23:   Surface utilization

5.4 Discussion

All participants readily understood the concept of personalized clipboards and were able to successfully complete copy and paste tasks independent of the identification method. They could instantly identify when and where required to immediately take advantage of the so afforded personalized interaction. We did not observe any fundamental difficulties in using either of the proposed methods. Despite their non-implicit identification approach, HandsDown and PhoneTouch facilitated fluid personalized interaction. In agreement, neither usability nor task load evaluation indicated difficulties, and the participants' ranking was balanced.

The collected qualitative and quantitative feedback does not suggest an overall preference for a single identification method, while individual participants naturally favored one or the other due to various reasons. For example, some appreciated the implicitness of IdWristbands, while others preferred HandsDown as it does not require additional devices for identification, or PhoneTouch as it uses familiar devices and provides additional display and interaction spaces.

5.4.1 General Task Approaches

Two strategies repeatedly emerged during the copy task (see Figure 5.2). First, some participant sorted items according to color before copying them. Secondly, some participants followed a structured copy order, such as picking up all items of a particular shape first. Applying or not applying either of these strategies was seemingly not a result of the identification method, but rather a personal preference. Sorting, for instance, was clearly separated from the actual copy task (which was particularly obvious for PhoneTouch, as phones were only picked up after sorting was completed). Further, only three participants sorted items in one condition, the remaining four did so in two or even all three conditions. Likewise, six out of 10 participants who followed a particular copy order did so in more than one condition.

Both copy strategies are mainly an artifact of the abstract task nature. Sorting requires an up-front understanding of which items have to be copied, while following a particular order was made possible by the clear task definition, which is arguably not present in less structured real-world tasks. Nevertheless, the fact that only two participants copied items following a particular order when using HandsDown (as opposed to eight participants for either IdWristbands and PhoneTouch) suggests a difference between these identification methods. Possibly, the larger areas occupied by hands and IdLenses lead to a reduced overview. Similarly, the abstract task introduced the notion of failed copies (i.e., attempts to copy duplicates). We banned duplicates to animate participants to reflect on the given task rather than blindly copying anything; as a side effect, it also increased the number of identified interactions. Despite not being significantly different, the smaller amount of failed copies for PhoneTouch, compared to either IdWristbands or HandsDown, suggests that participants had an increased awareness of their clipboard content, likely due to the additionally available phone screen.

Using HandsDown and PhoneTouch, participants had the option to either paste items one-by-one or in batches. While only two participants pasted multiple items at a time for PhoneTouch, all did so for HandsDown; some of them even pasted the entire clipboard content before arranging items. HandsDown took longer to identify before allowing for selecting items on the surface, which apparently lead to a stricter task division. In contrast, PhoneTouch, which allowed users to select items on the mobile screen before pasting them in a single step, resulted in fluidly interleaving phone and finger interaction. Note that by design IdWristbands was restricted to pasting items one-by-one.

5.4.2 Surface Utilization

Personalized interaction is location-dependent as it takes place in the context of specific targets on the interactive surface. As mentioned before (see Figure 5.23), the identification method had a significant influence on surface utilization with respect to identified interaction. Surface utilization was most limited for HandsDown, considering both the coverage of surface area as well as the vicinity to a participant's location around the table. In contrast, PhoneTouch resulted in the widest spread of interaction. Spatial differences were particularly apparent for paste interaction patterns, which clearly revealed the designated target locations for PhoneTouch and partially for IdWristbands, but not for HandsDown. Considering such differences is important when designing user-aware applications in order to inform suitable layouts of interface elements that require identification.

The utilization of surface space was influenced by different spatial and temporal requirements of the identification methods. Both IdWristbands and HandsDown require users to perform prolonged interactions on the surface, as they have to identify before choosing to copy or paste. At the same time, user interface elements such as context menus and clipboards take up surface space. In the case of HandsDown, copy-and-paste activities are coupled to IdLenses and in turn to the identified hand, which demands additional space and is arguably more difficult to perform than a simple finger touch. In contrast, PhoneTouch allows users to make selections on the phone in advance, independent of the surface application. Therefore, copying and pasting is reduced to a single touch on the surface, which is arguably quicker and easier to perform, even on the other side of the table. The results for IdWristbands are only applicable to a context-menu-based approach as used here. We assume that in the case of implicit, finger-based user identification as offered by IdWristbands the actual interface design primarily determines location preferences of identified interactions.

5.4.3 Method-Specific Insights

IdWristbands

Wearing wristbands did not impede interaction and participants did not feel bothered by it. We observed, however, that they performed interactions almost exclusively using the hand wearing a wristband. Such a limitation to single-handed interaction may be explained by the perception of having to interact with the instrumented hand—as it is equipped with a controlling device. Alternatively, it may be as well rooted in the unfamiliarity with large touch screens, or a general preference for interaction with a single hand. In particular, one user pointed out, though with respect to HandsDown, that people like keeping one hand available for doing other things, such as holding a beverage.

HandsDown

Despite the arguably less familiar interaction style of HandsDown, participants instantly grasped both its function for identification and the identification scope provided by IdLenses, which we saw readily adopted for the task at hand. Participants correctly understood hand gestures as a method for identification, not direct manipulation, and hence were typically not concerned about placing the hand on top of items (they were not interested in). Several participants used their dominant hand for identification, while others alternated between dominant and non-dominant hand; this has to be considered when implementing IdLenses in order to position them without conflicts. As expected, most participants respected the identification scopes of their group members; only few took items out of another user's lens. Overlapping of lenses was typically not an issue, primarily as a result of keeping identifications within one's own table half. However, this is largely dependent on the number of concurrent users, the surface size, and the application. Further, participants did not raise concerns about privacy issues of using biometrics, which is due in parts to the study environment, but also influenced by the perception of hand contours being less critical than fingerprints.

While participants identified primarily within their own table half, we observed two distinct approaches of combining HandsDown gestures with supplementary finger interaction in the copy task: Half the participants varied identification locations to get closer to items in question, while the other half preferred bringing items towards the identified hand by dragging them. Those who identified at different locations did so to define a coarse position for the fine-grained finger-based copy interactions to follow. The remaining participants regarded the identified hand rather as a static or fixed reference and fluidly moved items around it, thereby crossing arms if necessary. In the paste task, participants unanimously inserted items in batches, grouped closely together, and did not vary identification locations much. As these results show, the envisioned asymmetric bimanual concept (i.e., setting a coarse frame of reference for dexterous input with the other hand) was readily adopted. Locations for performing HandsDown gestures, however, varied less than anticipated. In fact, a large number of participants preferred a more static frame of reference (defined by the identified hand) at the cost of having to move items farther (using finger-based input). While such an approach is straightforward to apply for movable targets (such as the items in our study), application designers have to carefully consider interface layouts for fixed elements, such as buttons.

PhoneTouch

Our study confirmed the suitability of mobile phones for precise target selection in a stylus-like fashion. In the copy task, participants almost exclusively relied on phone touches for interaction with the surface, even in cases where items were partially occluded or located farther away. Likewise, they effortlessly inserted items directly at the designated target locations in the paste task. What is more, we did not receive any concerns with respect to potential phone or surface damage, but must keep in mind that participants were provided with devices that they did not own.

Interleaving phone and finger touches was readily adapted. In contrast to copying, pasting lent itself naturally to a tight coupling of phone touches (to paste) and finger touches (to arrange), which resulted in a fluid mixture of phone and finger interaction. Despite frequently alternating the phone between hands for different kinds of input, there was no negative impact on task completion time or on the perceived mental load; participants seamlessly switched hands apparently without being aware of it. These observations suggest that phone and finger touches can be combined without difficulties, as users are able to readily alternate between modalities. Assigning different tasks to phone and finger touches was easily understood. Such a division can help to structure tasks, similar to using different tools in everyday environments.

The phone's screen offered additional display and interaction space, which complemented the surface-centered task and was explicitly mentioned as an advantage of PhoneTouch. For copying, it provided unobtrusive and permanent feedback about the clipboard content, which was readily visible to participants as they held phones generally with the screen facing them. This behavior allowed to verify that an item was indeed copied, as for example an undesired color could easily be spotted. Furthermore, it provided information about how many items had already been copied at a glance. For pasting, the phone allowed participants to inspect both remaining items and available targets at the same time, without occupying the primary work space. As selections were made directly on the phone, the actual paste interaction on the surface consisted of a single phone touch.

5.4.4 Limitations

To better control the experiment while reducing its complexity and time requirements, we conducted a laboratory- rather than a field-based study. Although laboratory settings may weaken the ecological validity of a study, a comparison by Kjeldskov et al. suggests that a laboratory setting cannot only identify all critical usability problems but can actually reveal more problems than the corresponding field setting [80]. We designed the general study setup (i.e., two users interacting with a commercial surface device) to resemble a real-world setting, such as encountered at home or the workplace. The study task itself, however, did not match a real-world application, but was specifically designed to identify interaction characteristics and usability problems instead.

We carefully designed our task to evaluate different identification methods, using individual clipboards as an example for personalized interaction. The nature of our task was abstract on purpose to make it easy to understand and execute. Nevertheless, this design decision influenced interactions, which became for example apparent through different copy strategies (as discussed above). Further, personal clipboards and the surrounding copy-and-paste activities cannot cover personalized interaction in general, but rather provide insights focused on applications that require frequent and instantaneous but not necessarily continuous user identification.

Interaction design and user identification method are highly interwoven, as exemplified by IdLenses for HandsDown. Especially for implicit identification methods like IdWristbands there exist various alternative design options, which may impact the resulting interaction. It was not a goal of this study, however, to determine a single-best method, but to illustrate benefits of personalized interaction and to shed light onto interaction particularities and adoption by users.

Using a prototype system, several participants encountered detection-related problems, which influenced the user experience as well. Such problems, however, were not connected to a particular method. In the case of IdWristbands, despite replicating the default Windows 7 press-and-tap gesture for accessing context menus, several participants had initial difficulties performing it. Others encountered some difficulties using HandsDown as their hand was not always recognized immediately. We also observed participants for which phone touches were not always registered correctly.

5.4.5 Implications

Building user-aware applications requires their designers to consider spatial and temporal requirements of identification methods, as they impact the preferred utilization of surface space. Such requirements, in turn, are determined by the identified entities (e.g., hand versus phone) and their integration with surrounding touch interaction. Using HandsDown and PhoneTouch, we showed that implicit user identification is by no means a requirement for fluid personalized interaction on interactive surfaces; participants successfully completed the given task with either of the two non-implicit methods.

While PhoneTouch directly allows for fine-grained identified input, HandsDown makes use of IdLenses to expand the identification scope provided by a coarse hand gesture for dexterous finger input. It is important to keep in mind the extended spatial requirements of the HandsDown gesture and the surrounding IdLens. Further, unlike regular finger touches, HandsDown gestures are more difficult to perform and should hence be limited to easily accessible areas close-by. As a consequence, targets for identified interaction must be in physical reach, or it must be straightforward to bring them into reach (like in our study, where it was possible to move items for copying). Otherwise, users may have to change their position around the surface, which is inconvenient. Overlapping of lenses may happen, especially in presence of multiple users and on smaller surfaces, which has to be taken into account during the design process. Likewise, it is important to design for hand-independent interactions. In general, hand preferences for interaction vary and may change even during the course of interaction. With respect to PhoneTouch, we found that outsourcing information to the phone's display worked well to provide an unobtrusive but always accessible awareness of application states as well as to facilitate side by side inspections of different content without occupying surface space or interfering with other users.

As users preferred to perform HandsDown gestures close-by, future IdLenses extensions could allow for dragging identified touches out of the lens, rather than moving items inside it. For example, to access a fixed button at the other side of the table (i.e., out of reach of a HandsDown gesture), users may identify locally, and then start a finger movement inside the lens, which ends on top of said button, thereby providing user identity for it. While we evaluated IdLenses with HandsDown as provider for user identity, other sources may readily be used. For example, an IdLens could be attached to an uniquely identifiable tangible object as long as it placed on the surface. In doing so, a user would have both hands available for interaction on the surface. At the same time, some of the advantages offered by HandsDown, such as not requiring additional tools for identification, would be lost.

5.5 Summary

We showed that instantaneous user identification makes it possible to transfer the well-known clipboard concept from single-user to multi-user shared surface applications. Participants readily understood the provided personal clipboards and individual copy-

and-paste activities. At the same time, we demonstrated that IdWristbands, HandsDown, and PhoneTouch facilitate such personalized interaction for surface computing—despite their different interaction styles and identification granularities. During the course of the study, we gathered valuable insights into interaction particularities and user preferences, which may guide the decision for a particular method and inform the implementation of user-aware applications. Finally, we demonstrated that all proposed identification methods can be implemented with an off-the-shelf interactive surface. In the case of PhoneTouch, we additionally used unmodified iPhones, and for IdWristbands custom-built wristbands.

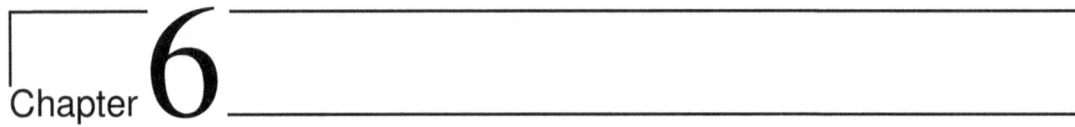

Chapter **6**

Conclusions

We set out to overcome the prevailing unawareness of different users on interactive surfaces by facilitating user identification and exploring personalized interaction. Following these aims, we introduced three novel methods of *instantaneous user identification* and explored the opening design space of *personalized interaction on shared surfaces*.

6.1 Contributions

The contribution of this thesis is three-fold:

1. We contribute three methods that apply yet unexplored strategies for instantaneous user identification in surface computing: IdWristbands, HandsDown, and Phone-Touch. All methods effortlessly integrate with typical multi-touch interaction styles. In their own way, each of them enables users to instantaneously and simultaneously identify at arbitrary locations on a direct-touch surface. Particularly relevant is the ability to make precise selections on the surface that can be attributed to individual users, without interrupting ongoing workflows. What is more, hardware requirements of the proposed methods are modest, as they rely on common vision-based touch detection techniques. Additionally needed equipment is either available off-the-shelf (in case of PhoneTouch) or consists of cheap components (in case of IdWristbands). We implemented each method as fully-functional prototype. These prototypes did not only allow us to evaluate identification performances, but they also paved the way for exploring user-awareness on the level of interaction and applications.

2. We explored the design space of personalized interaction for surface computing on the basis of HandsDown and PhoneTouch by introducing a wide range of user-aware interaction techniques. After framing the concept of personalized interaction, we first analyzed the specific input and output spaces of HandsDown and PhoneTouch on a conceptual level. This analysis provided an in-depth understanding of interaction requirements and opportunities, which guided the creative design of novel interaction techniques. Populating the design space of personalized interaction, the proposed techniques illustrate advantages of user-awareness across various levels, such as dynamically enforcing authorization or providing immediate access to personal data

in a shared environment. Our techniques timely address current issues in surface computing without being application-specific. In the case of PhoneTouch, our exploration further demonstrated the potential of complementing shared surfaces with personal handheld devices to realize numerous synergy effects.

3. By introducing personal clipboards for surface computing, we demonstrated that instantaneous user identification facilitates interaction concepts that are otherwise not obvious to realize. At the same time, we showed that IdWristbands, HandsDown, and PhoneTouch are suitable methods to facilitate such personalized interaction. Our qualitative analysis revealed interaction particularities and user preferences with respect to the three methods and their distinct user identification strategies, which can help to inform the design of user-aware applications. We further found that implicit identification of individual finger touches is not a requirement per se for fine-grained personalized interaction on interactive surfaces.

   In the appendix, we present design and implementation guidelines for multi-touch tables as a minor contribution on its own.

An alternative perspective on this work readily presents itself by considering IdWristbands, HandsDown, and PhoneTouch individually—from identity detection to interaction techniques to evaluation. Following such a system- rather than methodology-centric structure, our contribution lies in introducing three novel systems for instantaneous user identification on shared surfaces:

- *IdWristbands*, small wrist-worn devices, allow for implicitly identifying individual finger touches. Using light-emitting diodes (LED), they continuously transmit identifiers in the infrared spectrum, which are associated to corresponding touches. We showed their feasibility for such transparent identification, and further demonstrated their integration into a personal clipboard task: To independently copy and paste on a shared surface, users could immediately access their clipboards in context by performing a particular finger gesture with the instrumented hand.

- *HandsDown*, a light-weight biometric identification method, enables users to spontaneously identify by placing their bare hand flat on the surface; the extracted hand contour information is then matched against a database of registered users. We showed that HandsDown is a suitable identification method for group sizes typically encountered around a shared surface. To allow for fine-grained user-aware input, we proposed IdLenses, a novel interaction concept that extends the identification scope provided by HandsDown gestures. Following an asymmetric bimanual strategy, IdLenses allows for setting a coarse frame of reference with the identifying hand for supplementary dexterous finger input with the other hand. All touches inside a lens are attributed to the corresponding user, while all that is seen through the lens is dynamically personalized, for example by automatically translating labels to the user's native language. We demonstrated HandsDown with IdLenses as suitable enabler for personalized copy-and-paste activities on a shared surfaces. Our study showed that participants preferred to perform HandsDown gestures in their vicinity, but could rely on supplementary finger input with the other hand for reaching targets farther away.

- *PhoneTouch* adopts mobile devices as proxies for their users and allows for stylus-like direct-touch interaction. We demonstrated that the underlying detection mechanism—based on independent and distributed sensing of touch events—is suitable for small groups of co-located users. Phones, being personal and mobile devices, are a compelling complement to larger shared surfaces. We analyzed the opening interaction space in terms of input and output attributes enabled by the phones' capabilities, such as providing private displays. Based on this analysis, we proposed a wide range of novel interaction techniques that not only facilitate personalized interaction but that also realize various synergies between personal and shared devices, helping to address common issues in surface computing, such as providing fluid access to personal data. Based on PhoneTouch, we implemented individual copy-and-paste for shared surfaces, using the mobiles's screen to permanently display clipboards without occupying the main work space or interfering with other users. Our study revealed that this additionally available screen was readily adopted and served as an instant feedback channel. Further, users could precisely select targets with their phone, and showed no difficulties in fluidly interleaving phone and finger touch interaction.

Using the example of an emergency response system as discussed in the introduction (see page 5), we illustrate in the following how the three proposed systems integrate differently with the same application. An emergency response system (e.g., to manage disaster recovery) benefits from interactive surfaces as all team members can interact simultaneously with the same interface. Not all team members, however, are allowed to access all available functions. For instance, dispatching a unit in the real world by touching a button on the surface may only be initiated by a supervisor with sufficient rights.

As IdWristbands implicitly identifies finger touches, an authorized team member can issue a command simply by touching the "dispatch" button of the corresponding unit. The system registers the touch, which is already identified at this point. It can therefore immediately verify if this user is allowed to perform the selected function and execute it, or display an error message otherwise.

Using HandsDown, team members who wish to dispatch units need to place their hand next to the corresponding icon first. After successful identification, the interface shows a lens. Touching a "dispatch" button through this lens provides the necessary identity information for the system to decide weather the user has sufficient rights to perform the action or not. The lens disappears once the hand is lifted off the surface. HandsDown relies on social protocols to be in place, as anyone could perform a touch inside the lens while it is open. Note that all other, unrestricted functions of the user interface are still accessible by common multi-touch interaction without prior identification.

Similarly, PhoneTouch allows for finger-touch interaction with interface elements that do not require identification. To dispatch a unit, team members touch the "dispatch" button with their phone. Phone touches are always associated with the device identifier and the user in turn. Therefore, the system can assert that a user is authorized before issuing any command. In addition, PhoneTouch allows for specifying parameters on the phone. For instance, a team member may enter a message on the phone before touching the surface (i.e., without occupying space on the surface) to be send to the dispatched unit.

6.2 Further Considerations

We presented a comprehensive survey of enabling methods for user identification on interactive surfaces, and proposed three novel methods of our own. This collection of methods, however, can only serve as a snapshot of current technologies. With upcoming touch sensing techniques, existing identification methods will be refined and new methods will emerge. Nevertheless, the diversity of approaches and identification strategies are likely to prevail. We believe that future identification methods will still differ in the identified entity (e.g., biometric versus token-based) and the agent of control (e.g., stylus versus finger). What is more, various identification methods may provide additional benefits that go beyond just identifying users (such as PhoneTouch does by fluidly integrating personal data and providing a private interaction space).

Implicit user identification methods, which immediately associate indivual finger touches to users, are not likely to take hold as the single-best solution to user-awareness. Despite their distinct advantages, implicit methods are not suitable for all application scenarios alike, for instance due to hardware restrictions or privacy concerns (in case of biometrics). Especially in public settings, people may want to explicitly control when they reveal their identity to the system versus when to stay anonymous. They may refuse an identification method outright if sharing certain information (e.g., fingerprints) is out of question—a touch screen that instantly knows who you are may be a scary vision to some of us.

In summary, it will be a combination of application and environmental factors that decide on the suitability of a user identification method. In certain scenarios, additional devices may be acceptable, while other scenarios call for stand-alone solutions. Biometric-based identification gets by without additional devices, but users may be skeptical towards providing sensitive information in environments they do not consider trustworthy. The targeted user population plays an important role as well. For example, young children may not have a phone readily available for interaction. Therefore, system designers have to carefully balance different requirements before deciding for a user identification approach.

6.3 Future Directions

Despite the number of existing identification methods, there remains room for novel approaches that explore further modalities. For example, gaze-tracking is a promising candidate to associate touch input to users, as it is natural to look at one's hand during interaction. While this allows for user differentiation only, a combination with eye-based biometrics or face recognition could fill the gap to also provide user identification.

While IdWristbands, HandsDown, and PhoneTouch vary widely with respect to their identification approaches and interaction styles, we set out to integrate them into a general software framework that provides a unified, event-driven interface for user-aware applications, supplying user identity as additional input parameter. This framework proved to be helpful in prototyping applications, such as the personal clipboard task in the presented study (which was implemented for all three identification methods without having to change the core application). Expanding and generalizing this framework for user-aware surface computing, including current and upcoming user identification methods, will help to make user identification more widely available in order to build richer applications faster.

We looked at user-aware interactions mostly for parallel but individual use on the same surface. As suggested by the notion of overlapping IdLenses for example, seamlessly combining identified interactions of different users opens up a compelling design space, which we did not consider further up to this point. Designing for interwoven and overlapping user-aware interactions poses new questions with respect to suitable interaction and visualization concepts.

This thesis accompanied the proposed identification methods with in-depth analysis of the surrounding interaction spaces, and introduced an extensive range of user-aware techniques. Our decision of exploring user-awareness in a predominantly application-independent manner, however, leaves room for investigating the transferability to concrete applications. It is not obvious which interaction techniques are most suitable for specific application areas, or how they will be appropriated in a varying context.

We explored user-awareness in laboratory-based studies with small groups of users. How the proposed methods and techniques scale to a real-world context in possibly public environments with larger numbers of fluctuating users remains an open question. While we discussed issues with respect to the supported number of users and suitable application domains, it is not clear what new questions and challenges will arise from a larger scale deployment. More work is required to confirm our results in the context of real-world scenarios in different domains, and to investigate how the identified benefits transfer to actual applications. In addition, future work needs to address challenges with respect to deployment, robustness, and user account management.

If user identification became available on a broader scale, it will have the potential to transform how surface applications function and how they are perceived. New applications that were not or only difficult to realize without user-awareness will emerge. This may lead to a faster adoption of surface computing as a shared platform, which is currently limited to predefined content and does not easily allow for integrating personal data. In this context, questions of security and privacy arise, as it is not obvious how users will accept and appropriate identification in different usage scenarios.

Glossary

B

Bluetooth technology for wireless data exchange over short distances

D

direct-touch integration of input and output spaces that enables users to interact directly with the graphical user interface (GUI)

E

EndLighten acrylic that contains small reflective particles to diffuse light uniformly across its surface

G

groupware computer-based systems that support groups of people engaged in a common task (or goal) and that provide an interface to a shared environment [43]

H

HandsDown a user identification method based on biometric hand contour analysis

I

IdLenses an interaction concept that provides dynamic lenses for personalized input and output on a shared surface

IdWristbands a user identification method based on wristbands that continuously emit infrared identifiers

interactive surface a device whose GUI is operated through direct multi-touch input to promote natural interaction, potentially by multiple users at the same time

M

multi-touch ability of a touch-enabled input device to detect multiple contact points at the same time

P

PhoneTouch a user identification method that facilitates stylus-like direct-touch interaction between mobile devices (e.g., smart phones) and an interactive surface

PixelSense touch sensing technology integrated with a liquid crystal display (LCD); individual pixels sense not only finger contacts but also arbitrary objects [94]

S

shared surface see interactive surface

surface computing an interaction paradigm for GUI that promotes natural and gestural interaction using direct touch input

W

Wifi technology for wireless data exchange over a computer network

Windows 7 personal computer (PC) operating system by Microsoft

Acronyms

A

AC alternating current
AUC area under curve

D

DI diffused illumination
DIY do-it-yourself
DSI diffused screen illumination

E

EMG electromyography

F

FTIR frustrated total internal reflection

G

GUI graphical user interface

H

HCI human-computer interaction

I

IR infrared

L

LCD liquid crystal display
LED light-emitting diode
LLP laser light plane

N

NBC naive Bayes classifier
NFC near field communication
NUI natural user interface

P

PC personal computer
PDA personal digital assistant
PWM pulse-width modulation

R

RFID radio-frequency identification
ROC receiver operating characteristics

S

SDG single display groupware
SDK software development kit
SVM support vector machines

U

URL uniform resource locator

W

WP7 Windows Phone 7
WPF Windows Presentation Foundation

Bibliography

[14] Amnesia. Razorfish Connect. 02 March 2011. `http://www.amnesiarazorfish.com.au/2011/01/`. [cited on page 125]

[15] M. Annett, T. Grossman, D. Wigdor, and G. Fitzmaurice. Medusa: A proximity-aware multi-touch tabletop. In *Proc. UIST*, pages 337–346, 2011. [cited on pages 32 and 33]

[16] T. Augsten, K. Kaefer, R. Meusel, C. Fetzer, D. Kanitz, T. Stoff, T. Becker, C. Holz, and P. Baudisch. Multitoe: High-precision interaction with back-projected floors based on high-resolution multi-touch input. In *Proc. UIST*, pages 209–218, 2010. [cited on pages 40 and 45]

[17] R. Balakrishnan, T. Baudel, G. Kurtenbach, and G. Fitzmaurice. The Rockin'Mouse: Integral 3D manipulation on a plane. In *Proc. CHI*, pages 311–318, 1997. [cited on pages 123 and 134]

[18] R. Ballagas, M. Rohs, and J. Borchers. Sweep and Point & Shoot: Phonecam-based interactions for large public displays. In *CHI Ext. Abstracts*, pages 1200–1203, 2005. [cited on page 81]

[19] H. Benko, T. Saponas, D. Morris, and T. Desney. Enhancing input on and above the interactive surface with muscle sensing. In *Proc. ITS*, pages 93–100, 2009. [cited on pages 40 and 45]

[20] X. Bi, Y. Shi, X. Chen, and P. Xiang. uPen: Laser-based, personalized, multi-user interaction on large displays. In *Proc. Multimedia*, 2005. [cited on pages 38 and 44]

[21] E. Bier and S. Freeman. MMM: A user interface architecture for shared editors on a single screen. In *Proc. UIST*, pages 79–86, 1991. [cited on pages 17 and 18]

[22] E. A. Bier, M. C. Stone, M. C. Pier, W. Buxton, and T. D. DeRose. Toolglass and Magic Lenses: the see-through interface. In *Proc. Computer Graphics and Interactive Techniques*, pages 73–80, 1993. [cited on pages 111 and 114]

[23] G. Boreki and A. Zimmer. Hand geometry: A new approach for feature extraction. In *Proc. Auto. Identif. Adv. Techn.*, pages 149–154, 2005. [cited on pages 65 and 70]

[24] S. Boring, D. Baur, A. Butz, S. Gustafson, and P. Baudisch. Touch projector: Mobile interaction through video. In *Proc. CHI*, pages 2287–2296, 2010. [cited on page 81]

[25] Bosch Rexroth. Products & solutions. 01 December 2011. http://www.boschrexroth.co.uk/country_units/europe/united_kingdom/en/products_solutions/linear_motion_assembly_technologies/products/index.jsp. [cited on page 191]

[26] G. Bradski. The OpenCV Library, 2000. [cited on page 69]

[27] W. Buxton. Multi-touch systems that I have known and loved. 19 March 2012. http://www.billbuxton.com/multitouchOverview.html. [cited on page 20]

[28] W. Buxton. A three-state model of graphical input. In *Proc. INTERACT*, pages 449–456, 1990. [cited on page 121]

[29] X. Cao, A. Wilson, R. Balakrishnan, K. Hinckley, and S. Hudson. ShapeTouch: Leveraging contact shape on interactive surfaces. In *Proc. TableTop*, pages 129–136, 2008. [cited on pages 3 and 4]

[30] C. Chang and C. Lin. *LIBSVM: A library for support vector machines*, 2001. [cited on pages 69, 74, and 76]

[31] K. Cheverst, A. Dix, D. Fitton, C. Kray, M. Rouncefield, J. Sheridan, and G. Saslis-Lagoudakis. Exploring mobile phone interaction with situated displays. In *PERMID workshop at Pervasive*, 2005.

[32] Circle Twelve. DiamondTouch flier. 01 December 2011. http://www.circletwelve.com/circle12/images/file/DTflier-web.pdf. [cited on pages 35 and 190]

[33] G. Cozzolongo, B. De Carolis, and S. Pizzutilo. Supporting personalized interaction in public spaces. In *Proc. AIMS*, pages 64–70, 2004. [cited on page 99]

[34] C. Dang, M. Straub, and E. André. Hand distinction for multi-touch tabletop interaction. In *Proc. ITS*, pages 101–108, 2009. [cited on page 34]

[35] A. De Luca and B. Frauendienst. A privacy-respectful input method for public terminals. In *Proc. NordiCHI*, pages 455–458, 2008. [cited on page 133]

[36] R. Diaz-Marino, E. Tse, and S. Greenberg. Programming for multiple touches and multiple users: A toolkit for the DiamondTouch hardware. In *Adj. Proc. UIST*, 2003. [cited on page 16]

[37] P. H. Dietz and D. Leigh. DiamondTouch: A multi-user touch technology. In *Proc. UIST*, pages 219–226, 2001. [cited on pages 35, 36, 44, 47, and 48]

[38] K. C. Dohse, T. Dohse, J. D. Still, and D. J. Parkhurst. Enhancing multi-user interaction with multi-touch tabletop displays using hand tracking. In *Proc. ACHI*, pages 297–302, 2008. [cited on page 34]

[39] R. Downs. Using resistive touch screens for human/machine interface. *Analog Applications Journal*, 3Q:5–10, 2005. [cited on page 28]

[40] F. Echtler, A. Dippon, M. Tönnis, and G. Klinker. Inverted FTIR: Easy multitouch sensing for flatscreens. In *Proc. ITS*, pages 29–32, 2009. [cited on page 24]

[41] F. Echtler, S. Nestler, A. Dippon, and G. Klinker. Supporting casual interactions between board games on public tabletop displays and mobile devices. *Pers. and Ubiq. Comp.*, 13:609–617, 2009. [cited on page 81]

[42] S. Egelman, A. Bernheim Brush, and K. Inkpen. Family accounts: A new paradigm for user accounts within the home environment. In *Proc. CSCW*, pages 669–678, 2008. [cited on pages 4 and 6]

[43] C. Ellis, S. Gibbs, and G. Rein. Groupware: Some issues and experiences. *Comm. ACM*, 34(1):39–58, January 1991. [cited on pages 15 and 16]

[44] B. Eoff and T. Hammond. Who dotted that 'i'?: Context free user differentiation through pressure and tilt pen data. In *Proc. GI*, pages 149–156. Canadian Information Processing Society, 2009. [cited on pages 41, 45, and 47]

[45] K. Everitt, C. Shen, K. Ryall, and C. Forlines. Modal spaces: spatial multiplexing to mediate direct-touch input on large displays. In *CHI Ext. Abstracts*, pages 1359–1362, 2005. [cited on page 130]

[46] Evonik Industries. PLEXIGLAS EndLighten. 03 Decemeber 2011. `http://www.plexiglas.net/product/plexiglas/en/products/solid-sheets/endlighten/pages/default.aspx`. [cited on page 24]

[47] T. Fawcett. ROC graphs: Notes and practical considerations for researchers, 2004. [cited on page 73]

[48] G. Fitzmaurice. Situated information spaces and spatially aware palmtop computers. *Comm. ACM*, 36:39–49, 1993. [cited on page 80]

[49] S. Greenberg, M. Boyle, and J. Laberge. PDAs and shared public displays: Making personal information public, and public information personal. *Pers. and Ubiq. Comp.*, 3:54–64, 1999. [cited on pages 80 and 81]

[50] D. Grolaux, J. Vanderdonckt, and P. Van Roy. Attach me, detach me, assemble me like you work. In *Proc. INTERACT*, pages 198–212, 2005. [cited on page 129]

[51] Y. Guiard. Asymmetric division of labor in human skilled bimanual action: The kinematic chain as a model. *Journal of Motor Behavior*, 19:486–517, 1987. [cited on page 112]

[52] J. Han. Low-cost multi-touch sensing through frustrated total internal reflection. In *Proc. UIST*, pages 115–118, 2005. [cited on page 23]

[53] M. Hancock, C. Shen, C. Forlines, and K. Ryall. Exploring non-speech auditory feedback at an interactive multi-user tabletop. In *Proc. GI*, pages 41–50, 2005. [cited on pages 122 and 133]

[54] R. Hardy and E. Rukzio. Touch & Interact: Touch-based interaction of mobile phones with displays. In *Proc. MobileHCI*, pages 245–254, 2008. [cited on page 81]

[55] C. Harrison, H. Benko, and A. Wilson. OmniTouch: Wearable multitouch interaction everywhere. In *Proc. USIT*, pages 441–450, 2011. [cited on page 28]

[56] C. Harrison, M. Sato, and I. Poupyrev. Capacitive Fingerprinting: Exploring user differentiation by sensing electrical properties of the human body. In *Proc. UIST*, pages 537–544, 2012.

[57] C. Harrison, J. Schwartz, and S. Hudson. TapSense: Enhancing finger interaction on touch surfaces. In *Proc. UIST*, pages 627–634, 2011. [cited on page 29]

[58] S. G. Hart and L. E. Stavelan. Development of NASA-TLX (task load index): Results of empirical and theoretical research. *Human Mental Workload*, 1:139–183, 1988. [cited on page 152]

[59] B. Hartmann, M. Morris, H. Benko, and A. Wilson. Augmenting interactive tables with mice & keyboards. In *Proc. UIST*, pages 149–152, 2009. [cited on page 20]

[60] T. Hesselmann, N. Henze, and S. Boll. FlashLight: Optical communication between mobile phones and interactive tabletops. In *Proc. ITS*, pages 135–138, 2010. [cited on page 81]

[61] O. Hilliges, S. Izadi, A. Wilson, S. Hodges, A. Garcia-Mendoza, and A. Butz. Interactions in the air: Adding further depth to interactive tabletops. In *Proc. UIST*, pages 139–148, 2009. [cited on page 27]

[62] J. Hincapié-Ramos, E. Tabard, and J. Bardram. Mediated tabletop interaction in the biology lab: exploring the design space of the rabbit. In *Proc. UbiComp*, pages 301–310, 2011. [cited on pages 39 and 44]

[63] K. Hinckley. Synchronous gestures for multiple users and computers. In *Proc. UIST*, pages 149–158, 2003. [cited on page 81]

[64] U. Hinrichs and S. Carpendale. Gestures in the wild: studying multi-touch gesture sequences on interactive tabletop exhibits. In *Proc. CHI*, 2011. [cited on pages 3, 4, 5, and 7]

[65] S. Hodges, S. Izadi, A. Butler, A. Rrustemi, and W. Buxton. ThinSight: Versatile multi-touch sensing for thin form-factor displays. In *Proc. UIST*, pages 259–268, 2007. [cited on page 26]

[66] R. Hofer, D. Naeff, and A. Kunz. FLATIR: FTIR multi-touch detection on a discrete distributed sensor array. In *Proc. TEI*, 2009. [cited on page 27]

[67] L. Holmquist, F. Mattern, B. Schiele, P. Alahuhta, M. Beigl, and H. Gellersen. Smart-Its friends: A technique for users to easily establish connections between smart artefacts. In *Proc. UbiComp*, pages 116–122, 2001. [cited on page 81]

[68] C. Holz and P. Baudisch. The generalized perceived input point model and how to double touch accuracy by extracting fingerprints. In *Proc. CHI*, pages 581–590, 2010. [cited on page 42]

[69] J. Hourcade and B. Bederson. Architecture and implementation of a Java package for multiple input devices (MID). Technical Report 99-08, University of Maryland, HCIL, May 1999. [cited on page 19]

[70] W. Hutama, P. Song, F. Chi-Wing, and W. B. Goh. Distinguishing multiple smart-phone interactions on a multi-touch wall display using tilt correlation. In *Proc. CHI*, 2011. [cited on pages 38, 44, 46, 48, 49, 80, 81, and 94]

[71] M. Iida, T. Naemura, Y. Shirai, M. Matsushita, and T. Ohguro. Lumisight Table: An interactive view-dependent tabletop display. *IEEE Comp. Graph. and App.*, 25:48–53, 2005. [cited on page 30]

[72] S. Izadi, H. Brignull, T. Rodden, Y. Rogers, and M. Underwood. Dynamo: A public interactive surface supporting the cooperative sharing and exchange of media. In *Proc. UIST.*, pages 159–168, 2003. [cited on pages 17 and 18]

[73] S. Izadi, S. Hodges, S. Taylor, D. Rosenfeld, N. Villar, A. Butler, and J. Westhues. Going beyond the display: A surface technology with an electronically switchable diffuser. In *Proc. UIST*, pages 269–278, 2008. [cited on pages 5, 27, and 111]

[74] A. K. Jain, A. Ross, and S. Pankanti. A prototype hand geometry-based verification system. In *Proc. AVBPA*, pages 166–171, 1999. [cited on page 64]

[75] S. Jordà, G. Geiger, M. Alonso, and M. Kaltenbrunner. The reacTable: Exploring the synergy between live music performance and tabletop tangible interfaces. In *Proc. TEI*, pages 139–146, 2007. [cited on pages 3, 4, and 5]

[76] M. Kaltenbrunner and R. Bencina. reacTIVision: A computer-vision framework for table-based tangible interaction. In *Proc. TEI*, pages 69–74, 2007. [cited on page 22]

[77] A. Karnik, D. Plasencia, W. Mayol-Cuevas, and S. Subramanian. PiVOT: Personalized view-overlays for tabletops. In *Proc. UIST*, pages 271–280, 2012.

[78] H. Kato, M. Billinghurst, I. Poupyrev, K. Imamoto, and K. Tachibana. Virtual object manipulation on a table-top AR environment. In *Proc. ISAR*, pages 111–119, 2000. [cited on page 22]

[79] D. Kim, P. Dunphy, P. Briggs, J. Hook, J. Nicholson, J. Nicholson, and P. Olivier. Multi-touch authentication on tabletops. In *Proc. CHI*, pages 1093–1102, 2010. [cited on pages 5, 6, 7, 42, 45, 47, 122, 132, and 133]

[80] J. Kjeldskov, M. Skov, B. Als, and R. Høegh. Is it worth the hassle? exploring the added value of evaluating the usability of context-aware mobile systems in the field. In *Proc. MobileHCI*, pages 61–73, 2004.

[81] D. Klinkhammer, M. Nitsche, M. Specht, and H. Reiterer. Adaptive personal territories for co-located tabletop interaction in a museum setting. In *Proc. ITS*, pages 107–110, 2011. [cited on page 32]

[82] H. Koike, Y. Sato, and Y. Kobayashi. Integrating paper and digital information on EnhancedDesk: A method for realtime finger tracking on an augmented desk system. *ACM TOCHI*, 8:307–322, 2001. [cited on page 21]

[83] M. Krueger, T. Gionfriddo, and K. Hinrichsen. VIDEOPLACE—an artificial reality. In *Proc. CHI*, pages 35–40, 1985. [cited on page 21]

[84] J. R. Lewis. IBM computer usability satisfaction questionnaires: Psychometric evaluation and instructions for use. *Int. J. Hum.-Comp. Interact.*, 7:57–78, 1995. [cited on page 152]

[85] P. Lopes, R. Jota, and J. Jorge. Augmenting touch interaction through acoustic sensing. In *Proc. ITS*, pages 53–56, 2011. [cited on page 29]

[86] N. Marquardt, J. Kiemer, D. Ledo, S. Boring, and S. Greenberg. Designing user-, hand-, and handpart-aware tabletop interactions with the TouchID toolkit. In *Proc. ITS*, 2011. [cited on pages 36, 44, and 48]

[87] MATLAB. *Version R2009b*. The MathWorks Inc., Natick, Massachusetts, 2009. [cited on page 69]

[88] M. Matsushita, M. Iida, and T. Ohguro. Lumisight table: A face-to-face collaboration support system that optimizes direction of projected information to each stakeholder. In *Proc. CSCW*, pages 274–283, 2004. [cited on pages 5 and 30]

[89] N. Matsushita and J. Rekimoto. HoloWal: Designing a finger, hand, body, and object sensitive wall. In *Proc. UIST*, pages 209–210, 1997. [cited on page 21]

[90] R. Mayrhofer and H. Gellersen. Shake well before use: Intuitive and secure pairing of mobile devices. *IEEE Trans. Mob. Comp.*, 8:792–806, 2009. [cited on page 81]

[91] N. Mehta. A flexible machine interface. Master's thesis, Department of Electrical Engineering, University of Toronto, 1982. [cited on page 20]

[92] Microsoft. Microsoft Surface 2.0 platform. 13 December 2011. `http://www.microsoft.com/surface/en/us/gettingstarted.aspx`. [cited on page 90]

[93] Microsoft. Physical features of a Microsoft Surface unit. 02 April 2012. `http://technet.microsoft.com/en-us/library/ee692114.aspx`. [cited on pages 24 and 190]

[94] Microsoft. The power of PixelSense™. 02 April 2012. `http://www.microsoft.com/surface/en/us/pixelsense.aspx`. [cited on page 26]

[95] Microsoft. Surface Mobile Connect. 02 March 2011. `http://www.microsoft.com/downloads/en/details.aspx?FamilyID=0DAEC49D-8B97-419B-BF96-96FC4AD787F4`. [cited on page 125]

[96] Microsoft. Using touch gestures. 27 April 2012. `http://windows.microsoft.com/en-US/windows7/Using-touch-gesture`. [cited on page 147]

[97] D. Mills. Internet time synchronization: The network time protocol. *IEEE Trans. Comm.*, 39:1482–1493, 1991. [cited on page 84]

[98] K. Miyaoku, S. Higashino, and Y. Tonomura. C-Blink: A hue-difference-based light signal marker for large screen interaction via any mobile terminal. In *Proc. UIST*, pages 147–156, 2004. [cited on page 81]

[99] J. Moeller and A. Kerne. ZeroTouch: An optical multi-touch and free-air interaction architecture. In *Proc. CHI*, pages 2165–2174, 2012. [cited on page 26]

[100] M. Möllers and J. Borchers. TaPS widgets: Interacting with tangible private spaces. In *Proc. ITS*, pages 75–78, 2011. [cited on page 30]

[101] M. Morris, A. Cassanego, A. Paepcke, T. Winograd, A. Piper, and A. Huang. Mediating group dynamics through tabletop interface design. *IEEE Comp. Graph. and App.*, 26(5):65–73, September 2006. [cited on page 35]

[102] M. Morris, A. Huang, A. Paepcke, and T. Winograd. Cooperative gestures: multi-user gestural interactions for co-located groupware. In *Proc. CHI*, pages 1201–1210, 2006. [cited on page 35]

[103] M. Morris, J. Lombardo, and D. Wigdor. WeSearch: Supporting collaborative search and sensemaking on a tabletop display. In *Proc. CSCW*, pages 401–410, 2010. [cited on page 16]

[104] M. Morris, D. Morris, and T. Winograd. Individual audio channels with single display groupware: effects on communication and task strategy. In *Proc. CSCW*, pages 242–251, 2004. [cited on pages 122 and 133]

[105] M. Morris, K. Ryall, C. Shen, C. Forlines, and F. Vernier. Beyond "social protocols": Multi-user coordination policies for co-located groupware. In *Proc. CSCW*, pages 262–265, 2004. [cited on page 35]

[106] S. Murugapaan, Vinayak, N. Elmqvist, and K. Ramani. Extended multitouch: Recovering touch posture and differentiating users using a depth camera. In *Proc. UIST*, pages 487–496, 2012.

[107] B. A. Myers. Using handhelds and PCs together. *Comm. ACM*, 44:34–41, 2001. [cited on pages 80 and 81]

[108] B. A. Myers, R. Bhatnagar, J. Nichols, C. H. Hong, D. Kong, R. Miller, and A. C. Long. Interacting at a distance: Measuring the performance of laser pointers and other devices. In *Proc. CHI*, pages 33–40, 2002. [cited on page 81]

[109] B. A. Myers, H. Stiel, and R. Gargiulo. Collaboration using multiple PDAs connected to a PC. In *Proc. CSCW*, pages 285–294, 1998. [cited on pages 17, 18, and 116]

[110] T. Nakajima and I. Satoh. A software infrastructure for supporting spontaneous and personalized interaction in home computing environments. *Pers. and Ubiq. Comp.*, 10:379–391, 2006. [cited on page 99]

[111] L. O'Gorman. Comparing passwords, tokens, and biometrics for user authentication. *Proc. of the IEEE*, 91:2021–2040, 2003. [cited on page 6]

[112] A. Olwal and S. Feiner. Spatially aware handhelds for high-precision tangible interaction with large displays. In *Proc. TEI*, pages 181–188, 2009. [cited on page 81]

[113] A. Olwal and A. Wilson. SurfaceFusion: Unobtrusive tracking of everyday objects in tangible user interfaces. In *Proc. GI*, pages 235–242, 2008. [cited on pages 39, 44, and 47]

[114] J. Paradiso, C. Leo, N. Checka, and K. Hsiao. Passive acoustic sensing for tracking knocks atop large interactive displays. In *Proc. Sensor*, pages 521–527, 2002. [cited on page 29]

[115] G. Partridge and P. Irani. IdenTTop: A flexible platform for exploring identity-enabled surfaces. In *Proc. CHI 2009 EA*, pages 4411–4416, 2009. [cited on pages 40 and 45]

[116] U. Pawar, J. Pal, and K. Toyama. Multiple mice for computers in education in developing countries. In *Proc. ICTD*, pages 64–71, 2006. [cited on pages 4 and 7]

[117] N. Pears, D. Jackson, and P. Oliver. Smart phone interactions with registered displays. *IEEE Perv. Comp.*, 8:14–21, 2009. [cited on page 81]

[118] D. Pinelle, T. Stach, and C. Gutwin. TableTrays: Temporary, reconfigurable work surfaces for tabletop groupware. In *Proc. TableTop*, pages 41–48, 2008. [cited on page 144]

[119] R. Ramakers, D. Vanacken, K. Luyten, K. Coninx, and J. Schöning. Carpus: A non-intrusive user identification technique for interactive surfaces. In *Proc. UIST*, 2012.

[120] J. Rekimoto. Pick-and-Drop: A direct manipulation technique for multiple computer environments. In *Proc. UIST*, pages 31–39, 1997. [cited on page 125]

[121] J. Rekimoto. A multiple device approach for supporting whiteboard-based interactions. In *Proc. CHI*, pages 344–351, 1998. [cited on page 129]

[122] J. Rekimoto. SmartSkin: An infrastructure for freehand manipulation on interactive surfaces. In *Proc. CHI*, pages 113–120, 2002. [cited on page 29]

[123] J. Rekimoto. SyncTap: Synchronous user operation for spontaneous network connection. *Pers. and Ubiq. Comp.*, 8:126–134, 2004. [cited on pages 82 and 83]

[124] J. Rekimoto and M. Saitoh. Augmented surfaces: A spatially continuous work space for hybrid computing environments. In *Proc. CHI*, pages 378–385, 1999. [cited on pages 22 and 80]

[125] S. Richter, C. Holz, and P. Baudisch. Bootstrapper: Recognizing tabletop users by their shoes. In *Proc. CHI*, 2012. [cited on pages 40, 41, 45, and 47]

[126] J. Rick, Y. Rogers, C. Haig, and N. Yuill. Learning by doing with shareable interfaces. *Children, Youth and Environments*, 19:321–342, 2009. [cited on pages 3 and 5]

[127] M. Ringel, K. Ryall, C. Shen, C. Forlines, and F. Vernier. Release, relocate, reorient, resize: Fluid techniques for document sharing on multi-user interactive tables. In *Proc. CHI EA*, pages 1441–1444, 2004. [cited on page 19]

[128] M. Rofouei, A. D. Wilson, A. Bernheim Brush, and S. Tansley. Your phone or mine? fusing body, touch and device sensing for multi-user device-display interaction. In *Proc. CHI*, 2012. [cited on pages 39, 44, and 48]

[129] S. Ronkainen, J. Häkkilä, S. Kaleva, A. Colley, and J. Linjama. Tap input as an embedded interaction method for mobile devices. In *Proc. TEI*, pages 263–270, 2007. [cited on page 84]

[130] V. Roth, P. Schmidt, and B. Güldenring. The IR Ring: authenticating users' touches on a multi-touch display. In *Proc. UIST*, 2010. [cited on pages 37, 44, 46, 48, 49, and 94]

[131] D. Russell and A. Sue. Large interactive public displays: Use patterns, support patterns, community patterns. In K. O'Hara, M. Perry, E. Churchill, and D. Russell, editors, *Public and situated displays: Social and interactional aspects of shared display technologies*, chapter 1, pages 3–17. Kluwer, 2003. [cited on pages 39, 44, and 47]

[132] L. Rutledge, L. Aroyo, and N. Stash. Determining user interests about museum collections. In *Proc. WWW*, pages 855–856, 2006. [cited on page 99]

[133] K. Ryall, A. Esenther, K. Everitt, C. Forlines, M. R. Morris, C. Shen, S. Shipman, and F. Vernier. iDwidgets: parameterizing widgets by user identity. In *Proc. INTERACT*, pages 1124–1128, 2005. [cited on pages 17, 122, and 130]

[134] K. Ryall, A. Esenther, C. Forlines, C. Shen, S. Shipman, M. Morris, K. Everitt, and F. Vernier. Identity-differentiating widgets for multiuser interactive surfaces. *IEEE Comp. Graph. and App.*, 26(5):56–64, 2006. [cited on page 17]

[135] N. Sae-Bae, K. Ahmed, K. Isbister, and N. Memon. Biometric-tich gestures: A novel approach to authentication on multi-touch devices. In *Proc. CHI*, 2012. [cited on pages 41, 45, and 47]

[136] D. Saffer. *Designing gestural interfaces: Touchscreens and interactive devices.* O'Reilly Media, Inc., December 2008. [cited on page 20]

[137] R. Sanchez-Reillo, C. Sanchez-Avila, and A. Gonzalez-Marcos. Biometric identification through hand geometry measurements. *IEEE Trans. Pat. Anal. and Mach. Int.*, 22(10):1168–1171, 2000. [cited on page 65]

[138] J. Schöning, M. Rohs, and A. Krüger. Using mobile phones to spontaneously authenticate and interact with multi-touch surfaces. In *Workshop on designing multi-touch interaction techniques for coupled public and private displays*, pages 41–45, 2008. [cited on pages 5, 38, 44, and 48]

[139] S. Scott, S. Carpendale, and S. Habelski. Storage bins: Mobile storage for collaborative tabletop displays. *IEEE Comp. Graph. and App.*, 25:58–65, 2005. [cited on page 144]

[140] S. Scott, S. Carpendale, and K. Inkpen. Territoriality in collaborative tabletop workspaces. In *Proc. CSCW*, pages 294–303, 2004. [cited on page 108]

[141] C. Shen, K. Everitt, and K. Ryall. UbiTable: Impromptu face-to-face collaboration on horizontal interactive surfaces. In *Proc. UbiComp*, pages 281–288, 2003. [cited on page 36]

[142] C. Shen, K. Ryall, C. Forlines, A. Esenther, F. Vernier, K. Everitt, M. Wu, D. Wigdor, M. Morris, M. Hancock, and E. Tse. Informing the design of direct-touch tabletops. *IEEE Comp. Graph. and App.*, 26:36–46, 2006. [cited on pages 122 and 129]

[143] C. Shen, F. Vernier, C. Forlines, and M. Ringel. DiamondSpin: An extensible toolkit for around-the-table interaction. In *Proc. CHI 2004*, pages 167–174, 2004. [cited on page 36]

[144] A. Shirazi, T. Döring, P. Parvahan, B. Ahrens, and A. Schmidt. Poker surface: combining a multi-touch table and mobile phones in interactive card. In *Proc. MobileHCI*, 2009. [cited on pages 3, 4, and 5]

[145] G. Shoemaker and K. Inkpen. Single Display Privacyware: Augmenting public displays with private information. In *Proc. CHI*, pages 522–529, 2001. [cited on page 30]

[146] Smart Technologies, Inc. DViT. 19 May 2012. `http://www.smart-technologies.com/dvit.html`. [cited on page 26]

[147] M. Spindler, S. Stellmach, and R. Dachselt. PaperLens: Advanced magic lens interaction above the tabletop. In *Proc. ITS*, pages 77–84, 2009. [cited on page 111]

[148] J. Stewart, B. B. Bederson, and A. Druin. Single Display Groupware: A model for co-present collaboration. In *Proc. CHI*, pages 286–293, 1999. [cited on pages 16 and 19]

[149] N. Streitz, J. Geißler, T. Holmer, S. Konomi, C. Müller-Tomfelde, W. Reischl, P. Rexroth, P. Seitz, and R. Steinmetz. i-LAND: An interactive landscape for creativity and innovation. In *Proc. CHI*, pages 120–127, 1999. [cited on page 144]

[150] M. Strohbach, G. Kortuem, H. Gellersen, and C. Kray. Using cooperative artefacts as basis for activity recognition. In *Proc. EUSAI*, pages 49–60, 2004. [cited on pages 81 and 82]

[151] W. Stuerzlinger, O. Chapuis, D. Phillips, and N. Roussel. User interface façades: Towards fully adaptable user interfaces. In *Proc. UIST*, pages 309–318, 2006. [cited on page 131]

[152] A. Sugiura and Y. Koseki. A user interface using fingerprint recognition: Holding commands and data objects on fingers. In *Proc. UIST*, pages 71–79, 1998. [cited on pages 42 and 45]

[153] Q. Sun, C. Fu, and Y. He. An interactive multi-touch sketching interface for diffusion curves. In *Proc. CHI*, pages 1611–1614, 2011. [cited on pages 3, 4, and 5]

[154] Y. Takeoka, T. Miyaki, and J. Rekimoto. Z-touch: An infrastructure for 3d gesture interaction in the proximity of tabletop surfaces. In *Proc. ITS*, pages 91–94, 2010. [cited on page 25]

[155] N. Tanaka. New touch panel specifies who is touching it. 19 March 2012. http://techon.nikkeibp.co.jp/english/NEWS_EN/20120219/205050/. [cited on page 35]

[156] A. Tang, M. Tory, B. Po, P. Neumann, and S. Carpendale. Collaborative coupling over tabletop displays. In *Proc. CHI*, pages 1181–1190, 2006.

[157] E. Tse and S. Greenberg. Rapidly prototyping single display groupware through the SDGToolkit. In *Proc. AUIC*, pages 101–110, 2004. [cited on page 19]

[158] B. Ullmer and H. Ishii. The metaDESK: Models and prototypes for tangible user interfaces. In *Proc. UIST*, pages 223–232, 1997. [cited on page 22]

[159] T. Vu, A. Ashok, A. Baid, M. Gruteser, R. Howard, J. Lindqvist, P. Spasojevic, and J. Walling. Demo: User identification and authentication with capacitive touch communication. Demo MobiSys, 2012. [cited on pages 37 and 44]

[160] B. Walther-Franks, M. Herrlich, M. Aust, and R. Malaka. Left and right hand distinction for multi-touch displays. In *Proc. SG*, pages 155–158, 2011. [cited on page 34]

[161] B. Walther-Franks, L. Schwarten, J. Teichert, K. M., and M. Herrlich. User detection for a multi-touch table via proximity sensors. In *Proc. TIS*, 2008. [cited on page 32]

[162] F. Wang, X. Cao, X. Ren, and P. Irani. Detecting and leveraging finger orientation for interaction with direct-touch surfaces. In *Proc. UIST*, pages 23–32, 2009. [cited on page 34]

[163] N. Weibel, A. Fouse, E. Hutchins, and J. Hoolan. Supporting an integrated paper-digital workflow for observational research. In *Proc. IUI*, pages 257–266, 2011. [cited on page 152]

[164] P. Wellner. Interacting with paper on the DigitalDesk. *Comm. ACM*, 36:87–96, 1993. [cited on pages 21 and 22]

[165] A. Wilson. PlayAnywhere: A compact interactive tabletop projection-vision system. In *Proc. UIST*, pages 83–92, 2005. [cited on pages 22 and 23]

[166] A. Wilson and H. Benko. Combining multiple depth cameras and projectors for interactions on, above and between surfaces. In *Proc. UIST*, pages 273–282, 2010. [cited on page 28]

[167] A. Wilson and R. Sarin. BlueTable: Connecting wireless mobile devices on interactive surfaces using vision-based handshaking. In *Proc. GI*, pages 119–125, 2007. [cited on pages 37, 44, 47, 80, 81, 122, and 125]

[168] M. Wu and R. Balakrishnan. Multi-finger and whole hand gestural interaction techniques for multi-user tabletop displays. In *Proc. UIST*, pages 193–202, 2003. [cited on page 134]

[169] E. Yörük, E. Konukoglu, B. Sankur, and J. Darbon. Shape-based hand recognition. *IEEE Trans. Img. Proc.*, 15(7):1803–1815, 2006. [cited on pages 65 and 95]

[170] H. Zhang, X. Yang, B. Ens, H. Liang, P. Boulanger, and P. Irani. See Me, See You: A lightweight method for discriminating user touches on tabletop displays. In *Proc. CHI*, 2012. [cited on page 34]

[171] R. L. Zunkel. *Hand geometry based verification*, chapter 4, pages 87–101. Springer, 2002. [cited on page 64]

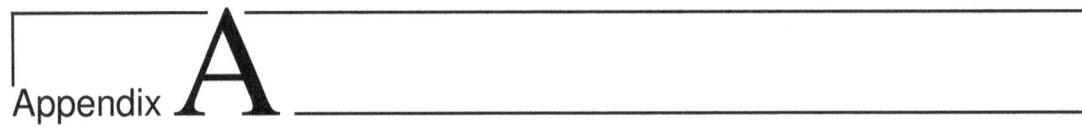

Appendix A

Prototype Platform

To develop and evaluate IdWristbands, HandsDown, and PhoneTouch, we designed two interactive table structures—one stationary and one portable—as flexible prototype platforms to test different camera and illumination configurations. Our efforts resulted in three vision-based interactive surfaces: Two based on the stationary structure (the first aimed at HandsDown, the second at both IdWristbands and PhoneTouch) and one based on the portable structure (designed as demonstrator for PhoneTouch outside the lab).

A.1 Introduction

Developing new user identification methods for surface computing calls for systems that support exploring different hardware configurations. Touch detection and user identification are closely connected, as the identifying information needs to be derived in real-time together with touch input. It is not apparent up-front, however, which sensors and techniques work best. Therefore, a suitable development platform provides open access and full control over its components.

At the time of commencing this research, the few interactive surfaces commercially available were closed-box solutions. Changing their hardware configuration, for instance to use faster cameras, was not feasible. It was further not clear if the required full access to raw sensor data was possible.

Therefore, we chose to design and implement custom-built interactive surfaces to support rapid prototyping. Inspired by the growing do-it-yourself (DIY) community and its plethora of resources[1], we set out to define specific system requirements leading to a set of design decisions that in turn informed our development efforts. We designed and implemented three interactive tabletops enabling us to prototype new concepts, test different components, and eventually arrive at suitable configurations that facilitate the kind of user identification we envision.

A.1.1 Requirements Analysis

We identified the following requirements to be met by an interactive surface that supports exploring novel user identification methods.

---

[1]For example, the natural user interface (NUI) group forums at `http://nuigroup.com/forums` cover a wide range of topics on building interactive surfaces.

1. *Direct multi-touch.* The interactive surface must support direct-touch by providing a shared input as well as output space, and must track multiple finger touches simultaneously.

2. *Co-located collaboration.* To support multi-user scenarios, the interactive surface must be sufficiently large to accommodate up to four co-located users simultaneously.

3. *Flexible setup.* As suitable hardware components are not known up-front, the interactive surface must be adaptable and modular to allow for a flexible exploration of different configurations.

4. *Reliable built.* To withstand user studies and demonstration sessions, the interactive surface must be robust and reliably supporting ongoing research usage.

5. *Feasibility.* The components used in the system must be readily available off-the-shelf, and building the system must be feasible with the resources at hand.

A.1.2 Design Decisions

Based on the above requirements analysis, we arrived at the following design decisions to guide our development efforts.

1. *Vision-based touch sensing.* Vision-based solutions do not only scale to large sizes, are affordable, and can be realized without industrial manufacturing processes, they are also capable of providing rich input that goes beyond finger contacts.

2. *Projector-based output.* Projectors allow for flexibly choosing a display size and are straightforward to integrate with cameras for vision-based touch sensing. In contrast to LCD-based solutions, they do not require any potentially complicated hardware modifications.

3. *Form factor.* We analyzed existing surface systems[2] and found 91 cm × 57 cm (using the 16:10 aspect ration of modern projectors) to be a suitable size for a maximum of four simultaneous users. Taking into consideration the space required underneath the surface for projector and cameras, this size allows for common table heights of about 70 cm.

4. *Modular base structure.* To facilitate a modifiable configuration of varying hardware components, we use a modular aluminum profile system to build the table's base structure.

A.2 Hardware Design and Implementation

Guided by our design decisions, we first introduce two stationary tables, using the same underlying frame structure, but different sensor configurations. One table provides rich input by detecting arbitrary object shapes, while the other is geared towards detecting input events at high sampling rates. Secondly, we present a portable table for exposing our approaches to users outside the lab. Table A.1 provides a side by side comparison of the three systems.

---

[2]Microsoft Surface [93] has an active area of 70 cm × 46 cm, and DiamondTouch [32] of 86 cm × 65 cm.

	Stationary		Portable
	Rich Input	**Low Latency**	**Low Latency**
Target	HandsDown	IdWristbands & PhoneTouch	IdWristbands & PhoneTouch
Technique	DSI	FTIR	FTIR
Surface	EndLighten & diffuser	Clear & compliant & diffuser	Clear & compliant & diffuser
Area	91 cm × 57 cm	91 cm × 57 cm	60 cm × 45 cm
Height	70 cm	92 cm	103 cm
Camera	Point Grey Dragonfly2 (DR2-HIBW-CSBOX) 1024 pixel × 768 pixel 30 Hz	Point Grey Grasshopper (GRAS-03K2M-C) 640 pixel × 480 pixel 200 Hz	Point Grey Grasshopper (GRAS-03K2M-C) 640 pixel × 480 pixel 200 Hz
Lens	Edmund optics varifocal (1.8 mm to 3.6 mm)	Eneo A0314M1 (3.4 mm)	Eneo A04Z12M-NFS (4 mm to 12 mm)
Projector	Toshiba TDP-EW25 1280 pixel × 800 pixel	BenQ MP782 ST 1280 pixel × 800 pixel	LG HX300G 1024 pixel × 768 pixel

Figure A.1: Comparison of interactive table systems

A.2.1 Stationary Tables

The main frame of the stationary table consists of aluminum profiles manufactured by Bosch Rexroth [25]. This profile system allows for a light-weight yet robust structure, which is straightforward to assemble and disassemble and can easily be modified or extended. Figure A.2 shows the table's main frame, which we use as foundation to add functional components step-by-step in the following. We use 40 mm × 40 mm profiles for this structure, and 30 mm × 30 mm profiles for some of the interior mountings. A complete parts list of all components and an extended set of technical drawings is included at the end of this section (staring from page 162).

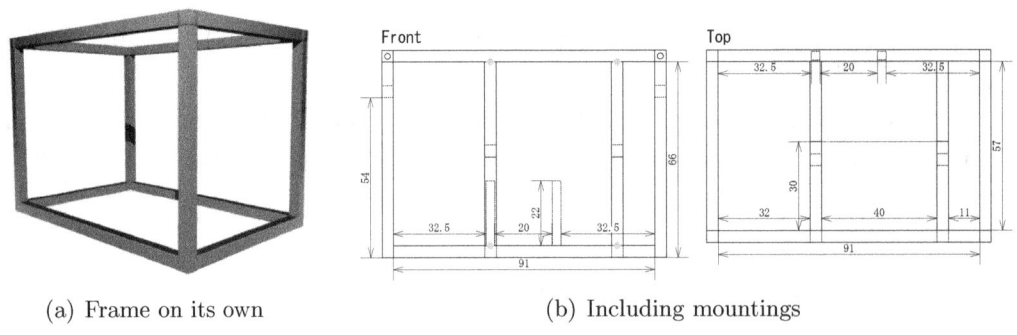

(a) Frame on its own   (b) Including mountings

Figure A.2: Stationary main frame as basis for two table variants

We use an acrylic sheet (94 cm × 60 cm × 1 cm) as table surface, which is held by an aluminum border fixed atop the main frame. This border also contains an infrared light-emitting diode (LED) ribbon (wave length: 850 nm, LED spacing: 3.83 cm, brightness: 658 mW/m), which is attached around the sheet's edges, and provides the required background illumination for touch detection. The main frame can integrate different projector and sensing configurations. Further, depending on the configuration, we use different acrylic materials.

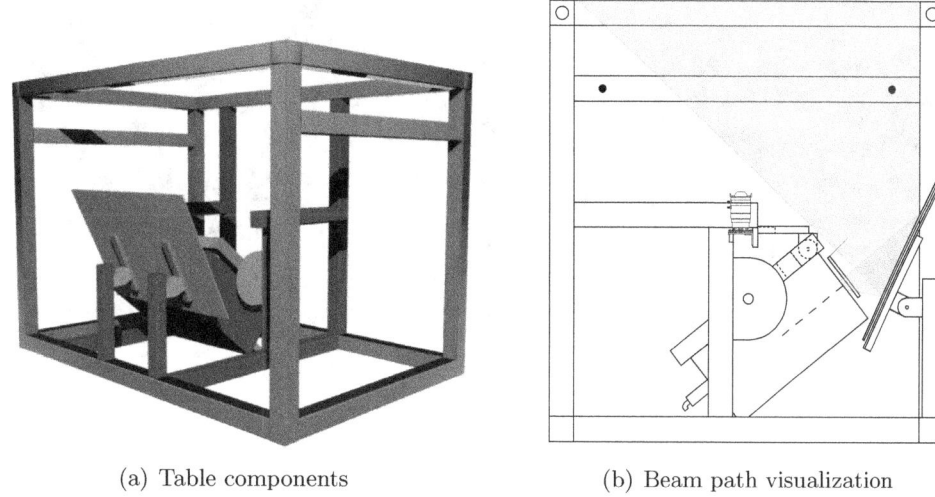

(a) Table components   (b) Beam path visualization

Figure A.3: Folding the projector's beam to reduce the overall table height

Despite using a short-throw projector, the targeted table height of 70 cm requires a mirror to fold the projection beam. We use a first surface mirror with a size of 40 cm × 25 cm. Projector and mirror mounting, as well as an illustration of the folded beam path is depicted in Figure A.3. To alternatively allow for standing operation, the table legs can easily be extended by adding aluminum profiles with attached feet.

Variant I: Rich Input for HandsDown

Biometric identification based on HandsDown requires rich information in order to extract sufficient hand features, and in turn a touch detection technique that sees more than just finger contacts. Diffused illumination (DI) is a suitable approach, which illuminates the surface from below (see section 2.2.1). The emitted infrared light is reflected off any object that comes close to the surface, and is captured by a camera. After initial experiments with DI, however, we switched to diffused screen illumination (DSI), a related approach that uses the same sensing principle, but allows for a simplified setup. While achieving a uniform light distribution across the entire surface with DI proved to be challenging, it is easy to achieve with DSI. At the same time, DSI allows for a more compact setup as no bulky light installations are required below the surface. To implement DSI, we use an acrylic sheet made of EndLighten, a material that contains small reflective particles to diffuse light uniformly across the surface. On top of it, we added a thin diffusing layer, which serves as projection surface and limits the visibility of the camera, thus facilitating the detection of touch events close to the surface.

On the sensor side, we initially followed a dual approach using two independent cameras, one mounted below the surface and one ceiling-mounted, but abolished the upper camera after initial experiments (see section 3.3.4). Our camera, a Point Grey Dragonfly2 (DR2-HIBW-CSBOX), captures black and white images at 30 Hz with a resolution of 1024 pixel × 768 pixel and is equipped with a varifocal (1.8 mm to 3.6 mm) lens. We added an infrared 850 nm band-pass filter between sensor and lens to block

(a) Open   (b) Walls attached

Figure A.4:   Stationary DSI table

visible light emitted by the projector and from the environment (the projected images become invisible to the camera and do not interfere with the touch detection). To avoid stray light interfering with the detection process, we surrounded the table with 3 mm thick black acrylic sheets. The final setup is shown in Figure A.4.

Variant II: Low Latency for IdWristbands & PhoneTouch

Our second table is based on the same main frame, but uses a different sensing and projection configuration (Figure A.5(a)). To allow for time-based matching of events from independent sources (PhoneTouch) and decoding identifiers sent through light (IdWristbands), we aim at a fast detection of input events. Instead of a high-resolution camera with a low frame rate as before, we use a faster camera with a lower resolution. The Point Grey Grasshopper (GRAS-03K2M-C) captures black and white images at a 200 Hz with a resolution of 640 pixel × 480 pixel, and is equipped with a Eneo A0314M1 lens (3.4 mm). Again, the same infrared band-pass filter as before is added to block visible light. Further, this setup uses a BenQ MP782 ST projector without beam-folding, resulting in an increased table height of 92 cm.

As higher frame rates imply shorter exposure times, an increased contrast is required to detect touches reliably. Therefore, we use frustrated total internal reflection (FTIR) instead of DSI (see section 2.2.1), but stay with the same edge-mounted infrared LED ribbon. Infrared light inside the acrylic sheet is internally reflected by default; that is, the surface appears dark as no light escapes. Once a finger gets in contact with the surface, however, the light is frustrated and hence produces a bright and clearly visible spot. We use a standard clear acrylic sheet and added a silicone layer as compliant surface in between acrylic and diffuser film (Figure A.5(b)). The silicone layer is rolled onto the diffuser film and substantially reduces the pressure one has to exert to achieve the FTIR effect.

(a) Complete setup   (b) Acrylic with compliant surface

Figure A.5: Stationary FTIR table

A.2.2 Portable Table

This setup is considerably smaller and lighter to serve as portable demonstrator for PhoneTouch at conference venues. It is based on the same camera and touch detection as the stationary FTIR table, but uses smaller $30\,\text{mm} \times 30\,\text{mm}$ aluminum profiles, Eneo A04Z12M-NFS lens ($4\,\text{mm}$ to $12\,\text{mm}$), and the portable LG HX300G projector with a resolution of $1024\,\text{pixel} \times 768\,\text{pixel}$ (Figure A.6); the active surface area measures $60\,\text{cm} \times 45\,\text{cm}$ at a height of $103\,\text{cm}$.

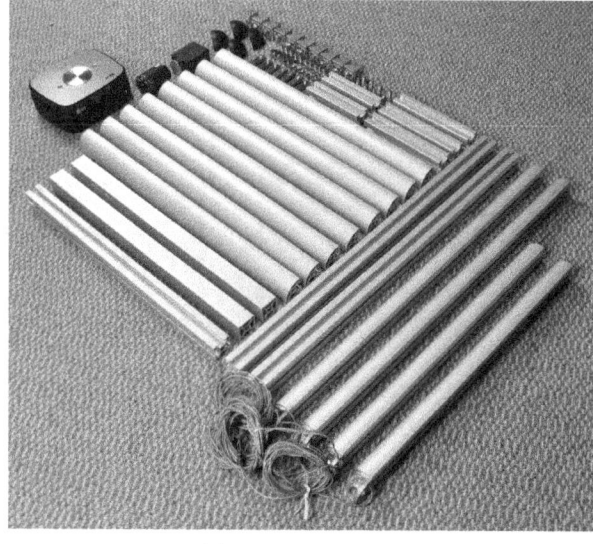
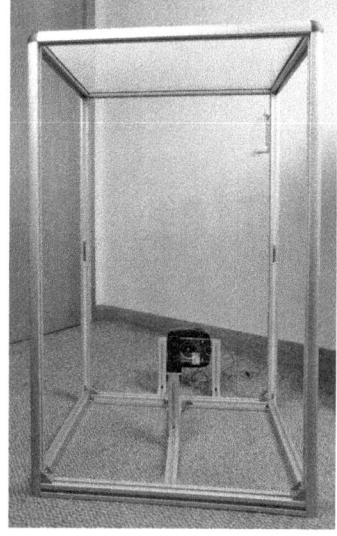

(a) Individual parts   (b) Assembled table

Figure A.6: Portable FTIR table

A.3 Summary

The table designs introduced in this section served as reliable and flexible research platforms to support our exploration of IdWristbands, HandsDown, and PhoneTouch. Moreover, our technical report [2], which illustrates these designs and gives detailed building instructions, proved to be a valuable contribution to the research community. To our knowledge, there existed no complete document that described the entire process of building an interactive surface beforehand. Our report was not only used as guiding framework for two follow-up publications on building interactive surfaces ([13, 12]), but was also valued by other research labs: A table based on the stationary design is used at the AmiLab of the Universidad Autónoma de Madrid, Spain[3] while the portable design was implemented at the Mobile HCI research group of the University of Duisburg-Essen, Germany[4].

---

[3]http://amilab.ii.uam.es
[4]http://www.mhci.uni-due.de

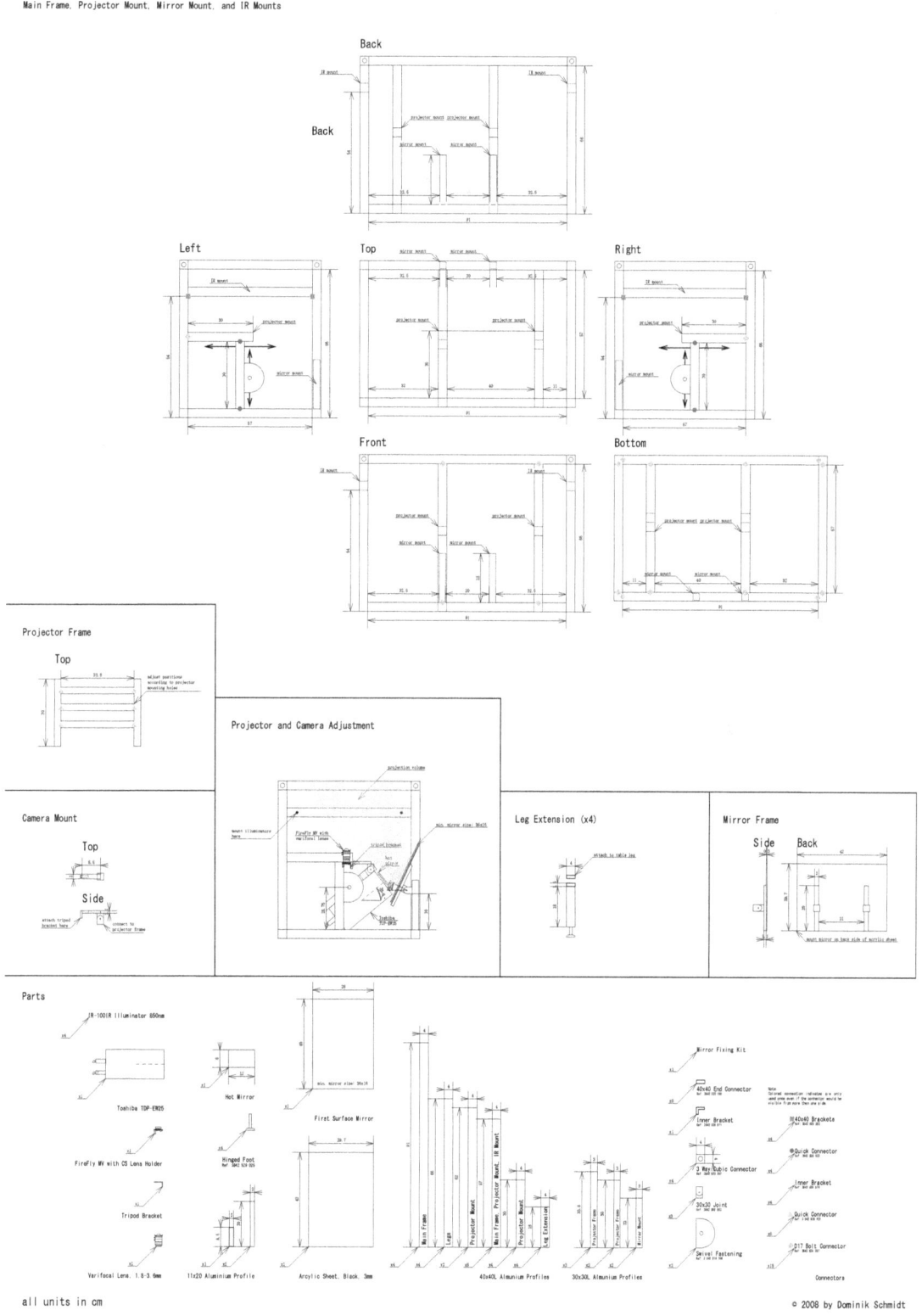

Figure A.7: Stationary frame with camera, projector, and IR mounts

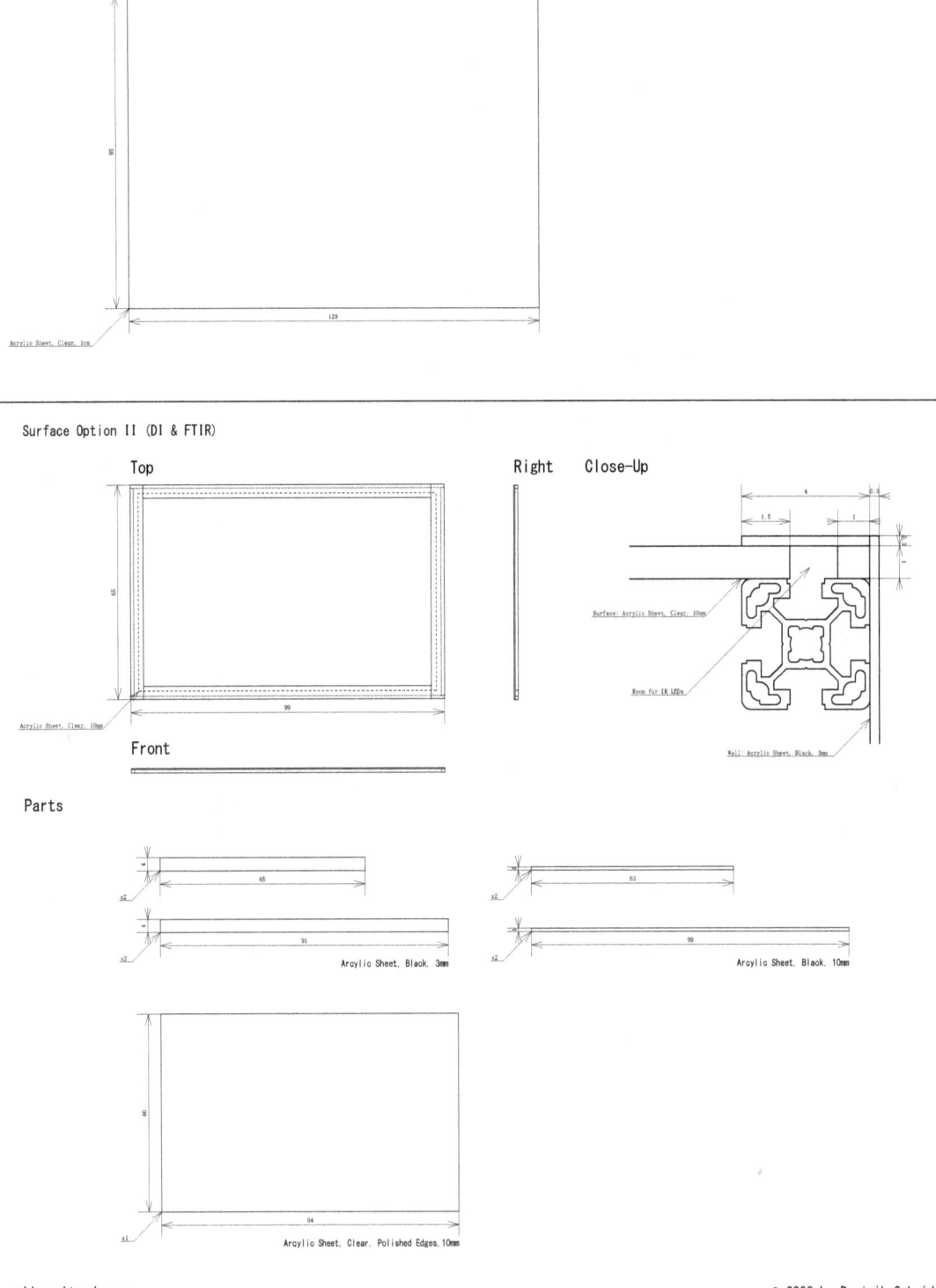

Figure A.8: Surface options for stationary tables

Walls

Top

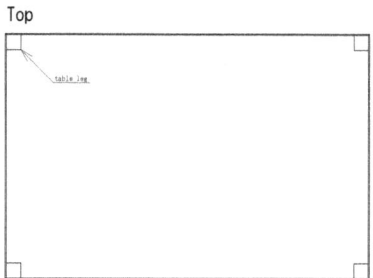

table leg

General Parts

M4x40 Machine Screw   12cm Fan

x16   x4

M4 T Nut   12cm Dust Filter Cover

x24   x4

M4x12 Machine Screw   12cm Fan Guard

x24   x4

Parts for Surface Option I

Acrylic Sheet, Black, 3mm

Parts for Surface Option II

Acrylic Sheet, Black, 3mm

Figure A.9: Enclosing for DI or DSI table

Quantity	Make	Item	Function	Supplier	Reference #
4	kjn	40x40L profile, 910mm	top/bottom frame	kjn	KJN 993 120
4	kjn	40x40L profile, 660mm	legs	kjn	KJN 993 120
2	kjn	40x40L profile, 620mm	projector support mount	kjn	KJN 993 120
8	kjn	40x40L profile, 570mm	top/bottom frame, IR & projector mount	kjn	KJN 993 120
4	kjn	40x40L profile, 300mm	projector mount	kjn	KJN 993 120
4	kjn	40x40L profile, 180mm	leg extension	kjn	KJN 993 120
3	kjn	30x30L profile, 338mm	projector frame	kjn	KJN 990 720
2	kjn	30x30L profile, 300mm	projector frame	kjn	KJN 990 720
2	kjn	30x30L profile, 220mm	mirror mount	kjn	KJN 990 720
1	Bosch Rexroth	11x20 profile, 85mm	camera mount	kjn	3 842 992 476
2	Bosch Rexroth	11x20 profile, 200mm	mirror mount	kjn	3 842 992 476
4	Bosch Rexroth	40x40 3 way cubic connector	top frame	kjn	3 842 529 397
18	Bosch Rexroth	D17 bolt connector	bottom frame, projector (support) mount	kjn	3 842 535 620
4	Bosch Rexroth	Quick connector 10mm	projector support mount	kjn	3 842 535 633
6	Bosch Rexroth	Quick connector 8mm	projector support mount	kjn	3 842 535 631
4	Bosch Rexroth	40x40 end connector	leg extensions	kjn	3 842 532 196
4	Bosch Rexroth	40x40 bracket with fittings	IR mount	kjn	3 842 529 383
3	Bosch Rexroth	Inner bracket 10 mm with fixings	camera mount, fan controller mount	kjn	3 842 535 571
3	Bosch Rexroth	Inner bracket 8-10mm with fixings	frame mount connection	kjn	3 842 535 576
2	Bosch Rexroth	Swivel fastening	frame mount connection	kjn	3 842 516 706
3	Bosch Rexroth	30x30 joint with fastenings	camera mount, mount acrylic connection	kjn	3 842 502 683
3	Bosch Rexroth	M4 T nut 8mm	frame projector connection	kjn	KJN 501 751
24	Bosch Rexroth	M4 T nut 10mm	wall mount	kjn	KJN 530 281
12	Bosch Rexroth	M5 T nut 10mm	illuminator mount	kjn	KJN 530 283
4	Bosch Rexroth	Hinged foot	feet	kjn	3 842 529 025
3–6	n/a	M4 washer	frame projector connection	RS Components	189-636
24	BZP	Machine screw M4x12	wall mount	Screwfix	28806
19	BZP	Cap screw M4x40	frame projector connection, fan mount	RS Components	483-8253
12	n/a	Cap screw M5x16	illuminator mount	Screwfix	77044
1	Fischer	Mirror fixing kit	acrylic mirror connection	Screwfix	46116
16	BZP	M4 nut	fan mount	Screwfix	13138
2	n/a	Brackets	PSU mount	n/a	n/a
2	n/a	Acrylic sheet, 420 × 297 × 3mm	mirror mount, additional illuminators	Retail Engineering Design	n/a
1	n/a	Acrylic sheet, clear, 1290 × 950 × 10mm	surface (option I)	Alternative Plastic	n/a
2	n/a	Acrylic sheet, 650 × 700 × 3mm	wall (option I)	Alternative Plastic	n/a
2	n/a	Acrylic sheet, 996 × 700 × 3mm	wall (option I)	Alternative Plastic	n/a
1	n/a	Acrylic sheet, clear, 940 × 600 × 10mm	surface (option II)	Alternative Plastic	n/a
2	n/a	Acrylic sheet, 650 × 710 × 3mm	wall (option II)	Alternative Plastic	n/a
2	n/a	Acrylic sheet, 996 × 710 × 3mm	wall (option II)	Alternative Plastic	n/a
2	n/a	Acrylic sheet, 990 × 10 × 10mm	rim (option II)	Alternative Plastic	n/a
2	n/a	Acrylic sheet, 630 × 10 × 10mm	rim (option II)	Alternative Plastic	n/a
2	n/a	Acrylic sheet, 910 × 40 × 3mm	rim (option II)	Alternative Plastic	n/a
2	n/a	Acrylic sheet, 650 × 40 × 3mm	rim (option II)	Alternative Plastic	n/a
1	PastHorizons	Drafting film roll, 841mm × 20m	diffuser (option I/II)	PastHorizons	DF003
1	Evonik	Plexiglas EndLighten sheet, 940 × 600 × 8mm	surface (option III)	Plexiglas-Shop	0N002 XL
1	Evonik	Plexiglas RP sheet, 930 × 590 × 5mm	diffuser (option III)	Plexiglas-Shop	7D006 RP
2	n/a	Cardboard sheet, A1, white	wall cover	The Paper Mill Shop	n/a
2	n/a	Cardboard sheet, A1, black	floor cover	The Paper Mill Shop	1453303
1	Toshiba	TDP-EW25	projector	E-Plenish	n/a
1	Knight Optical	Hot mirror, 120 × 80mm	Knight Optical	Knight Optical	730FHQ12080-C
1	Point Grey	Dragonfly2	camera	Point Grey	n/a
1	Knight Optical	IR band-pass filter 850nm	visible light block	Knight Optical	850FAP5050
1	Knight Optical	First surface mirror, 400 × 280 × 3mm	mirror	Knight Optical	MGE400280-C
1	Edmund Optics	Varifocal 1.8-3.6mm lens	lens	Edmund Optics	NT55-254
12	n/a	IR illuminators, 99 LEDs, 850nm	main illuminators (standard DI)	RF Concepts Ltd	1781
1	Vishay	IR LEDs, 850nm	additional illuminators (standard DI)	Farnell	TSHA5201
1	n/a	IR LED ribbon, 850nm, 3.83cm spacing, 308cm	illuminations (DSI and FTIR)	Environmental Lights	irrf850-reel
1	n/a	Connector ribbon to cable	current supply (DSI and FTIR)	Environmental Lights	rf2-to-cable
8	n/a	Wire lead	current supply	n/a	n/a
4	Pro Power	Fan power power connectors	current supply	Farnell	n/a
4	Kaze Jyuni	Fan 120mm	fan	QuietPC	CS11200
4	Fansis	Dust filter 120mm	outer fan protection	QuietPC	n/a
4	n/a	Fan guard 120mm	inner fan protection	QuietPC	n/a
1	Xilence	PC powers supply unit (PSU)	powering IR and fans	QuietPC	XP420-12R
1	Zalman	Fan controller	driving fans	QuietPC	ZM-MFC2

Table A.2: Summarized parts list (stationary DI or DSI table)

Appendix B

Supplementary Material

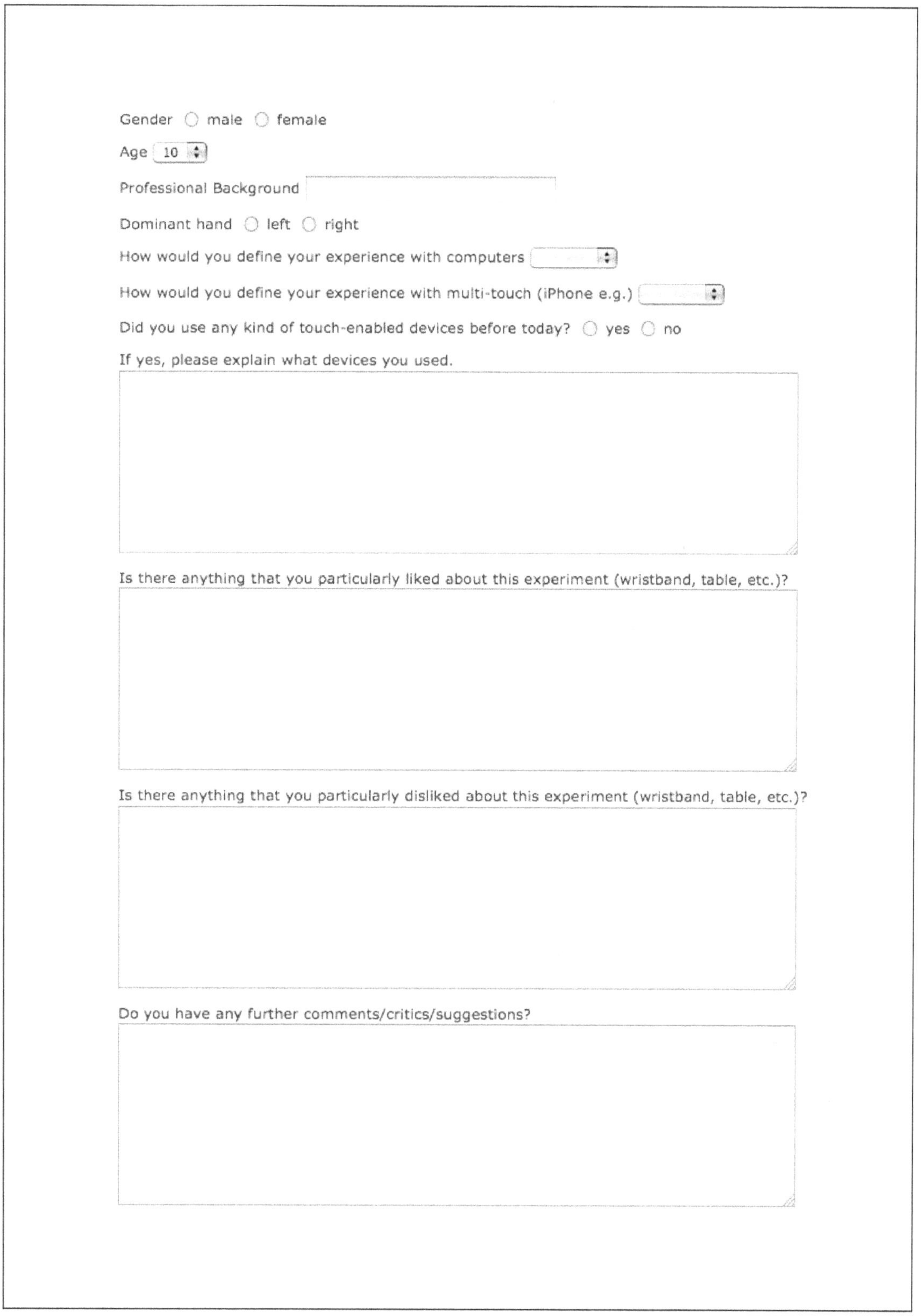

Gender ○ male ○ female

Age [10 ⬍]

Professional Background [_____]

Dominant hand ○ left ○ right

How would you define your experience with computers [⬍]

How would you define your experience with multi-touch (iPhone e.g.) [⬍]

Did you use any kind of touch-enabled devices before today? ○ yes ○ no

If yes, please explain what devices you used.

Is there anything that you particularly liked about this experiment (wristband, table, etc.)?

Is there anything that you particularly disliked about this experiment (wristband, table, etc.)?

Do you have any further comments/critics/suggestions?

Figure B.1: Questionnaire for IdWristbands study (section 3.2)

Participant:

1. Positive aspects of the system

2. Negative aspects of the system

3. Further comments

4. Age:
5. Sex: ☐ Male ☐ Female
6. Professional background:
7. Dominant hand: ☐ Left ☐ Right
8. Do you own a mobile phone? ☐ Yes ☐ No

		None	*Poor*	*Medium*	*High*	*Expert*
8.	How would you define your experience with computers?	1	2	3	4	5
9.	How would you define your experience with mobile phones?	1	2	3	4	5
10.	How would you define your experience multi-touch (IPhone e.g.)?	1	2	3	4	5

11. Is there anything you particularly liked about this experiment?

12. Is there anything you particularly disliked about this experiment?

13. Do you have any further comments?

Figure B.2: Questionnaire for PhoneTouch study (section 3.4)

		Strongly agree	Moderately agree	Slightly agree	Neither agree nor disagree	Slightly disagree	Moderately disagree	Strongly disagree

Participant: **Date and Time:**   **Order:**

System: ☐ PhoneTouch ☐ HandsDown ☐ IdWristbands

Part A

		Strongly agree	Moderately agree	Slightly agree	Neither agree nor disagree	Slightly disagree	Moderately disagree	Strongly disagree
1.	It was simple to use the system.	1	2	3	4	5	6	7
2.	I was able to complete the tasks quickly using this system.	1	2	3	4	5	6	7
3.	I was able to efficiently complete the tasks using this system.	1	2	3	4	5	6	7
4.	I felt comfortable using this system.	1	2	3	4	5	6	7
5.	It was easy to learn to use this system.	1	2	3	4	5	6	7
6.	I believe I could become productive quickly with this system.	1	2	3	4	5	6	7
7.	I liked using the interface of this system.	1	2	3	4	5	6	7
8.	Overall, I am satisfied with this system.	1	2	3	4	5	6	7

Part B

		Very low	Moderately low	Slightly low	Undecided	Slightly high	Moderately high	Very high
1.	*Mental demand* How much mental and perceptual activity was required (e.g., thinking, deciding, calculating, remembering, looking, searching, etc.)? Was the task easy or demanding, simple or complex, exacting or forgiving?	1	2	3	4	5	6	7
2.	*Frustration level* How insecure, discouraged, irritated, stressed and annoyed versus secure, gratified, content, relaxed and complacent did you feel during the task?	1	2	3	4	5	6	7

		Very good	Moderately good	Slightly good	Neither good nor poor	Moderately poor	Slightly poor	Very poor
3.	*Performance* How successful do you think you were in accomplishing the goals of the task set by the experimenter? How satisfied were you with your performance in accomplishing these goals?	1	2	3	4	5	6	7

Part C

1. Positive aspects of the system

2. Negative aspects of the system

3. Further comments

Study "Personalized Clipboards on Multi-Touch Surfaces"

Figure B.3: Method-specific questionnaire for personal clipboard study (Chapter 5)

Participant: Date and Time: Acquaintances:

Part A

1. Age:
2. Sex: ☐ Male   ☐ Female
3. Current occupation:
4. Dominant hand: ☐ Left   ☐ Right

	None	Poor	Medium	High	Expert
5. How would you define your experience with computers?	1	2	3	4	5
6. How would you define your experience with touch interfaces?	1	2	3	4	5

7. Which touch devices do you regularly use (e.g., smart phone or tablet)?

8. a. Have you used large multi-touch surfaces before?
        ☐ Yes   ☐ No
    b. If yes, in what context?

Part B

1. a. Please rank the systems according to your overall preference (1: best – 3: worst)
        ☐ PhoneTouch ☐ HandsDown ☐ IdWristbands
    b. Reasons for system preference

2. With which systems do you think you were faster (1: fastest – 3: slowest)?
    ☐ PhoneTouch ☐ HandsDown ☐ IdWristbands
3. With which systems do you think you were most efficient (1: most – 3: least efficient)?
    ☐ PhoneTouch ☐ HandsDown ☐ IdWristbands
4. Which systems were most enjoyable to use (1: most – 3: least enjoyable)?
    ☐ PhoneTouch ☐ HandsDown ☐ IdWristbands
5. Which systems were easier to learn (1: easiest – 3: hardest to learn)?
    ☐ PhoneTouch ☐ HandsDown ☐ IdWristbands
6. Which systems behaved more responsive (1: most – 3: least responsive)?
    ☐ PhoneTouch ☐ HandsDown ☐ IdWristbands

Part C

1. Is there anything you particularly liked about this experiment?

2. Is there anything you particularly disliked about this experiment?

3. Do you have any further comments?

Study "Personalized Clipboards on Multi-Touch Surfaces"

Figure B.4:   General questionnaire personal for clipboard study (Chapter 5)